*Mapping Morality in Postwar German Women's Fiction*

*Studies in German Literature, Linguistics, and Culture*

# Mapping Morality in Postwar German Women's Fiction

## Christa Wolf, Ingeborg Drewitz, and Grete Weil

Michelle Mattson

CAMDEN HOUSE
Rochester, New York

Copyright © 2010 Michelle Mattson

*All Rights Reserved.* Except as permitted under current legislation,
no part of this work may be photocopied, stored in a retrieval system,
published, performed in public, adapted, broadcast, transmitted,
recorded, or reproduced in any form or by any means,
without the prior permission of the copyright owner.

First published 2010
by Camden House

Camden House is an imprint of Boydell & Brewer Inc.
668 Mt. Hope Avenue, Rochester, NY 14620, USA
www.camden-house.com
and of Boydell & Brewer Limited
PO Box 9, Woodbridge, Suffolk IP12 3DF, UK
www.boydellandbrewer.com

ISBN-13: 978-1-57113-443-1
ISBN-10: 1-57113-443-3

**Library of Congress Cataloging-in-Publication Data**

Mattson, Michelle.
 Mapping morality in postwar German women's fiction : Christa Wolf, Ingeborg Drewitz, and Grete Weil / Michelle Mattson.
   p. cm. — (Studies in German literature, linguistics, and culture)
 Includes bibliographical references and index.
 ISBN-13: 978-1-57113-443-1 (acid-free paper)
 ISBN-10: 1-57113-443-3 (acid-free paper)
  1. German literature—Women authors—History and criticism. 2. German fiction—20th century—History and criticism. 3. Literature and morals—History—20th century. 4. Ethics in literature. 5. Wolf, Christa—Criticism and interpretation. 6. Drewitz, Ingeborg—Criticism and interpretation. 7. Weil, Grete, 1906–1999—Criticism and interpretation. I. Title. II. Series.
 PT167.M38 2010
 833'.91409353—dc22

                                                              2010004488

A catalogue record for this title is available from the British Library.

This publication is printed on acid-free paper.
Printed in the United States of America.

*To my parents, who provided
excellent models of what
it means to care for others*

# Contents

| | |
|---|---|
| Acknowledgments | ix |
| Introduction | 1 |
| 1: The Individual, Memory, and History | 11 |
| 2: Feminism, the Self, and Community | 38 |
| 3: Ingeborg Drewitz: Families, Historical Conflict, and Moral Mapping | 61 |
| 4: Christa Wolf: Rehearsing Individual and Collective Responsibility | 96 |
| 5: Grete Weil: The Costs of Abstract Principles | 142 |
| Conclusion | 185 |
| Bibliography | 193 |
| Index | 209 |

# Acknowledgments

I AM GRATEFUL TO MANY colleagues and friends for their input on this project. First and foremost, I'd like to thank Matthias Kaelberer, who patiently and thoughtfully read numerous drafts of the manuscript. I am also grateful to my colleagues at Rhodes College who have listened intently and commented insightfully on different portions of this work. Karen Carr, Mark Rectanus, Sabine von Dirke, Monika Shafi, Russell Berman, and Andreas Huyssen also offered helpful suggestions at key points in the process. Additionally, I would like to thank Jim Walker, whose careful reading and editing of the manuscript have made the book clearer and more reader-friendly.

I thank Kurt D. Hollomon for allowing me to use his art on the cover of this book. The cover is based on his image "Land Survey Map No. 4." I also appreciate the willingness of several journals to let me reprint portions of articles that are included in the chapters of this book. Parts of chapters 2, 3, and 4 appeared, in earlier form, in "Mothers Care? Models of Motherhood and their Ethical Implications in post-WWII German literature," in *National Women's Studies Association Journal* 21.1 (Spring 2009): 101–30 (copyright © 2009 *NWSA Journal*) and are reprinted with permission of the Johns Hopkins University Press. Sections of chapter 3 were also published as "History, Politics, the Individual: Ingeborg Drewitz's Novels *Gestern war heute* and *Eis auf der Elbe*" in *German Quarterly* 76.1 (Winter 2003): 38–55. Parts of chapter 5 are based on "Classical Kinship and Personal Responsibility: Grete Weil's *Meine Schwester Antigone*," published in *Seminar* 37.1 (2001): 53–72, and "Grete Weil: A Jewish Author?," published in *German Studies Review* 27.1 (February 2004): 113–27.

# Introduction

THIS BOOK CENTERS ON several novels by Christa Wolf (1929–), Ingeborg Drewitz (1923–86), and Grete Weil (1906–99). In particular, the study examines their attention to questions of moral responsibility in the second half of the twentieth century. All three writers seek to illustrate how our understanding of the historical present, informed as it is by our personal and our shared memories, shapes how we see our moral responsibilities in a world with increasingly porous and shifting community boundaries. They anchor their exploration of individual and collective responsibility within the family, moving out along different routes through local, national, and finally international communities. With little certainty, but a considerable sense of urgency, they attempt to map the moral geography of western European society in the second half of the twentieth century. In all three cases, furthermore, the inquiry is driven by their reflection on the individual's place within broader historical developments.

Why focus on these particular writers and these questions? The issue of responsibility played a considerable role in much of postwar German literature — one need only think of such writers as Heinrich Böll, Martin Walser, Max Frisch, Wolfgang Borchert, Hans Magnus Enzensberger, Rolf Hochhuth (to name just a few) to realize that questioning responsibility is not unique to the three writers at the heart of this study. Nonetheless, my readings within German Studies have drawn my attention increasingly to these authors. Although they all come from different social and political backgrounds and thus offer distinct socio-political perspectives, they share a focus on questions of personal responsibility within the context of family. In fact, they use those primary human relationships to interrogate ever expanding issues of ethical responsibility. Furthermore, they cannot separate these issues from questions of historical imbrication.[1] In other words, they approach ethical responsibility not from an abstract, atemporal position, but rather always as embedded in specific historical contexts and within family structures.

More specifically, I chose the work of these three writers because it met three important criteria that are at the heart of my own scholarly and philosophical interests. First, while the Second World War naturally features prominently in all of the literary texts on which the study focuses, my interest does not lie in the war or the Holocaust directly. Rather, I am concerned with how reflections on the past inform our sense of moral responsibility in the present. For this reason, the study excludes literary works that do not address social and political conflicts and issues relevant to the postwar period. Second, I seek to understand how broadly we can construe personal or collective responsibility. How far does it go beyond our immediate personal relationships? Does it include community responsibility? National (or even international) responsibility? All three of these writers ask these questions as well. I chose not to include texts that do not look at issues of responsibility beyond the personal or the local community. Finally, I wish to think through the way our various responsibilities compete with one another and make upholding responsibilities to one person or group quite difficult — if not downright impossible. For this reason, I was eager to deal with literary texts that thematized such competition. This made works that focused on characters within broad relational networks (extended families, schools, circles of friends, business communities, etc.) particularly attractive, but especially those that showed how our immediate responsibilities to family often conflict with what we perceive to be our possible obligations to individuals and communities more removed from us.

Of course, male writers also look at issues of responsibility. However, women of the same age cohort as these three writers underwent different kinds of socialization than men and asked questions about responsibility that men generally did not.[2] Thus, their primary focus on living life within their families provided numerous examples of how we must balance competing responsibilities, think through the sometimes conflicting moral choices we face, and try to locate ourselves within any number of intersecting moral communities.

One might also ask why the study does not include younger writers or, for that matter, the growing body of literature by writers with recent immigration backgrounds. Indeed, this latter group often addresses similar topics.[3] The answer to this question is partially a matter of pragmatism: there is only so much ground one book can cover. However, Wolf, Weil, and Drewitz have common concerns and perspectives on the central questions of the book that later writers do not share — at least not to the same degree. For Germans who grew up shortly before and during the Third Reich, the presence of history in the making loomed large. Although the connections are neither transparent nor undisputed, it is clear in the context of this particular time period that individuals played significant roles in how the Nazi regime cemented power in Germany and how the destruction process developed.[4] Furthermore, after sufficient time had elapsed to begin processing memories of the war, the urge to understand how a highly cultured society such as Germany could have descended to such levels of cruelty and depravity grew in intensity.[5] In contrast, the larger social and political roles of the individual during periods of relative stability are not as easy to specify.

However, what attracted me to these writers was also their insistence on drawing connections between Germany's pre-war and Nazi past and the socio-political realities of postwar Germany. For them, and for me, it is crucial to see the social spaces individuals occupy — both intentionally and unintentionally; self-reflectively and naively — in historical developments not only in moments of tremendous human crisis, but always. Doing this involves acknowledging and exploring how different historical settings in different social surroundings imbricate individuals in a variety of ways.

There are many writers whose work intersects thematically and chronologically with the novels in this study. For instance, there were a number of autobiographical texts published by women within roughly the same time frame that dealt with many similar issues. Eva Zeller, Ruth Rehmann, and Carola Stern[6] are three examples of writers whose autobiographical texts also offer well crafted, critically self-reflective works of literature that explore how women of the same generation as Wolf and Drewitz grew into the young adults they were at the end of the war. They examine the relationships within families in great detail and also the broader social pressures from friends and social institutions that influenced their perspectives and personal decisions. One could mention many other such texts with less literary ambition here as well.[7] Furthermore, since virtually all of the works by Wolf, Drewitz, and Weil that I discuss in this book bear strong autobiographical traces, one could choose to examine them as part of a large body of autobiographical texts written by women after the Second World War. However, I have not found that these other autobiographical texts address the postwar period as extensively as Drewitz, Weil, and Wolf do, to say nothing of political and social concerns that go beyond central Europe. While they merit and have received scholarly attention,[8] they do not fit into the parameters of this study.[9]

There are most probably relevant works by other writers that I have excluded, but this book's focus on Wolf, Drewitz, and Weil yields substantial insights into its central questions, since they present many commonalities but also important differences. Additionally, their novels offer a rich vein of material with which to explore issues of vital significance to human existence both at the end of the twentieth and at the beginning of the twenty-first century.

Christa Wolf is Germany's most prominent female writer and thus requires little introduction here. She has been the subject of numerous scholarly works and the center of an extended literary controversy in Germany in the aftermath of German unification.[10] However, beginning with *Moskauer Novelle* (Moscow Novella, 1961)[11] and continuing all the way up through *Leibhaftig* (In the Flesh, 2002),[12] she has integrated questions about the individual's place in history and the various forms of personal and social responsibility into all of her works. As someone who was a citizen of the former East Germany, she also offers a historical and political perspective that diverges markedly from that of West German writers. While this study could focus on a number of her novels and autobiographical texts, the issues central to this book crystallize most clearly in *Kindheitsmuster* (Patterns of Childhood, 1976).[13] Of course, *Kindheitsmuster* grew out of her previous works and had an impact on later ones, so the analysis will also draw in material from such novels as *Nachdenken über Christa T.* (The Quest for Christa T., 1968)[14] and *Kassandra* (Cassandra, 1983).[15]

Ingeborg Drewitz wrote numerous plays, essays, and biographies. She is, however, best known in literary circles for her involvement in both the German central committee of the international writers' association, PEN,[16] and in the organization and founding of the Verband deutscher Schriftsteller (The Association of German Writers) as well as for her work as a chronicler of twentieth-century German cultural history in several novels. She repeatedly demonstrates her characters' embeddedness in the historical struggles of their immediate present, and how they emerge from a longer-running historical drama, which preshapes — but does not predetermine — the way they view their own time. Drewitz's novels from *Wer verteidigt Katrin Lambert?* (Who Will Defend Katrin Lambert? 1974)[17] to *Gestern war heute* (Yesterday was Today, 1978)[18] and finally *Eis auf der Elbe* (Ice on the Elbe, 1982)[19] also reflect how her own thinking on individual and collective responsibility changed over time from an early emphasis on a moral perspective unique to women to one that is more inclusive.

Grete Weil, whose literary efforts have increasingly been the topic of scholarly work in German Studies, was a German Jewish writer. Born and raised in Germany, she was forced to leave her home during the Third Reich. However, she returned to Germany as soon after the war as she could, and worked through her experiences and her ambivalences about living as a Jew in Germany in her literary works. Weil's inclusion in this study may puzzle some readers, since her experiences as a victim of the Holocaust set her apart in many ways from Wolf and Drewitz. Indeed, the analysis of her work requires a somewhat different set of analytical tools than the analysis of either Wolf's or Drewitz's novels. Both *Meine Schwester Antigone* (My Sister Antigone, 1980)[20] and *Der Brautpreis* (The Bride Price, 1988)[21] — the two novels at the center of my analysis — query the rupture of historical perception that the Holocaust survivor experiences. For Weil, the Holocaust becomes an unavoidable filter to all questions asked of history, both the history that came before the Holocaust and the history that came after it. In contrast to the non-Jewish Germans Drewitz and Wolf, whose space within German history remained unquestioned, the Jewish German writer Weil can no longer find a secure footing from which to examine history. From this unstable terrain, however, Weil persistently interrogates the nature of individual responsibility within political and social developments that seem largely beyond individual control.

Furthermore, Weil strongly identified herself as a German writer. Indeed both *Meine Schwester Antigone* and *Der Brautpreis* recount the struggles of her narrative stand-ins to see herself meaningfully as anything but German. While she accepts the fact that the Nazis and even her contemporaries see her always as German and Jewish, she also feels this is the result of a process of violence formalized by the Nazis' arbitrary definitions of Jewishness. Thus, although serious biographical differences distinguish her from Drewitz and Weil, I believe that the thematic and stylistic similarities warrant her inclusion. I would also like to echo Pascale Bos's frustration with a widespread tendency to isolate the study of German Jewish literature from other branches of literary study rather than to see it as an integral part of German literary production.[22] Of course, studies of German Jewish literature *as* German Jewish literature remain valuable. On the other hand, Weil's markedly different experiences and her distinctive approach to the two questions that are key to this study — the questions of individual historical positioning and of moral responsibility — create new angles from which to view the issues that all three of the writers considered here address.

In sum, the work of these three authors creates an intersection of two very important questions. First, how do individuals see themselves in relation to their historical present? The second question rests of necessity on the answer to the first. Namely, how do they then explore the extent of their personal responsibilities to their families and friends, and as part of both local groups and intersecting global communities? All three women take up the major political and social issues that Germany and Western Europe faced after the Second World War and follow them forward into the present. They zero in on the questions of competing political systems during the Cold War, on terrorism, political repression, the emerging social movements of the '60s and '70s, and address the implications of an increasingly heterogeneous German population. Together they speak to virtually all of the major events of twentieth-century German and European history. Furthermore (as noted above), all of them represent the lives of individuals as located not only generally within a set of intersecting interpersonal relationships, but also specifically within families. They explore how these relationships of immediate personal responsibility co-determine the spectrum of actions available to individuals and shape the way that they define and defend their choices.

This study looks at the literary tools Wolf, Drewitz, and Weil use to approach answers to these questions. It also shows how they use literature as a moral laboratory, locating within the extended narrative structures of the novel the conceptual spaces to map out a discourse on ethics. This will prove key to combining the discussion of plotting the individual's place in history — or histor*ies* — and determining from there how individuals negotiate and understand their ethical responsibilities, both as individuals and as members of social collectives. As Peter and Renate Singer point out,

> It is surely true that the detailed and creative exploration of a situation that can emerge from a good novel can help us to understand more about ourselves, and how we ought to live. In contrast to the examples discussed in works of philosophy, discussions of ethical issues in fiction tend to be concrete, rather than abstract, and to give a rich context for the distinctive moral views or choices that are portrayed. Literature therefore often presents a more nuanced view of character and circumstances than is to be found in the works of philosophers.[23]

Narrative, the act of telling stories, is also the most plastic point at which ethics, philosophy, and literature intersect. Margaret Urban Walker argues in her book *Moral Understandings* that narrative plays an essential role in the formation of our moral understandings of ourselves and others. She points out that the "resolution of a moral problem itself takes a narrative form, the form of a transition which links past moral lives (individual, interpersonal, and collective) to future ones in a way not completely determined by where things started, and open to different continuations that may yet affect what the resolution means."[24] It is through narrative that we test the validity of our moral precepts and come to an understanding of ourselves.

Traditionally in Western philosophy, ethicists have tended to use short, situational examples — generally rather sparing of detail, nuance, or socio-historical context — to illustrate possible moral conflicts and to reason through their resolutions. Feminist ethicists, however, have long recognized that the contextualization necessary to address a situation of need requires rich narrative, a full description of the factors that pertain to the dilemma at hand. Fiction offers us the narrative spaces to weave even broader tapestries of relationships and to expand the landscape of our moral experimentation and the thought processes we engage when deciding how we can best act. For this reason, literary texts can give us the chance to play through ethical models to test our satisfaction with their relational results. Indeed, they can do so even before the philosophers lay these models out in more abstract form.

Drewitz, Wolf, and Weil offer good examples of how literature can function in this way. In particular, their narrative experiments in thinking through moral paradigms pertain directly to the two main questions that I pursue in this book. To approach these questions, the book draws on two areas of academic discourse that — with few exceptions — have remained isolated from one another. The first deals with the intersection of collective and individual memory. The second engages feminist discussions of ethics to explore conceptual frameworks that acknowledge the myriad articulations of responsibility in contemporary society. Together, these two academic discourses provide tools with which to examine the central questions of the book. For this reason, the study opens with two chapters that introduce these theoretical discussions broadly, but also begin to weave in how the theoretical issues relate to and help clarify the literary texts of Drewitz, Wolf, and Weil. Chapters on each of the three writers follow the discussion of the theoretical and philosophical questions.

From the middle of Europe, these three writers attempt to map the connections between the lives of their characters and events happening in areas geographically remote from them: in Vietnam, Chile, and Japan to name only a few examples. The characters ask themselves what their relationship is to these distant events and places and wonder just how "distant" they really are. Based on their always-provisional conclusions, each writer offers us views on individual agency in a world that seems somehow too big.

All three writers use their exploration of history to think about issues of moral responsibility in the present. While they acknowledge the shifting boundaries of the spaces that individuals occupy socially and geographically, they insist that understanding how individuals experience and impact their historical present builds a foundation for thinking about the spectrum of human responsibility. Wolf, Weil, and Drewitz ultimately cannot specify exactly how individuals "fit in" to history or what the parameters of individual and collective responsibility should be. This is so precisely because moral understandings are subject to collaborative negotiation and thus change over time and space. However, these writers can and do offer their readers pathways to examining how human beings struggle with themselves and with others to answer these two questions.

## Notes

[1] Technically, the word imbrication applies to a geometrical pattern in which objects overlap. However, when discussing the individual's relationship to historical developments and or the impact that history has on individuals, the term implies more the multiple, overlapping layers on/in which individuals are implicated in historical developments. It thus conjures up an image of a web of relationships and interdependence.

[2] Weil was born in 1906 and was, thus, much older than either Drewitz or Wolf. However, because she had to go into hiding during the Nazi period, she established her public and professional identities at roughly the same time as did the two younger writers.

[3] Early plans for this book, for instance, included the work of Emine Sevgi Özdamar. I was at the time particularly interested in incorporating Özdamar's

*Das Leben ist eine Karawanserei. hat zwei Türen, aus einer kam ich rein, aus der anderen ging ich raus* (Cologne: Kiepenheuer & Witsch, 1999). However, the very different cultural and historical context of this work would have required a considerably different interpretive framework.

4 Raul Hilberg describes the systematic murder of Europe's Jews as a "destruction process," made up of a "series of administrative measures that must be aimed at a definite group." The term "process" thus indicates the breadth and scope of activities involved in destroying such a large number of individuals from such a great variety of countries. See Raul Hilberg, *The Destruction of the European Jews. Student Edition* (New York: Holmes & Meier, 1985), 27.

5 This dynamic is discussed in greater detail in chapter 1, below.

6 Eva Zeller, *So lange ich denken kann* (Stuttgart: Deutsche Verlagsanstalt, 1981) and *Nein und Amen* (Stuttgart: Deutsche Verlagsanstalt, 1986); Ruth Rehmann, *Der Mann auf der Kanzel* (Munich: Hanser, 1979); Carola Stern, *In den Netzen der Erinnerung* (Reinbek bei Hamburg: Rowohlt Verlag, 1986) and *Doppelleben* (Cologne: Kiepenheuer & Witsch, 2001).

7 For instance, Margarethe Hannsmann, *Der helle Tag bricht an: Ein Kind wird Nazi* (Hamburg: A. Knaus, 1982), Renate Finckh, *Mit uns zieht die neue Zeit* (Baden-Baden: Signal Verlag, 1978), and Melita Maschmann, *Fazit: Kein Rechtfertigungsversuch* (Stuttgart: Deutsche Verlagsanstalt, 1963).

8 See for instance, the volume edited by Elaine Martin, *Gender, Patriarchy, and Fascism in the Third Reich* (Detroit: Wayne State UP, 1993), which contains individual contributions that focus on several of these writers.

9 Several colleagues who have read portions of this work in earlier versions have suggested including a deliberate discussion of feminist autobiography theory in the interpretation of Wolf, Drewitz, and Weil's texts. This suggestion has some merit, since all three writers borrowed heavily from their own life experiences to write them. Furthermore, their literary efforts have all been variously characterized as autobiographical in both their popular and their scholarly reception. This characterization is not completely incorrect, but it is problematic. Weil was, in fact, the only one of the three to write a work that she herself labeled an autobiography, although this work, *Leb ich denn, wenn andere leben,* did not appear until 1998, one year before her death. A fairly recent dissertation on Grete Weil by Carmen Giese, *Das Ich im literarischen Werk von Grete Weil und Klaus Mann: Zwei autobiographische Gesamtkonzepte* (Frankfurt am Main: Peter Lang, 1997), devotes considerable energy to convincing us to see Weil's work as autobiography. On the other hand, in an interview appended to the dissertation, Weil addresses directly some of the aspects of her life that she changed in her literary texts and why this was important to her. She also emphasizes that until her 1998 autobiography her works were novels, and however much autobiographical material they contained, they were independent works of fiction. Although Christa Wolf's *Kindheitsmuster* has been read as an autobiography, the book begins with an explicit disclaimer that all the characters are inventions of the narrator. Thus, although there is ample evidence that Wolf is in fact relating to the reader much of her own biography, the writer quite clearly does not wish us to make any facile equations between the narrator, Nelly, and Christa Wolf herself. Similarly, readers familiar with Ingeborg

Drewitz's life will know that many of the characters in her book resemble people from the writer's own family. Nonetheless, she chose to edit and mold the material from her life into a less explicitly autobiographical form. Part of the problem with calling any of these writer's works autobiographies lies in the generic designation itself. To a great extent owing to feminist work on autobiography, but also as a result of general shifts in the conception of the subject beginning around the turn of the nineteenth to the twentieth century, the genre of autobiography has undergone vast redefinition. Various reformulations of the term: autography, autogynography, and auto/biographical practices — to name just three — have arisen to address from a feminist perspective the inadequacies of the term "autobiography" as it had been understood. While I have no objection to calling any of these works autobiographical, I am not convinced that doing so really furthers the analysis this book pursues.

[10] For a collection of the contributions to the public controversy over Christa Wolf, see Thomas Anz, ed., *"Es geht nicht um Christa Wolf": Der Literaturstreit im vereinten Deutschland* (Munich: Spangenberg, 1991).

[11] Christa Wolf, *Moskauer Novelle* (Halle: Mitteldeutscher Verlag, 1961).

[12] Christa Wolf, *Leibhaftig* (Darmstadt: Luchterhand, 2002).

[13] Christa Wolf, *Kindheitsmuster* (Berlin and Weimar: Aufbau Verlag, 1976). All quotations from the German are from this edition and will be indicated by chapter and page number in parentheses. Whenever possible, English translations of such passages will be from *Patterns of Childhood*, trans. Ursule Molinaro and Hedwig Rappolt (New York: Farrar, Straus, and Giroux, 1976). Occasionally, Wolf's translators chose to leave certain passages out of the English translation. When this occurs, the note will indicate that the translation is my own.

[14] Christa Wolf, *Nachdenken über Christa T.* (Darmstadt: Luchterhand Verlag, 1971). All quotations are from this edition and will be indicated by chapter and page number. English translations of such passages will be from *The Quest for Christa T.*, trans. Christopher Middleton (New York: Farrar, Straus, and Giroux, 1970).

[15] Christa Wolf, *Kassandra* (Darmstadt: Luchterhand, 1983).

[16] PEN is an international literary and human rights organization. The acronym PEN was derived from the three words "Poets, Essayists, and Novelists."

[17] Ingeborg Drewitz, *Wer verteidigt Katrin Lambert?* (Stuttgart: Verlag Werner Gebühr, 1974). All quotations from the German are from this edition. All English translations of passages from the work are my own.

[18] Ingeborg Drewitz, *Gestern war heute. Hundert Jahre Gegenwart* (Düsseldorf: Claassen Verlag, 1978). All quotations from the German are from this edition. All English translations of passages from the work are my own.

[19] Ingeborg Drewitz, *Eis auf der Elbe* (Düsseldorf: Claassen, 1982). All quotations from the German are from this edition. All English translations of passages from the work are my own.

[20] Grete Weil, *Meine Schwester Antigone* (Zurich: Benziger, 1980). All quotations from the German are from this edition. Whenever possible, all English citations will come from *My Sister, My Antigone*, trans. Krishna Winston (New York: Avon

Books, 1984). Occasionally, I have had to retranslate a passage or alter one. The endnotes will reflect such exceptions.

[21] Grete Weil, *Der Brautpreis* (Zurich: Nagel & Kimche, 1988). All quotations from the German are from this edition. All English translations of passages from the work are from *The Bride Price*, trans. John Barrett (Boston: David R. Godine Publisher, 1991).

[22] Pascale Bos, *German-Jewish Literature in the Wake of the Holocaust: Grete Weil, Ruth Klüger, and the Politics of Address* (New York: Palgrave Macmillan, 2005), 12–13.

[23] Peter Singer and Renata Singer, eds., *The Moral of the Story: An Anthology of Ethics Through Literature* (Oxford: Blackwell, 2005), xi.

[24] Margaret Urban Walker, *Moral Understandings: A Feminist Study in Ethics* (New York: Routledge, 1998), 69. Indeed, care ethics (an outgrowth of feminist ethics that I outline in greater detail in chapter two) in particular has recognized the centrality of narrative in considering moral questions because it is a contextually-driven approach to moral understanding rather than simply the application of particular moral dictates. In order to improve a situation before us, we must first understand it in all of its complexities.

# 1: The Individual, Memory, and History

Drewitz, Wolf, and Weil's literary projects delve explicitly into how individuals construe their relationship to their historical present.[1] Therefore, this chapter begins by gathering the tools to approach the issue theoretically. However, because individual perception of one's own imbrication in history, rather than a historiographical record of events, stands central to the inquiry, an attempt to discern the actual role of the individual in history is unnecessary. In other words, this analysis examines individuals' subjective processing of their place in history. Thus, the chapter explores various ways to conceive of our historical *self*-emplotment. Memory is one of the processes that individuals activate in their efforts to locate their place in history, but what is memory? What is individual memory? What is collective memory? How do individuals relate one to the other? After an examination of possible answers to such questions, the focus shifts to the links between memory and history. Finally, the chapter briefly discusses how these issues pertain to Drewitz, Wolf, and Weil.

## On Memory: Definitions and Puzzles

A basic definition of memory would include the following: the ability to reproduce or recall what one learns and the collection of things that individuals retain from an activity or experience.[2] Such a basic definition, however, does not reveal why people remember certain things and forget others. It does not tell us how we remember things. It also does not give any indication of what external factors influence what we remember, and it says nothing about the relationship between personal and collective memories of shared experiences. Such a definition also cannot adequately explain the importance of memory. The writers at the center of this study are eager to understand these different facets of memory. The narrator in Christa Wolf's *Kindheitsmuster*,[3] for instance, asks the following questions:

> Wieviel und was von dem, was du jetzt erlebst, wird einst — in zwanzig Jahren — des Erinnerns wert sein? Welches Bild von heute wird sich eingeprägt haben, unauslöschlich wie die Anordnung jener Wehrmachtsbaracken unter märkischen Kiefern, an der Nelly erfuhr, wie die Bedrohung durch das Allergewöhnlichste einem den Atem abschneiden kann? (397)

> [How much of your present experiences will be worth remembering in twenty years? Which of today's images will be impressed on the memory, as indelibly as the layout of the army barracks under the Brandenburg firs, where Nelly learns that the most commonplace can be so menacing as to take your breath away? (304)]

Wolf's narrator in this passage (and in numerous others) speaks directly to the questions of what we remember, why we remember, and when we remember. She also links those questions explicitly to the process of understanding the sociopolitical events that have happened in our historical present and how individuals relate themselves to those events. As a writer, Wolf approaches these questions through complex literary forms.

Scholars explore these same questions through — at times — equally complex theoretical discussions. But their efforts can provide different ways to understand abstractly the issues that Wolf's fictional characters also face. The scholarly discussion of memory mushroomed toward the end of the twentieth century and into the twenty-first. Indeed, although scholars have theorized the nature of memory over the centuries, studies of the topic seemed to become an academic industry as the last century closed. What is at stake in such interest? Why did the topic seize our attention? Andreas Huyssen argues that at the turn from the twentieth to the twenty-first century we are obsessed with memory because we find ourselves in a crisis over the structure of temporality. Memory has become our vehicle of choice to slow down the process of integrating information into consciousness. In an era of readily accessible and rapidly changing sensory and intellectual input, memory allows us "to claim some anchoring space in a world of puzzling and often threatening heterogeneity, non-synchronicity, and information overload."[4] Huyssen hopes that the recent interest in memory is a positive sign that we are looking to memory as a means to resist being cut off from the past as a place to which we can secure our sense of the present.[5] In other words, we look to memory to help us situate ourselves in the world both diachronically and synchronically.

An important voice in this discussion belonged to the historian Pierre Nora, editor of the expansive *Realms of Memory: Rethinking the French Past*.[6] Nora's introduction to this collection of essays is widely cited by scholars working on many different aspects of historical consciousness and collective memory. His theory of memory and *lieux de mémoire*, specifically, has been cited and discussed in works on topics as diverse as politics and war in Central America, the history of the American civil rights struggle, and public commemorations and contested memories of the Holocaust.[7] His influential work offers both intriguing definitions of memory and history and many points for possible contention. This chapter lays out his definitions and how they are productive for this study, but also indicates where they become problematic and overly constraining.

Nora, for instance, sees the resurgent interest in memory as a sure sign that it has faded away: "Memory is constantly on our lips because it no longer exists" (1). Nora's definition of memory is admittedly both intentionally provocative and quite idiosyncratic. He sees memory as a function in society that transmitted values from generation to generation, with both individual and collective benefits. It was located within traditional institutions, which, he argues, no longer perform the way they used to. Memory once provided "[e]very one of our acts, down to the most quotidian . . . an intimate identification of act and meaning, as a religious repetition of sempiternal practice" (3). Since the demise of the nation as an organic, *holy* entity (which, in France at least, he dates back to the 1930s), history has assumed a separate function from memory. It has, in Nora's view, supplanted memory, as he defines it, in our minds. Memory, a function Nora sees as driven by the present, constantly reaffirmed our relationship to our past, imbuing our lives with a continuity of meaning. We have, however, put distance between ourselves and the past through a very different vehicle, namely history. How memory and history relate to each other is the subject of discussion later in this chapter. At this juncture, the emphasis is rather on memory's function for the individual and for society.

Both Huyssen and Nora agree that memory is not solely — or even primarily — about the past. Instead, memory serves the needs of the present. We call upon memories of the past to help us respond to the demands of our present. Indeed, we need to use past experiences in order to interpret present ones.[8] As Raphael Samuel puts it,

> memory is historically conditioned, changing colour and shape according to the emergencies of the moment; that so far from being handed down in the timeless form of "tradition" it is progressively altered from generation to generation. . . . Like history, memory is inherently revisionist and never more chameleon than when it appears to stay the same.[9]

Samuel's description of memory gets at both aspects of the term, that is, memory as an activity and as what human beings actually remember. What he stresses here is that human beings can remember the same event at different times and yet slant memory to serve different purposes in the present. The remembered event may not appear to have changed, but has been recontextualized or reinterpreted. Samuel is not alone in his understanding of the term. Although the specific definitions that scholars give of the term memory and the way they use it may vary, there is a broad consensus that memory is not static, but rather changes fundamentally over time.

Any history of memory in the European tradition will demonstrate that, from the world of the ancient Greeks through to the present, human understanding of memory has taken remarkably different forms.[10] This study is particularly concerned with the relationship between individual and collective memory. At the intersection of the two, people query their understanding of history and where they fit into it. The following passage from Drewitz's *Gestern war heute*, in which the main character's grandfather reflects on his own childhood, provides a literary instance of when individual and collective memory conflict.

> Sie haben ihn stehen lassen damals, weil er sich weigerte, ein Gedicht für den Sedantag zu lernen; weil er vom Vater anderes wußte über Paris, über die Franzosen, über den Aufstand, den sie gemacht hatten, nachdem ihr Kaiser Sedan verloren hatte, und weil sein Vater gesagt hatte, auch der deutsche Kaiser wird sein Sedan haben. (10–11)

> [They left him standing then because he refused to learn a poem about the Day of Sedan; because from his father he knew different things about Paris, the French, the revolt that they instigated after their Kaiser had lost Sedan, and because his father had said, the German Kaiser will have his Sedan some day too.]

The chapter is told in the third person, but from the grandfather's perspective. In his reflections about the impending birth of his granddaughter and the historical conditions into which she will be born, he recalls the contradiction in his life between officially sanctioned public memories of Germany's victory over the French, the institutional demands to celebrate it, and the stories his own father had told him of the French people and the war between the two countries. He also refers to the impact that his refusal to participate in the collective staging of Germany's military and national superiority had on his social standing.

The point here is to connect the way the literary texts in this study approach the relationship between individual and collective memory to more theoretical or abstract work on memory. The above passage from Drewitz, for instance, offers a good illustration of how the sociologist Maurice Halbwachs understood the way memory functions, as expressed in his posthumously published and widely-cited *The Collective Memory*. Despite the rather belated reception of his work,[11] Halbwachs has undoubtedly become one of the most influential scholars of memory. Like Nora's *Realms of Memory*, Halbwachs's volume has generated so much interest among scholars of memory that a discussion of individual and collective memory would be unthinkable without an attempt to understand his contribution to the topic. This might seem surprising since his radical and at first glance incredible thesis is that memory is *always* collective. Since it is obvious that only individuals can remember, his basic assertion of memory's collective nature requires some explanation.

Halbwachs argues that even when we experience something alone, we process all experiences through structures learned within various social collectives. These can be any number of potentially overlapping social groupings, as small as families and as large as national populations — just as we see the conflicting narratives of German nationhood expressed in the above passage from *Gestern war heute*. Halbwachs argues that when individuals experience something apart from others, they are alone in appearance only, "because [their] thoughts and actions during even this period are explained by [their] nature as [social beings]." They never cease being part of some type of social network.[12] Following Émile Durkheim, Halbwachs maintains that we can experience nothing independently of the social structures in which we exist. In sum, memory is collective because: 1) We remember the past as part of an intersubjective context that we experience with other people; 2) Memory draws on social points of reference, such as ritual, ceremony, and social events; 3) People remember and share memories with others; and 4) Memory is based on language, which is a social convention.[13] Therefore, all memory is collective even if individuals continue to experience and remember things as individuals, indeed even if individual memories contradict collective memories.

If this is the case, what is the relationship between what we deem to be individual memories and collective memory? What do we make of the differences between memories that individuals have of the same events or event sequences? The following passage from Christa Wolf's *Nachdenken über Christa T.* indirectly points to how Halbwachs sees individual memories:

> Kostjas Brief spielt, in gebotener Zurückhaltung, auf die Vorgänge an, oder wie man es sonst nennen will, und ihr Zeugnis ist ihr [Christa T.'s] Tagebuch. In beiden allerdings haben die Ereignisse andere Spuren hinterlassen, auf andere Weise machen sich die geheimen Manipulationen und Ausflüchte der Erinnerung geltend, anders geht bei jedem die eilfertige, gefährliche Arbeit des Vergessens vor, so daß man, je nach dem Zeugen, dem man sich anvertraut, die Spuren leugnen oder sie übertreiben kann." (67–68)

> [Kostja's letter alludes, with due tact, to what occurred (or however one wants to put it); and Christa T.'s diary is her own witness. But the events left different traces in each; the secret manipulations and evasions of memory are shown in different ways, in each the rapid and dangerous workings of oblivion take a different course. Accordingly, one can exaggerate the traces or fail to find any, depending on which source you trust. (64)]

Wolf's narrator here — as in other works — often thinks through or speculates about how different individuals process the same event. Halbwachs himself describes individual memories as "viewpoints" on the memories of the various collectives to which we belong or of the varied positions we occupy within these collectives. Our individual viewpoints change when our social positionings shift. As we move from one social group to another, or as the influence of the different social groups on us varies, the structures through which we interpret both the past and the present change too, which explains also why our memories of the past do not remain the same over time (48). Memory as a process — rather than a storehouse of static images — configures moments of the past in order to respond to current situations. Individuals react to experiences, however, with different levels of intensity depending in part on the level of influence that various social groups have on them. Thus, individuals within similar social groups can experience the same events with dissimilar emphases and recall them later in distinct ways.

Collective memory is not, however, the sum total of the various viewpoints that individual members of a group hold. Halbwachs argues that the reality of a group "is not exhausted in an enumerable set of individuals who constitute the starting point for its reconstruction. On the contrary, what constitutes the essence of a group is an interest, a shared body of concerns and ideas" (119). What comes to the fore in collective consciousness represents a negotiation of shared interests, information is exchanged and recurrent themes arise. Collective memory probes the past at varying depths depending on what issues and conflicts confront a social group at any given time (43, 119–20). This, however, still does not explain adequately the relationship of the individual to collective memory.

To be more specific, individuals participate in collective remembrances of events that did not happen to them in at least two distinct ways. Halbwachs writes:

> On the one hand, he [the individual] places his own remembrances within the framework of his personality, his own personal life; he considers those of his own that he holds in common with other people only in the aspect that interests him by virtue of distinguishing him from others. On the other hand, he is able to act merely as a group member, helping to evoke and maintain impersonal remembrances of interest to the group. These two memories are often intermingled. (50)

The passage above creates the impression that these two forms of memory are distinguishable (if not always neatly separated) from each other — as if one could say, "these experiences are mine personally, whereas this other set belongs to the memory of the group/s to which I belong." Since individual perception is, however, processed through social structures, memories of individual experiences — ones not shared by a larger group in a specific form — are still shaped by the collective experiences of that group. But why draw out this particular point now?

The writers whose work is at the heart of this book are interested in the intersection of individual and collective memories of history. In what collective pool of historical experience do individuals partake, and what is the nature of such experience? One cannot answer such a question relying solely on one theorist's work on the topic. On the other hand, Halbwachs eloquently describes how collective historical experience is mediated to and through individuals. He highlights two ways in which individuals appropriate memories drawn from a collective historical background. First, individuals can consciously place themselves within a historical context broader than their individual experience would normally allow. Halbwachs explains this as follows:

> During my life, my national society has been theater for a number of events that I say I "remember," events that I know about only from newspapers or the testimony of those directly involved. These events occupy a place in the memory of the nation, but I myself did not witness them. (51)

Halbwachs refers to such memories as "borrowed" memories, memories to which we have access solely as members of a particular social group.

A second, more complex source of historical memory for the individual is one that is passed on indirectly through the generationally determined patterns of socialization that transmit values from our most recent ancestors (i.e. parents and grandparents). Halbwachs uses his own parents to illustrate how historical consciousness is mediated from generation to generation even before we become cognizant ourselves of the events happening around us. In the following passage he talks about how his parents' generation experienced France's defeat in the Franco-Prussian War and how that defeat influenced the cultural framework of that generation.

> I was always with my parents. . . . They were, in part, the people they were because they lived through that period, in a certain country under certain national and political circumstances. Perhaps I can find no trace of definite 'historical' events in their overt habits, in the general tone of their feelings. But there certainly existed in France during the ten-, fifteen-, or twenty-year period following the Franco-Prussian War of 1870–1871 a remarkable psychological and social atmosphere unique to this time. My parents belonged to this period; they acquired certain habits and characteristics that became part of their personality and made an early impression upon me. What is at issue here is no longer mere dates or facts. (56)

While they might not have passed on specific memories of the war, they did — so he argues — pass on the way their generation came to view their world after that point in time.

We have then as individuals at least three access points to our position within our own historical present: experiences we have as individuals, experiences we have as part of a larger social collective, and experiences that pre-date us, but are mediated to us through processes of socialization. Drewitz, Wolf, and Weil all attempt consciously to illustrate these different entry points. To give one example here, Drewitz begins her novel *Gestern war heute* with the reflections of three different generations on the historical developments that have led to their particular moment in time, and how those developments manifested themselves in their own lives and in the lives of those around them. In this way, she grounds the consciousness of her protagonist, Gabriele, within a collective, historical consciousness.

So far we have looked primarily at how we experience our historical present both directly and through various socialization processes. This will not suffice to explain either how individual experience is transferred to social groups, or how individuals effect or affect historical change — even when they are not members of the social groups historians have long treated as the makers of history, for instance political leaders, clerics, and soldiers, to name just a few. Both of these questions, however, are central concerns of this study.

The first of the two, namely how individual experiences come together in collective consciousness, is also at stake in the work of social psychologists on collective memory.[14] James Pennebaker points out that psychologists have long had primary interest in individual memories, but that sociologists (like Halbwachs) have been more concerned with collective memory.[15] If one's interest lies, however, in probing the connections between the two, one cannot do so by approaching only one of them. Instead, one needs to explore both how sociohistorical events generate individual reactions, and then how these individual reactions circulate and become part of a group's memory. The first step might be understanding what kinds of events generally lead to lasting memories — both personal and collective.

Some social psychologists stress several factors to explain what we remember and why. The first two are closely linked: 1) An event must be unique; and 2) It must also have a long-term and significant impact on our lives. Elaborating on the first two criteria, one can for instance, distinguish between the Second World War, the Vietnam War, and the Korean War as leaving differing degrees of memory in US culture. While the Second World War fundamentally changed the way American society viewed the world and the nature of human beings, and the Vietnam War left lasting schisms within American society itself, the Korean conflict resulted in few enduring changes to our collective experience. Collectively, our memories of the Second World War and the Vietnam War are much stronger than of the Korean War.

A third criterion for the generation of lasting memories is that we must "rehearse" the event both for ourselves and for others. One can rehearse or review an occurrence both "overtly" in communication with others, or "covertly" in one's own mind. However, in order for a memory to stick with us it must be something we care enough about to reflect on it, return to it intellectually and emotionally, or discuss with others fairly often. To stay with the above examples, both the Second World War and the Vietnam War have generated numerous public rehearsals — for instance, personal testimonies, movies, books, discussions, demonstrations, memorials, and so on, but there has been little such public rehearsal of the Korean War.

Interestingly, particularly for the Second World War in the German context, not only overt and frequent rehearsal of an event but also an active and sustained avoidance of such rehearsal will lead to a greater emphasis on that event in both individual and collective memory. James Pennebaker and Betsy Banasik refer to such a situation as a silent event, "one where people actively avoid talking about a major shared upheaval."[16] In such a case, the effort that goes into suppressing rehearsal sustains the memory. It may also, however, make it difficult for an individual or a collective to integrate or assess the impact of such an event.

Some scholars interpret the effects of "silent events" along Freudian lines.[17] That is to say, actively repressed events can lead to episodes of "acting out" as opposed to "working through" the experiences in a way that allows for an integration of the event into consciousness. Acting out repressed events does nothing to give the individual positive ways to deal with those events.[18] In contrast, working through is an analytical process that allows individuals to come to terms with repressed events and move beyond the control the events have over their lives.[19] While working through would be a positive way to rehearse traumatic or difficult past experiences, acting out leaves the subject to relive such experiences without being able to come to terms with them.

Other social psychologists find that repeated rehearsal of events — whether analytically or affectively driven — can lead to overwhelmingly negative assessments of a social collective by the individuals who consider themselves members of that collective.[20] Such negative self-assessment has detrimental consequences for group identity. In this context, the initial unwillingness of Germans to confront the personal and social implications of their participation in the Third Reich can be said to have led both to acting out and to a persistent negative self-definition of the German social collective. They remain today competing residual responses to the legacies of the Third Reich.

In contrast, the literary works of Drewitz, Wolf, and Weil offer examples of overt, productive rehearsal of Germany's troubled past and efforts to break down the barriers to such rehearsal. Even though the characters in the different novels achieve mixed results in working through their own memories and traumas, the novels themselves offer a venue for their readership to work through the still-open questions raised about individual and collective responsibility during the Nazi era.

In sum, the nature of an event in terms of a perceived uniqueness and a long-term significant impact coupled with frequent and public rehearsal will establish it in collective memory. The age cohort upon which sociopolitical events have the greatest effect represents a further factor in the way an incident generates lasting and broadly shared collective memories. Research in the field of social psychology supports the thesis that individuals between the ages of twelve and twenty-five are most likely to retain memories of events with substantial social significance.[21] This is important here because all three of the writers at the center of this study were within this age group during the years of the Third Reich. Individuals in this age range are the ones most likely later to record an account of the events in "official" or academic historiography or in public efforts to commemorate the events in question. They are also — given the formative character of experiences during these years — more likely to reflect on these events later in biographical and autobiographical accounts and other media.[22]

This relates also to the time span that it usually takes for influential studies and projects about significant historical events to capture attention in the public sphere. Generally, this occurs in twenty- to thirty-year cycles.[23] Indeed, Wolf's *Kindheitsmuster* (1976), Drewitz's *Gestern war heute* (1978), and Weil's *Meine Schwester Antigone* (1980) — to name three of the works to be examined here — were all written and published between thirty and thirty-five years after the end of the war.

However, my intent is not to apply simplistic schema to explain the publication of literary works about the Third Reich from a social-psychological perspective. In fact, in the case of the events occurring between circa 1933 and 1945, one should caution against applying such age-cohort distinctions too readily. The experiences of the Second World War and the Holocaust changed so many people's lives forever that it seems unnecessarily limiting to suggest that it would be primarily people of a certain age group that would be affected by or address them. Instead, social pyschological explanations of how individual and collective historical memory intersect describe the processes of remembering and the transference of memories between individuals and the collectives of which they are part. While they do help to explain why these three writers addressed specific historical memories when they did, they also provide a way for us to understand what Drewitz, Wolf, and Weil are trying to depict in their literary representations of how individuals establish a place for themselves in a collective narrative of the past.

The concept of rehearsal — both covert and overt — proves useful in examining Drewitz, Wolf, and Weil's contributions to a discussion of the individual's self-positioning in history. However, the notion of rehearsal needs further specification here. In an article titled "How Individual Emotional Episodes Feed Collective Memory," Bernard Rimé and Véronique Christophe describe the ways individual emotional responses circulate within groups and contribute to the range of experience that collective bodies can articulate and recognize as familiar and legitimate. While Rimé and Christophe restrict their focus to the distribution of emotions within social groupings, a brief discussion of the basic forms of rehearsal might shed light on other aspects of group experiences as well. The term rehearsal is admittedly broad; it can include something as common as conversations about past events or recent occurrences that attempt at least partially to re-enact the incident, or it can take place on a broader stage in public commemorations, films, institutional narratives of the past, to list only a few. The reason the term is helpful is because it indicates an intent to understand and possibly reinterpret the past by retelling it within a new context.

Rimé and Christophe argue that individuals tend to share with others their emotional responses to events that occur in their lives. They refer to this mediation of emotions as the primary social sharing process.[24] It pertains especially to intense emotions, such as reactions that are extreme, unusual, or new to the individual in question. Individuals tend to share their emotional responses with others, and to do so repeatedly. In other words, they rehearse them in interpersonal settings.

If one person's rehearsal of her or his emotional response has sufficient emotional impact on the listener, that person too is likely to go out and retell the first person's story — also repeatedly. Rimé and Christophe designate this as the secondary social sharing process. Of such sharing they write, "the net result of this double process is that the script of a private emotional episode is spread across the social group, feeding the collective mind with new social knowledge about emotions."[25] Furthermore, the store of collective information that is gathered through such sharing makes possible the formation of *schemata*, which allow us to process emotional information through established emotional rubrics. Although Rimé and Christophe restrict their focus to emotions, the process of mediating individual experiences into collective consciousness must work through similar processes with many different kinds of information.

All three writers illustrate this process of rehearsal explicitly within their literary works — not the simple, mechanical recitation of a pre-existing script, but the emotional and intellectual replaying of individual and social memories that remain conflicted and painful. Wolf, for instance, shares with the reader of *Kindheitsmuster* the many personal conversations her characters have about key experiences. However, she also goes beyond such intimate exchanges by including public responses to the book. While the novel was still in process, she gave several public readings of it and she builds portions of the audience discussions that followed many of those readings into the narrative. In this way, Wolf manages to capture forms of both private and public rehearsal of Nazi-era experiences.

To reiterate, collective memory lies in a body of shared experiences. Physically and emotionally we experience events as individuals. We process these experiences, however, intersubjectively. We communicate the memories we have to others through different kinds of interpersonal interaction. Depending on the intensity or broader significance of the experiences being rehearsed, certain events are shared extensively within larger groups, leading to their place in collective memory. The interplay between individual experience and the social framework available to make such experiences intelligible creates a fluid exchange between individual and collective memory. Furthermore, new interpretive frameworks with new vocabulary and new perspectives, become available to us as we move in time away from the events in question.

Michael Kinney, writing from the perspective of an anthropologist, attempts to map out this interaction in his article "A Place for Memory: The Interface Between Individual and Collective History." Kinney looks at how changing political climates affect the way individuals *can* recall events from the past and to what extent they can even approach past events as personal memories.[26] He uses three examples: the Yir Yoront aboriginal people in Australia, the Indian Schools in Canada, and Holocaust survivor trauma. His purpose is to demonstrate how developments in the intellectual and social climate of a given society lead to changes in the "frameworks through which memory and history are structured, thereby affecting memory itself and the way in which the meaning of the past is construed" (422).

He argues further that memories are accessed through stories, or narrative rubrics, through which particular kinds of experiences are articulated. At the time the events happen, only certain narrative frameworks are available. As new experiences arise, new rubrics become necessary. These, in turn, affect the way that we look back on past experiences — both individual and collective. Kinney's thesis explains gaps left by the three above-cited criteria according to which events will become part of individual or collective memory. He notes, for instance, that the massacre of the Yir Yoront at the hands of white settlers in 1864 left no traces in their collective memory. Surely an event of that magnitude should represent a unique event with far-reaching consequences for the people in question. One could, of course, argue that the Yir Yoront group in question either did not feel the event to be one with far-reaching consequences, or it did not rehearse the event with enough frequency for it to leave long-lasting traces in its collective consciousness.

Kinney, too, gives a number of possible explanations for why the Yir Yoront would not have remembered this event collectively. One explanation has to do with the fact that the Yir Yoront generally do not remember past events that are not pertinent to their current condition. Another has to do with how the Yir Yoront community broke down into factions over differing views on collaboration with the white settlers. A number of the Yir Yoront felt cooperation with the white colonists to be mutually advantageous. Possibly, this meant there was no consensus among the Yir Yoront on which to base a cohesive collective narrative. Whatever the cause, those members of the Yir Yoront alive at the time of the massacre did not pass collective memories of the events on to subsequent generations.

Kinney allows us to expand on our original three criteria (an event's unique status, its far-reaching impact, and frequent rehearsal) with context-specific material. Socioeconomic developments in Australia from the end of the nineteenth to the end of the twentieth century effected a change in the economic status of the aboriginal peoples and a concomitant change in ethno-national consciousness. The interpretation of mutual benefit became less compelling among the aboriginal population, and a new narrative of oppression and resistance gained in currency. Kinney argues that the new interpretive framework of oppression and resistance has no direct or necessary connection to the events that it re-tells and "is very much an ideological reflection of the present situation. It is no less 'true' for all that" (426). Newer discursive frameworks lead to a reconfiguration of past events, yielding an interpretation more responsive to the demands of the present. This is not simply an example of people viewing the past in light of their present situation. It underscores that historical developments make possible both a new way to evaluate what has happened in the past as well as new ways of articulating what happened. New vocabulary becomes available that can shed an entirely different light on a series of past events. This does not change what occurred, but it can change how later groups relate the past to the present.

Kinney subjects public responses to the history of the Indian Schools in Canada to similar scrutiny. In the Indian School project, the Canadian government resettled native Canadians in government funded, largely church-run schools, the mandate of which was to civilize the native Canadians for white Canadian society. Based on scholarly studies, public confessions by school administrators, and government studies, a reinterpretation of the school project in the late twentieth-century recontextualized the experience of the students in the schools in very public ways. This then had an impact on the way individuals understood their memories of life in the Indian Schools. Kinney writes:

> Awareness of this history both derives from and helps to create the memories of individuals. It was, after all, individuals who — depending on perspective — enjoyed, survived, or simply endured

the schools. But what one is to make of the schools depends very much on awareness of their history and the wider social context. The schools have come to *mean* something very different in the 1980s and 90s than they could have done in the 1940s and 50s. (431)

Kinney suggests that the new interpretive framework actually creates the memories themselves. Rather than simply clearing away past misperceptions, the new frameworks create discursive spaces or contexts in which different stories of the past can be told. Drawing together former residents of the Indian Schools, the exchange of memories within new story parameters effects a redistribution of the way both the individuals who experienced the Indian Schools and society approaches them, which then affects both individual and collective memory on numerous levels. The cases of the Yir Yoront and the Indian Schools of Canada are examples of the complex ways in which individual memories and collective memories intersect with each other, with changes in one eventually having an impact on the other.

How does this relate to the literary rehearsal of German experiences from the Nazi era? As mentioned above, social psychology tells us that decades must pass before overwhelming collective experiences can be adequately processed. This owes at least partially to the fact that it takes time for people to develop the tools for such processing. Wolf's narrator in *Kindheitsmuster*, for instance, thematizes explicitly her efforts to find the narrative strategies that can best undertake the memory work of the novel. One could see her efforts in this direction as participating in an attempt to generate new interpretive frameworks for understanding the Nazi past. Thus, Wolf as a writer participates consciously in the collective creation of such new frameworks.

It would be convenient to end this section with the optimistic assertion that this chapter has clarified entirely the relationship between individual and collective memory. Of course, it has not. It has provided, however, a few tools with which to explore the ways we engage memory in an attempt to situate individuals within collective historical consciousness. Many scholars currently conceive of memory as driven by the needs of the present and as based on a complex interaction between individual and collective experience, with social schemata offering the tools for understanding personal experiences. Social psychologists also have very concrete ideas about the social processes involved in the sharing of individual and collective experience.

Up to this point, however, the chapter has dealt primarily with the intersection of individual and collective historical memory, the part of collective memory that Jan Assmann refers to as "communicative memory."[27] This intersection will remain the focal point for most of this book's analyses of the literary texts. However, some sense of the way individuals position themselves along a historical trajectory that goes back well beyond their own lives and the lives of their parents will also contribute important insights into the interpretation of the individual writers in this study. This is where scholars like Halbwachs and Nora have traditionally opposed memory to history — or, more concretely, historiography. Rather than insist on this opposition, I would prefer to see how individuals can engage more remote historical events.

This will be particularly important for the chapters on Ingeborg Drewitz and Grete Weil. Drewitz, for instance, mobilizes hundreds of years of history through an appropriation of family lore. Weil, on the other hand, explores longstanding intellectual and aesthetic traditions and her place in them. She does this by examining the connections of her own generation to the cultures of ancient Greece and Rome through German culture's appropriation of the history of those civilizations. Late in her life she also attempts to establish such a link for herself between her identity as a German Jew and Jewish history.

For the moment, this chapter will approach the issue more theoretically. Specifically, the discussion now returns to the work of Maurice Halbwachs and his efforts to distinguish between the realm of memory and the tasks of historiography. It also revisits Pierre Nora and his insistence on history's usurpation of memory. Finally, a few examples of how these theoretical approaches can provide insight into representative texts by Drewitz, Wolf, and Weil draw us back into the literary-historical context of this book.

## On the Differences between Memory and History

Halbwachs believed that the concept of memory signified something very different and distinct from history. Although he acknowledged two different kinds of history, namely written and living, generally he felt that history begins its study of the past at the point where social memory begins to weaken. He writes:

> General history starts only when tradition ends and the social memory is fading or breaking up. So long as a remembrance continues to exist, it is useless to set it down in writing or otherwise fix it in memory. Likewise the need to write the history of a period, a society, or even a person is only aroused when the subject is already too distant in the past to allow for the testimony of those who preserve some remembrance of it. (78–79)

Clearly, this kind of strict chronological separation of history as an activity and memory is no longer serviceable. While having witnesses available creates its own difficulties for historians working on events from the recent past, this has not prevented them from tackling any number of topics for which there are still vibrant personal and collective memories.

Halbwachs also insists that history is an objective discipline that provides the world with a unitary and truthful account of events distant from living human beings. While he insists that collective memory is plural and highly subjective, history is a self-conscious, analytical, and self-reflective activity, which generates — if done well — a single delineation of historical developments. Not a "plaything of the emotions" for Halbwachs, history takes abstract reason as its foundational principle and offers empirical evidence for its claims.[28] But the twentieth century did irreparable harm to such an understanding of history. Historians can no longer claim immediate access to "what really happened." Additionally, the boundaries between what is past and what is present have become blurry. It has been repeatedly called into question how far back collective memory reaches and how objective history really is. In fact, Gerdien Jonker claims that Halbwachs's work on collective memory — which Halbwachs himself saw as being so distinct from history — has, in fact, had a tremendous impact on the study of history since his work found broad reception in the 1970s.[29] In this sense, Halbwachs's understanding of the distinction between memory and history gives us an opportunity both to problematize such a rigid separation and approach a more differentiated relationship between the two.

We find another, yet equally problematic view of the distinction between history and memory in Pierre Nora's introduction to *Realms of Memory*. For Nora, memory was, as we have seen, an unconscious, unreflected function of society. It tied individuals to their community's past and imbued the present with mythological significance. As human beings lived through the processes of modernization and increasingly left the countryside to seek opportunities in developing urban areas, they came to sever their ties to the land and to a simpler existence that had such tight bonds to the past. In Nora's view this process culminated in the first half of the twentieth century. In abandoning their landed roots (at least in France),[30] human beings lost the immediate connection with the past, and are now seeking to replace memory with history, which Nora defines as "the reconstruction, always problematic and incomplete, of what is no longer" (3).

Nora, too, sees history as reliant on critical analysis and emotional distance. Whereas memory was both collective and individual, plural and yet specific, history is supposed to be devoid of emotional attachment. As a discipline, he argues, history has entered a new phase, which he calls the "historiographic age," a stage that represents to him the final separation of history from memory (4). We have residues of memory that we instantiate in what Nora terms "lieux de mémoire" (sites of memory). Rather than spontaneous manifestations of memory practice, such places of memory serve as placeholders for collective memory. They protect us from what Nora sees as history's inexorable tendency to erase completely any vestiges of true communal memory. History in its present state "seize[s] upon memories in order to distort and transform them, to mold them or turn them to stone" (7). Yet the *lieux de mémoire* do not contain truly vibrant memories: they are merely vestiges of memory.

Indeed, because we fear being completely cut off from the past, we have started collecting what we consider to be evidence of history indiscriminately, to act in a sense as the historians of our own lives. Although Nora maintains that we look to history now not as a mirror for our current selves, but rather as a benchmark for what we no longer are, we nonetheless save and archive anything that might have even minor significance, hoping to secure for ourselves a place in a future collective past. Individuals preserve multiple grade reports for their children, annual pictures of all sorts, locks of hair, baby outfits, etc. Societies, too, are bent on preserving memories, assuming or hoping that they will provide a link between our current and our future selves. A good example of this would be the Story Corps project, samples of which are frequently aired on National Public Radio. The project encourages individuals to stop by the project's touring recording booths to elicit memories that they believe will be collectively significant.[31] Nora argues that the inaccessibility of the past for us has caused a growing nostalgia for things past: "The whole dynamic of our relation to the past is shaped by the subtle interplay between the inaccessible and the nonexistent" (11–12). Because we no longer have direct access to what was significant from the past, we collect everything, hoping to prevent a loss of the present in the future (8).

Nora at times seems dismissive of ordinary people who believe their lives to be historically significant. While historical records traditionally came from society's dominant institutions (for example, royal families, the church, and the state), today both the sources of archival material as well as the material itself have expanded beyond our ability to control the input and process the information. Nora notes with disdain how "everyone has gotten into the act" (10). He sees the efforts to record oral testimonies as a "deliberate and calculated compilation of vanished memory" (10). And yet, other interpretations of what Nora calls the "terroristic effect of historicized memory" are possible, and Nora is well aware of this.

For instance, until the second half of the twentieth century, history rarely considered the role of women and minority population groups in historical developments. Once content to let historians tell them what was or was not historically significant, women and minorities of various cultures have now set out to find where they were or are in history.[32] They have been intent not only to distinguish themselves from what they found in traditional representations of the past, but also to find both the continuities with those traditional representations and the changes that have occurred in their social roles in today's societies. Since professional historians generally did not consider such lives to be historically meaningful, the quest for clues to the past took new paths, centered on new objects. This has resulted at least partially in the changes within the discipline of history that Nora's massive collection of studies in *lieux de mémoire* examines so diligently. And, in fact, Nora locates the many-volumed *Realms of Memory* at the intersection of a change in historiography and the "end of a tradition of memory" (6). Although his work as a historian offers alternative approaches to collective memory, his assessment of the nature of memory and history fails to explain satisfactorily the many ways in which individuals invest parts of their lives with memory and historical significance or locate themselves within broader historical structures.

The problem in productively engaging Nora's theories of memory and history in our context is his definition of the term memory. While it is intriguing to conceive of memory as a social function embedded in social institutions that provide a collective and unreflected link to a more traditional past, using the term this way narrows it unnecessarily. On an everyday level, we as individuals have numerous memories: I know what I did yesterday because of memory;[33] I have appropriated family memories of my grandmother's childhood on a farm in northwestern Iowa; and, similarly, I can participate in a collective memory that both draws out the broader cultural significance of historical events (such as the Reformation, the American struggle for independence, and the American Civil War) that pre-date me as an individual by centuries and invest them with personal significance. The objection that these are not memories, but rather historical data is not compelling. They can legitimately be considered part of our collective memory because, in our various reconstructions of them, they still have an impact on our collective and also personal identities. This may be at least partially what Nora thinks his *lieux de mémoire* do, but distinguishing them from memory itself (as he defines it) negates in my opinion two very important things: 1) the mutability of memory over and through history; and 2) the creative reconfiguration and reengagement of memory. A statement like, "memory is constantly on our lips because it no longer exists" has a great deal of rhetorical force, yet using "memory" in this very restricted sense closes off options of looking at it in new, potentially more inclusive ways. Rather than thinking of memory as the passage of traditional lifestyles from one generation to the next, it will be more helpful to see memory as an engagement with the past on the part of both individuals and groups.

While I reject Nora's very specific definition of memory, this does not mean that his other arguments on the subject are not compelling. His contention that we are unsure of what is worth remembering is persuasive, that in the age of information overflow we seem to be floundering in an at-times-threatening sea of material potentially worthy of preservation for both collective and private purposes. However, we can return to Huyssen's hope that our renewed interest in memory is a sign that we are actively working on stemming the explosion of information and preserving private and public spaces for "acts of memory."[34] The processes of remembering respond to the demands of the present. Memory is not gone; it is only in the throes of yet another social reconfiguration.

Since this chapter, along with the next one on feminist literary theory, is part of a two-part theoretical foundation for the literary analyses that follow, my intention so far has been to explore discussions of memory to establish a common framework for the analyses of the three writers' works. The chapters on the individual writers explore further the approaches to and definitions of memory that are operative in the work of Ingeborg Drewitz, Christa Wolf, and Grete Weil. It will nonetheless be helpful to preview briefly at this point some of the ways the preceding discussion of memory is productive for our case studies.

## Ingeborg Drewitz and the Family "Archive"

Early on in Drewitz's *Gestern war heute* the main character's, Gabriele's, great-grandmother pulls her aside when she is around six years old to tell her about her great-uncle Paul's life. She shows Gabriele pictures of her mother and her uncle and tells her of the various places he lived during his young adult years: Paris, London, and St. Petersburg. The narrator relates the child's fear of her ancient great-grandmother, the unpleasant smells that she associated with the woman's aging body, the traces of age on her skin, and the sense of revulsion that Gabriele felt toward her. In this physically and mentally stressful setting, Gabriele hears for the first time the story of her great-uncle Paul and his compassion for the poor and suffering of St. Petersburg. The great-grandmother recounts to her how Paul himself related the events of January 1905:

> Von einem Januarsonntag und einem Zug von Tausenden, die ihre Bitten vorzutragen gekommen waren, und die Soldaten des Zaren schossen in die Menge auf dem weiten Platz. Paul war dabei. Neben ihm brach eine Frau zusammen. Er hat nicht weiterreden können, als er davon erzählt hat, hat dagesessen, geatmet, schwer geatmet. Wie sie die Menschen verachten können, wenn sie oben sind — ich verstehe nicht! Ja, das war so ein Satz, den er immer wieder gesagt hat. (57)

> [Of a Sunday in January and a march of thousands who had come to present their pleas, and the soldiers of the tsar shot into the crowds on the broad square. Paul was there. Next to him a woman collapsed. He couldn't continue speaking any longer after he told of it, he sat there, breathed, breathed heavily. How they can hate people

so, when they are on top — I don't understand it! Yes, that was a sentence that he said again and again.]

Gabriele's great-grandmother tells her how much she resembles her great uncle in appearance and personality, thus forging a link between the main character and her long-deceased relative. Gabriele never met him; he died young from tuberculosis. The events in St. Petersburg have blurred in the aftermath of much more far-reaching developments in twentieth-century history, and yet they assume significance in Gabriele's memory as part of a family history and as part of the political changes affecting all of Europe in the first decades of the twentieth century. Gabriele "rehearses" the memories of her great-uncle as passed down to her by her great-grandmother frequently throughout the novel; he becomes something of a *leitmotiv* in her life.

Eventually Gabriele passes the memory on to her daughter, Renate. Drewitz emplots this process in a scene in which Gabriele, her daughter, and Gabriele's sister Ulrike sift through the possessions of their recently deceased father. Ulrike selects a few, possibly valuable, porcelain items to keep for herself. Renate chooses a letter Paul had written from St. Petersburg. Gabriele focuses instead on the memories themselves and the stories attached to these physical items. As each woman settles her attention on different things, the narrative shows how each of us carries within us a conscious and an unconscious selection of the history that came before us (305–7). Indeed, not only do we generate personal connections to physical objects from a past that pre-dates us, but that history also to a certain extent prefigures the different ways in which we do this. Halbwachs's ideas that individual memories are viewpoints on collective memory and that our more immediate ancestors pass on to us both cultural structures and political philosophies provide an interpretive perspective for both the function of the Paul character and the scenes in which family members literally handle and select for themselves historical material.

How people appropriate aspects of history for their own personal uses reflects more than just the immediate historical context in which they do so, since each individual approaches and perceives the same historical era differently. The differences between Gabriele's approach to her father's estate and her sister Ulrike's approach to it, as well as the variations of meaning that the political activism of Gabriele's great-uncle assumes for Gabriele and her daughter Renate make this clear. While Gabriele and Ulrike — as sisters — share the same family history, they read its significance differently, leading Ulrike to look for items of monetary value and Gabriele to use the opportunity to revisit the family's past.

Gabriele and her daughter, on the other hand, share similar ethical and political beliefs, but the historical differences between their respective generations guide them to attach changing values to objects both of them treasure for similar reasons. Renate does not have the stories of Paul as her mother always has, or the sense that she has a special personal connection to this particular relative.[35] Instead, as an individual active in the protest culture of the late sixties and early seventies, she responds to the activism of her great-great-uncle, thus affirming a family tradition of social engagement for the politically oppressed. Renate may never have the facts of her distant relative's life readily accessible for recall, but she has incorporated aspects of his history into her own personal historical memory.

Following Nora, one could read this scene as illustrating an attempt to preserve or archive material that may be inessential, lest something important be lost. On the other hand, Renate's selection of her great uncle's letter represents a conscious individual choice of what to preserve from the past — not for an official or public archive, but as a personal memory link to the past. The letter may not be historically significant, but Renate's choice invests the item with personal meaning and allows her to generate a connection to an already-distant moment of history.

## Christa Wolf, Social Structures, and Historical Memory

Halbwachs's argument that we have access to collective memories of past times indirectly through the behavior and ideology of our parents, grandparents, and other close personal contacts also echoes Wolf's methodology in *Kindheitsmuster*. Wolf explores precisely such conduits, seeking to find in the behavior of the adults around Nelly, the main character, clues to the relative passivity of her environment to the Nazis' encroachment on human rights and freedoms. The text, for instance, highlights both commonplaces about German culture (its emphasis on obedience) and more subtle ways that the society in which her parents were socialized molded their behaviors. Twice in the first chapter, the narrator tells us that Nelly learned through her parents and other adults around her that she was expected to follow orders and that — even more significantly — she learned to associate obedience with parental love and social acceptance (13, 24).

Perhaps even more consequential is how social institutions like the family, schools, and churches instrumentalize and channel a specific notion of reason to force compliance with social norms. For instance, in chapter 5 Nelly is gradually disciplined into accepting the rules of German capitalization, despite the fact that she herself does not see the logic or reason behind the rules as her teacher explains them. Rather than engage the child through other explanations or through an acknowledgment of her objections to the teacher's dictates, Nelly's parents insist that she submit to reason. At the outset of the chapter, the narrator muses, "Die Schicksale der Vernunft — Vernunft als Übereinstimmung — über die Jahrzehnte hin. Vernunft als Dämpfer: Ein Regelungssystem, das, einmal eingebaut, hartnäckig darauf besteht, das Signal für 'Glück' nur im Zustand vernünftiger Übereinstimmung aufleuchten zu lassen" (123; "What has happened to reason throughout the decades, reason as grounds for approval. Reason as the damper. A regulating mechanism which, once installed, stubbornly insists on flashing the 'happiness' signal only under certain reasonable conditions": 91). Nelly demonstrates her successful compliance with the discipline of the community and comes into her own as an individual, a student, a speaker of German and a member of the community when she acquiesces to dictates of logic as determined by the community's institutions: "Einsicht haben und Vernunft haben. Auch: zu sich kommen" (124; "Understanding and listening to reason. Thus: to come to one's senses": 92).

Michael Kinney tells us that residents of the Canadian Indian Schools were not able to recognize as repressive the methods of socialization in the schools until social discourse on race provided a different interpretive framework for such a discussion. In a similar fashion, societies premised on the primacy of reason, which took hold in the wake of the European Enlightenment, were at least partially able after the extent of the Third Reich's horrors became known to see the destructive power wielded through an overly restrictive and normative concept of reason. Whether one looks at changes in scholarly discourse, such as represented by Adorno and Horkheimer's ground-breaking work *The Dialectic of Enlightenment*, or at systemic political changes (the emergence of a federalist democracy in West Germany, or the anti-fascist educational efforts of the early GDR), one can see various fissures in the predominance of a discourse based on individual submission to "logic" or "reason" as abstract, given qualities. The massive social and political upheavals in the first half of the twentieth century revealed the context-bound quality of terms like "logic" or "reason" and made it possible to recognize restrictive and socially homogenizing uses of the terms in very specific configurations of political and social power. Learning to apply such insights to one's own life requires a certain amount of critical, self-reflective distance, which we generally do not achieve until several years, if not decades, have passed. This is a process that *Kindheitsmuster* illustrates well. The ideological differences between the fascist past and the competing systems of Western capitalist democracies and Eastern socialist governments and the buffer zone created by the intervening thirty years make it possible for Wolf's narrator to revisit her childhood with a view to the demands she faces in the narrative present of *Kindheitsmuster*.

## Grete Weil's Attempts to (Re)inscribe Herself into Shared Pasts

Christa Wolf's multiply refracted autobiographical self explores issues of her own generation's history. Grete Weil does this too in *Der Brautpreis*, but also attempts to construct or restore ties to a very distant past — the beginnings of Jewish national history during the reign of King David. It is a past to which her narrator, also named Grete, does not feel any clear connection. Similarly, Weil's *Meine Schwester Antigone* seeks to regenerate a connection between the writer's narrative stand-in and the culture of classical antiquity, which, beginning in the eighteenth century, became part of the cultural heritage and collective memory of the educated German bourgeoisie in which Weil's assimilated family was firmly situated.

Weil consciously tries to weave a common fabric from the autobiographical reflections of Grete and Michal, David's first wife, and from her experiments with the Sophoclean heroine Antigone. Most assuredly, it is a loosely woven fabric, since Weil narrates both Michal's and Antigone's lives based on very little textual evidence.

As mentioned above, memory engages the past creatively in order to meet the demands of the present. Both Drewitz and Wolf can draw from a continuum of personal (familial) and collective (German/central European) memories in their efforts to understand the individual's place in history and to articulate new moral geographies. While they may question their own roles in that collective history, they don't doubt that they are a part of it. Weil as a German Jew, on the other hand, was literally and metaphorically exiled from that common tradition. At an earlier point in this chapter, I concluded that collective memory lies in a body of shared experiences. People experience events individually, but process them through social structures and discursive frameworks that social groups construct collectively. Weil's dislocation from the society in which she learned to understand and to contextualize experience leads her to complex attempts to re-embed her experiences in collective experience, reconnect to the cultural spaces from which she was exiled, and forge new connections to others.

In *Der Brautpreis*, she imaginatively renders the founding of Jerusalem as the center of the Jewish nation and writes herself into Jewish history. No doubt neither scholars of Jewish history nor many Israelis would accept her biblical narrative as adequate. However, it does respond quite directly to the conundrum Weil's Grete faces in coming to terms with her identity as a secular German Jew. She perceives a need to forge a connection to a collective Jewish past and a community to which she has never really felt any personal bond, but to which their common history of suffering draws her.

In *Meine Schwester Antigone*, on the other hand, Weil experiments with the character of the Greek princess to meet her narrative needs. Those needs were multiple, but certainly included using her place within the long cultural tradition of Germans appropriating Greek myth to think through the moral dilemmas before which her experiences as a Holocaust survivor placed her. Weil's Antigone steps in and out of her mythological narrative frame to test certain moral precepts and to reflect on her narrator's life choices. Weil's narrator cannot disconnect herself entirely from this cultural heritage — any more than the Nazis were able to do this to her, but she comes to reject what her classical model represents for her. Weil's work deals with many of the same issues as do Drewitz's and Wolf's, but because of her experiences as a victim of the Holocaust, she has a distinctly different approach to collective memory. The chapter on Weil explores how she engages with what she sees as two distinct cultural traditions and her place within them.

## Conclusion

Thinking about memory as an act in which both individuals and communities engage in order to fulfill the demands they see in the present brings us back to the question of why we remember. If memory represents (among other things) a response to current problems that we face, then what we hope to get out of memory is also an array of possible behavioral choices that could help us decide how to act. Generally speaking, the process of thinking through our options for action belongs within the realm of ethics. However, what we *ought to* do also depends on what we *can* do. That is to say, our decisions to act in one way or another are limited or enhanced by the social contexts in which we live.

All three of the writers at the heart of this study emphasize in their work the lives of women. Their interest in portraying women's lives starts with the ways society trains young girls to be women, to fulfill society's expectations of the way women are supposed to be. They follow their characters through adolescence and the discovery of sexual desires, underscoring the ways in which women are often torn between trying to explore those desires and retaining a sense of independence from their sexual partners. Wolf, Drewitz, and Weil also examine the issues of aging in cultures driven by youth and innovation. Thus, they look at all of the stages of human life from the perspective of women and girls.

They also do not include characters who live largely independent, unencumbered lives. Even Weil's aging narrators, who do live alone, do so mostly because they have outlived their families. The narrator of *Meine Schwester Antigone* goes so far as to beg her friends and acquaintances to take from her a bit of her independence, her freedom. Living as if one were free of all others, free of the need to react, respond, or reach out to others terrifies her. Of course, it is also an impossible fiction: human beings seldom find themselves in situations where no others constrain their choices. How the web of relationships in which we all live impacts our life choices constitutes one of the common and primary themes of all three writers under examination in this book.

This concern and others draw them into ongoing discussions among feminists. Although these writers might not be willing to call themselves feminists explicitly, their literary efforts presage, follow, and comment upon a whole spectrum of issues of direct concern for feminists in the last half of the twentieth century and the beginning of the twenty-first. For this reason, the next chapter looks at how feminist theory can help us to analyze how the literary characters of these three writers approach the issue of self in their communities as well as personal and collective responsibility. Specifically, chapter 2 looks at developments within the area of feminist ethics that address explicitly feminist contributions to a discussion of ethical choices.

## Notes

[1] Agnes Heller describes the historical present as follows: "Present history encompasses all events and happenings whose consequences are alternative in character, and also events which can threaten us or fill us with hope; events to which we can relate both practically and pragmatically. Historical present is the cultural structure that we are 'inside.'" Agnes Heller, *A Theory of History* (London: Routledge, 1982), 44. Heller also gives us a very good description of how we as individuals actually construe our own history: "But the statement that we cannot know our future and cannot change our past has only relative validity. Every recollection of what is bygone is an interpretation: we reconstruct our past. What we reconstruct, how we reconstruct it, what kind of sense we attribute to the reconstructed, all this changes with our experiences, with our interest, with the measure of sincerity and insincerity. In brief, we change our past via selective interpretation" (38).

[2] See e.g., Merriam Webster's Online Dictionary: http://www.merriam-webster.com/dictionary/memory (accessed September 2009).

[3] Christa Wolf, *Kindheitsmuster* (Berlin and Weimar: Aufbau Verlag, 1976). Subsequent citations are by chapter and page number in parentheses. English translations are from *Patterns of Childhood*, trans. Ursule Molinaro and Hedwig Rappolt (New York: Farrar, Straus, and Giroux, 1976). When Wolf's translators chose to leave certain passages out, the note will indicate that the translation is my own.

[4] Andreas Huyssen, *Twilight Memories: Marking Time in a Culture of Amnesia* (New York: Routledge, 1995), 7.

[5] Huyssen, *Twilight Memories*, 9.

[6] Pierre Nora, ed., *Realms of Memory: Rethinking the French Past*, vol. 1, trans. Arthur Goldhammer (New York: Columbia UP, 1996). Citations of this work will be followed by page number in parentheses.

[7] See, respectively, Judith Zur, *Memories: Mayan War Widows in Guatemala* (Boulder, CO: Westview Press, 2001); Kathleen Brogan, *Cultural Haunting: Ghosts and Ethnicity in Recent American Literature* (Virginia: U of Virginia P,

1998); and James Young, *At Memory's Edge. After-images of the Holocaust in Contemporary Art and Architecture* (New Haven: Yale UP, 2000).

[8] See Gerdien Jonker, *The Topography of Remembrance: The Dead, Tradition and Collective Memory in Mesopotamia* (Leiden: E. J. Brill, 1995), 6. Jonker writes: "The cognitive process makes 'an interest in the past' a compelling necessity, a *conditio sine qua non* for attaining perception in the present. . . . Only through the association of a particular 'signal' with an 'earlier signal' is interpretation possible."

[9] Raphael Samuel, *Theatres of Memory*, vol. 1: *Past and Present in Contemporary Culture* (London: Verso, 1994), x.

[10] For such a history, see Frances Yates, *The Art of Memory* (Harmondsworth: Penguin, 1978). See also Susannah Radstone, ed., *Memory and Methodology* (Oxford: Berg, 2000), 3.

[11] Halbwachs, a French Jew and active socialist, was captured by the Nazis in Paris after the invasion and deported to Buchenwald, where he died in 1945.

[12] Maurice Halbwachs, *The Collective Memory*, trans. Francis J. Ditter, Jr. and Vida Yazdi Ditter (New York: Harper Colophon Books, 1980), 34. All further citations of this work will be by page number in parentheses.

[13] Dario Paez, Nekane Basabe, and Jose Luis Gonzales, "Social Processes and Collective Memory: A Cross-Cultural Approach to Remembering Political Events," in *Collective Memory of Political Events: Social Psychological Perspectives*, ed. James Pennebaker, Dario Paez, and Bernard Rimé (Mahwah, NJ: Lawrence Erlbaum Associates Publishers, 1997), 152–53.

[14] James Pennebaker, Dario Paez, and Bernard Rimé, eds., *Collective Memory of Political Events: Social Psychological Perspectives*.

[15] See the following contributions to *Collective Memory of Political Events*: Pennebaker, "Introduction," *Collective Memory of Political Events*, x; James Pennebaker and Betsy Banasik, "On the Creation and Maintenance of Collective Memories: History as Social Psychology," 4–5; and George Gaskell and Daniel Wright, "Group Differences in Memory for a Political Event," 178.

[16] Pennebaker and Banasik, "Creation and Maintenance of Collective Memories," 7–11.

[17] See for instance, Pennebaker and Banasik, "Creation and Maintenance of Collective Memories," 10–11.

[18] J. Laplanche and J.-B. Pontalis, *The Language of Psycho-Analysis* (1967; New York: Norton, 1973), 4.

[19] Laplanche and Pontalis, *Language of Psycho-Analysis*, 488.

[20] See here Paez, Basabe, and Gonzales, "Social Processes and Collective Memory: A Cross-Cultural Approach to Remembering Political Events," 159, 162.

[21] For supporters of this thesis, see the following contributions to *Collective Memory of Political Events*: Pennebaker and Baskin, "Creation and Maintenance of Collective Memories," 14–16; Martin Conway, "The Inventory of Experience: Memory and Identity" 33–35; and Howard Schuman, Robert Belli, and Katherine Bischoping, "The Generational Basis of Historical Knowledge," 71–72. George Gaskell and Daniel Wright, the authors of "Group Differences in Memory for a Political

Event," could not find enough supporting evidence for the thesis. See Gaskell and Wright 187. They did not, however, seem in their own study to have controlled adequately for the second of our initial criteria for events to find a lasting space in memory, namely a long-lasting impact on the individuals or groups in question. Schuman, Belli, and Bischoping support the assertion that individuals between the ages of twelve and twenty-five are most likely to remember an event of tremendous personal or social significance, but they caution against applying this guideline too mechanistically (74). They suggest that "the generational hypothesis about knowledge must be converted from one based entirely on assumptions about the life cycle to one that incorporates the Weberian principle . . . that subjective meaning is crucial to the connection between events and their effects. It is not just an automatic registering of events that occur during impressionable years, but the way events connect with the lives of real people" (75). Conway also points out that the age factor is culturally variable, depending on the age a given culture sees as the transition phase from childhood/adolescence to adulthood (33).

[22] Pennebaker and Banasik, "Creation and Maintenance of Collective Memories," 15–16.

[23] Pennebaker and Banasik, "Creation and Maintenance of Collective Memories," 17.

[24] Bernard Rimé and Véronique Christophe, "How Individual Emotional Episodes Feed Collective Memory," in Pennebaker, Paez, and Rimé, eds., *Collective Memory of Political Events*, 144.

[25] Rimé and Christophe, "How Individual Emotional Episodes Feed Collective Memory," 133.

[26] Michael Kinney, "A Place for Memory: The Interface between Individual and Collective History," *Comparative Studies in Society and History* 41.3 (July 1999): 420–37.

[27] See e.g., Jan Assmann, "Collective Memory and Cultural Identity," trans. John Czaplicka, *New German Critique* 65 (Spring/Summer 1995): 126–33.

[28] See Raphael Samuel's description of Halbwachs's views on history. Samuel, *Theatres of Memory*, ix.

[29] Jonker, *Topography of Remembrance*, 23.

[30] Nora, as mentioned earlier in the chapter, speaks specifically about historical developments in France, yet indicates that much of the theoretical foundation in his work applies to other Western industrialized nations as well.

[31] See: http://www.npr.org/templates/story/story.php?storyId=4516989 (accessed September 2009).

[32] See Nora's comments about the impact minorities and women have had on historiography in the preface to the English edition, xxii.

[33] I understand that this particular example would, in French, more likely be described by the term "souvenir" rather than "mémoire," but it is just one possible counterexample to Nora's description of memory.

[34] I am borrowing this term from the title of Mieke Bal, Jonathan Crewe, and Leo Spitzer's edited volume, *Acts of Memory* (Dartmouth: Dartmouth College, 1999).

[35] At least the book does not give us this information.

## 2: Feminism, the Self, and Community

In Ingeborg Drewitz's *Gestern war heute,* Gabriele, the main character, tells a male friend that women greet the world with their arms wide open. She contrasts this explicitly with the way men approach life: "Vielleicht kann sich ein Mann nicht vorstellen, daß die Frau immer mit sorgend ausgebreiteten Armen lebt" (297: Perhaps a man cannot imagine that a woman always lives with her arms open to care). The primary difference Gabriele sees between women and men seems to lie in the word "sorgend." That is to say, men may set out to greet the world with open arms, but women's open arms are there to embrace those in need of care, whereas men's arms are open to new opportunities for self-realization.

In a gesture common to all of the female characters treated in this study, Gabriele's statement emphasizes her role as caring for others and de-emphasizes the importance of fulfilling her own wishes. All of the women characters have varying levels of difficulty using the pronoun "I" to refer to a self separate from others, distinct from the demands and desires of other individuals. From Christa Wolf's now-famous phrase in *Nachdenken über Christa T*: "Die Schwierigkeiten, 'ich' zu sagen" (173: The difficulties of saying "I.") to Drewitz's repeated explorations of the ramifications that an insistence on saying "I" can have, their readers find again and again an acknowledgement of how individual lives are caught up in a web of relationships. These relationships go beyond mutual friendship, intellectual respect, or the realization that as individuals we do not live on this planet alone. In addition to all of these possibilities, Wolf, Drewitz, and Weil's characters come to recognize not only that we are parts of interconnecting relationships, but also that these relationships entail differing and sometimes competing levels of interdependence and responsibility. How these differing levels of interdependence affect the spectrum of choices available to us as agents in any number of historical dramas constitutes a central question posed by all the works this book analyzes.

The still-emergent field of feminist ethics has always insisted on the relational character of human existence and has, in this vein, worked to develop both a critique of philosophical traditions that posit the autonomous individual as *the* moral subject and a theory of morality that centers on individual behavior within a variety of interpersonal relationships. Before we go on to discuss those feminist approaches to morality that address the same concerns as Drewitz, Weil, and Wolf, we must first lay out what feminist ethicists have challenged in the philosophical traditions of Euro-American moral philosophy and what they consider to be the implications of certain central tenets of such moral philosophy. From there, the chapter also looks at the early stages of feminist moral theory and how the field has developed since those efforts. The focus will then shift to explore the work of specific feminist ethicists who broach ethical issues similar to those Drewitz, Wolf, and Weil raise in the texts analyzed in the remaining chapters.

## Feminist Critiques of Euro-American Ethics

Feminist ethicists have critiqued many aspects of traditional Euro-American moral theory — particularly Kantian, neo-Kantian, utilitarian, and contractarian approaches,[1] but perhaps the most significant — in the sense that other points of their criticism relate back to it as well — is the traditional emphasis on the autonomous individual as the ethical subject. As Virginia Held succinctly puts it:

> Western liberal democratic thought has been built on the concept of the individual seen as a theoretically isolable entity. This entity can assert interests, claim rights, and enter into contractual relations with other entities, but is not seen as related to others in inextricable or intrinsic ways. He is assumed to be motivated primarily by a desire to pursue his own interests, though he can recognize the need to agree to contractual restraints on the ways others may pursue their interests.[2]

Although, as Held formulates it, the subject in traditional moral theory (conceived of as male) can enter into relationships of dependence, interdependence, or subordination, he can also choose not to do so. His motivation for doing so would be self-interest. Focusing on this kind of moral agent is, however, possible only if one excludes from the purview of moral theory all relationships among individuals that do not conform to the model, including almost all relations within the private sphere, not to mention any number of relationships that exceed the level of individual responsibility, but include individuals as members of a community.

Feminist ethical theory has seen the autonomous individual of traditional moral theory as a prerequisite for the establishment of universal codes and norms for ethical behavior that have been extracted from specific sociopolitical contexts and then generalized. These generalizations obscure in turn the embeddedness of such universal codes within very specific social formations; they deny their initial basis in certain kinds of human interaction and certain forms of society. This last issue will reappear later in the chapter. At this point, however, one example of the kind of ethical theory that feminist ethicists criticize would be helpful.[3]

Immanuel Kant's categorical imperative provides one of the most influential instances of such universalist principles. In its abbreviated form, Kant argues that one should decide if an action is moral or not based on whether the action under consideration could be made into a universal law. Kant tests this principle in *The Foundations of the Metaphysics of Morals* with four cases: the contemplation of suicide; making intentionally false promises; the choice not to develop one's natural talents; and a possible obligation to help less fortunate members of society.[4] In each case, Kant suggests that we must make the decision by considering whether the act can be consistently thought and willed when turned into a universal law. Kant's moral agent, the autonomous individual governed solely by what Kant deems to be the universal dictates of reason (as opposed to an individual's wants, needs, or instincts), should always be able to make the morally right choice independent of cultural context, possibly competing responsibilities, and actual outcomes of the action. While there are, of course, differences between Kantian ethics and later models of ethics, John Stuart Mill's utilitarianism and John Rawls' theory of justice also purport to offer objective principles that can be applied by any rational agent without recourse to our concrete embeddedness in any specific context.[5]

As the above citation from Held's *Feminist Morality* indicates, many Euro-American moral theories are based on a model of self-interest, non-interference,[6] and the voluntary and un-coerced contract between individuals. Feminist ethicists would argue that women, children, the elderly, the infirm, and the economically disadvantaged are all virtually absent from the picture painted here of representative social interaction. Taken together, surely these groups constitute the majority of human beings on earth, and yet they find no space as *agents* in the moral theories feminists have been contesting. In short, feminists argue that traditional moral philosophy sets up as the sole legitimate agent of moral behavior the autonomous individual, whose behavior is guided by a set of abstract universal codes. These codes do not account for variations in context and competencies, not to mention the physical embodiment of the human subject, and therewith its physical limits and vulnerabilities. The female characters in Drewitz's, Wolf's, and Weil's works — embedded as they are in relationships of varying dependencies — would not even register as moral subjects in such ethical frameworks, or would appear at best to be inferior moral agents. Indeed women in traditional moral theory as far back as Aristotle have been portrayed as incapable of becoming fully functioning moral subjects.

Of course, this is not an exhaustive representation of feminist challenges to traditional Euro-American moral theories, but it does give us several of the salient points to which feminist ethicists have objected and which all three novelists in this study reject. In addition to uncovering the tacit assumptions of such traditional moral philosophy, feminists have also been concerned to point out the ramifications of such assumptions. They underscore consistently that in the process of converting the experiences and social positioning of one specific class of individuals into universal moral codes, innumerable individuals who cannot meet such expectations — for any number of reasons — are marginalized, excluded, overlooked, or condemned as morally deficient.[7]

A leading voice in the development of feminist ethics, Margaret Urban Walker argues that much of traditional moral philosophy is premised on a model of human existence that sees the individual's life as a self-driven project, working toward some ultimate goal.[8] At some point individuals will be held to an accounting, asking them to review whether they stayed true to the goals set. Walker contends that a model of moral accountability founded in such a "whole" life project is bound to leave too many individuals with a sense of failure because their lives do not conform to that of the supposedly paradigmatic moral agent, who is free to choose which responsibilities and obligations he enters into (136–37). Selma Sevenhuijsen, another prominent feminist ethicist, makes a similar case when she suggests that setting the autonomous individual up as the moral agent implies that anyone who is dependent (children, the elderly, the infirm) is morally deviant or — at a minimum — morally deficient. Furthermore, when people become care providers, they too can no longer be considered "autonomous" moral agents.[9]

Needless to say, there is much more to this argument in both Walker's and Sevenhuijsen's work. However, fundamental to both is the acknowledgment of how our relationships with others affect our own lives in ways that are often beyond our control. The impact of relationships that we have with others is not something incidental to who we are as individuals, but rather of central importance to our identities. Such relationships can be entered into voluntarily (e.g., voluntary parenthood), or involuntarily as the result of coercion or accident (e.g., parenthood as a result of rape, or legal decisions of responsibility in case of accidents or illness). Feminist ethicists ask us to examine closely and critically the ways in which we are constituted as moral agents in and through our relationships to others, and the development of feminist ethics as a discipline has developed around the key concepts of relationality and responsibility.

So far, this brief overview of feminist work in ethics has highlighted what feminists have found deficient in many approaches to ethics within Euro-American philosophy. Of course, as the field has developed, feminist ethicists have also offered their own alternatives to a discipline that had historically been dominated by male philosophers. In her introduction to the volume *Feminist Ethics*, Claudia Card describes the earliest efforts in feminist moral theory as based largely on those experiences women believe previous moral theory had left out — namely, the experiences of women, children, and other social groups whose autonomy society restricts in a variety of ways and for a variety of reasons.[10] Influential early works based on women's experiences were Carol Gilligan's *In a Different Voice*,[11] Nel Noddings's *Caring*,[12] and Sara Ruddick's *Maternal Thinking: Toward a Politics of Peace*.[13] Card emphasizes particularly Carol Gilligan's work as the catalyst for much of the work on feminist ethics that began to blossom in the second half of the 1980s. However, since both Noddings's and Ruddick's approaches articulate similar concerns as do the literary works of Drewitz, Wolf, and Weil, the analysis begins with an overview of these two seminal works.

## Feminist Ethics: Mothers, Children, and Care

Jede Frau ist ICH und WIR zugleich. Keine Frau kann sagen: ICH DENKE, DAHER BIN ICH, weil jede Frau auch immer die mit den ausgebreiteten Armen ist und SORGEND ERFÄHRT, DASS SIE IST. (*Gestern war heute*, 298)

[Every woman is I and We at the same time. No woman can say: I THINK, THEREFORE I AM, because every woman is also always the one with the open arms and, CARING, EXPERIENCES THAT SHE IS.]

Although Drewitz wrote *Gestern war heute* before the earliest scholarly texts on care ethics appeared, the passage cited at the outset of this chapter and the above quote underscore the centrality of caring to Drewitz's understanding of the way women approach interpersonal relationships. Indeed, caring is a concept that underlies all of the literary texts analyzed in this book. Thus, a discussion of care as a theoretical foundation for feminist ethics is crucial to understanding the ethics discourse in which the novels participate.

One of the most prominent representatives of early care ethics is Nel Noddings, whose work lays out a model of ethics based on the principle of caring. Along with many other feminist ethicists, Noddings believes that ethical theories have traditionally been rule-based: dicta grounded in abstract situations and then universalized to apply in any roughly similar situation. Because relationships of dependence and the care they require are not at the foundation of such ethical systems and because women have been largely responsible for caregiving, she sees such ethical systems as representative of the "language of the father," within which the mother's voice is largely silenced. She proposes instead an ethics based on caring, which is an act (single, continuous, or serial) carried out by the "one-caring" and received by the "cared-for." While Noddings suggests that caring must have both an agent and a recipient, the emphasis is almost exclusively on the one-caring. In fact, the moral worth of the one-caring is measured by the reception of care in the cared-for: "How good *I* can be is partly a function of how *you* — the other — receive and respond to me" (6). Thus, a sense of self-worth and social approbation for the one-caring depends almost entirely on external validation. Furthermore, the caring relationship becomes "inauthentic" when the cared-for finds him- or herself needing to care for the one-caring (77). This is not to say that caring relationships do not exist between equals, but Noddings notes that imbalances of power are inherent in a caring relationship (66).

In caring, the one-caring opens herself up to the needs and wants of the cared-for. For Noddings this entails "engrossment" (a term she selected after rejecting "empathy") and a moving away from oneself (14–17). Both involve an intense emotional investment in the cared-for and a willingness to put aside one's own expectations in favor of understanding or attempting to understand fully the needs of the cared-for. For Noddings, caring is neither a system (i.e. codifiable), nor is it driven by principles that can be universalized (11). Its goals are generally the welfare, protection, or enhancement of the cared-for and responding to a specific individual in a concrete situation (23–24). It differs from traditional moral theory in its insistence on dealing with concrete situations described and analyzed in rich detail versus abstract conflicts that focus on general types of moral conflict and on the analysis of each given situation rather than the application of a general principle that may or may not be appropriate to the conflict or needs at hand.

In a similar fashion, all three of the writers whose works form the core of this book insist on the rich narrative contextualization of moral choices that care ethics demands and reveal their characters' positioning in multiple care relationships. Care is perhaps most important for Ingeborg Drewitz's early work. We have seen how it forms a key concept in Gabriele's sense of female ontology in *Gestern war heute*. In an earlier work, *Wer verteidigt Katrin Lambert?*, Drewitz even experimented with a female protagonist whose whole existence is founded in the principle of caring for others. The character's experiment fails, because — so the novel implies — Katrin's other-directedness leads to a dissolution of her own self. Although Noddings takes it for granted that, in order to care, the one-caring must devote similar energy and creativity to maintaining her own self (99, 105), she does construe the efforts of the one-caring as completely dependent upon the reaction of the one cared-for for confirmation and completion (4). Drewitz's initial attempts in *Katrin Lambert* to think through her own model of moral behavior based on caring yielded what appear to have been disappointing results for the author. The chapter on Drewitz's work will go into more detail on this issue, but it is important to note that her next works — particularly *Gestern war heute* and *Eis auf der Elbe* — explore modifications to this model that also prefigure in some ways how feminist ethicists responded to Noddings's work.

The ethicists that built on the early contributions of theorists like Noddings quickly became dissatisfied with what seemed to them efforts to found a moral theory on the basis of supposed feminine characteristics. One reason for this dissatisfaction was that despite Noddings's disclaimers, many feminists declared that her notion of an ethical system based on caring essentialized as feminine certain behavioral patterns and emotional responses that were learned, schooled, and contextually determined. Instead of challenging the construction of socialized gender roles in patriarchal society, Noddings's work represents simply an effort to switch the focus from so-called masculine norms to feminine norms.[14]

Noddings admits in the preface to the 2003 edition of *Caring* that she might have written things differently were she rewriting the book in the twenty-first century, but she does not specify what she would change. She also argues in her preface that she does not see caring or the gestures fundamental to it as excluding men (xvi). She nevertheless left the book replete with references to the one-caring as "she" and the cared-for as "he." Furthermore, she focuses almost exclusively on relationships that resemble those between mother and child (or teacher and student, whereby she codes the teacher as female and the student as male). This becomes more and more disconcerting the further one reads in the volume. Thus, while there is nothing about caring that should be exclusive to women, her constant gendering of the one-caring and the cared-for as she and he subverts her attempts to keep the concept of caring gender neutral.

## Sara Ruddick and Maternal Thinking

Sara Ruddick's *Maternal Thinking* echoes many facets of Noddings's work, but its purpose is more tightly focused. Specifically, Ruddick wrote this book at the time of the first Gulf War as a way to envision an ethical system that would avoid the inevitable loss of life that war brings with it. While she refers explicitly to Noddings's *Caring*, she also modifies or further specifies the concept of caring. Her suggestion is that we look at the praxis of motherhood — its goals and motivations — to see if we can find in it a way to move the politics of peace forward, to make the notion of peacemaking more "robust" (137) and to end the senseless loss of life. She identifies in the practice of motherhood certain ideals to which women dedicate themselves once they have consciously accepted the commitment to care for their children (68). For her, mothering entails three overarching goals: protecting, nurturing, and training the child for social acceptance (17). One notes that these goals do not differ substantively from Noddings's three goals of caring: welfare, protection, and enhancement, nor from the way both Wolf and Drewitz represent maternal practices.

As does Noddings, Ruddick asserts that the goals of mothering make the abstract principles of traditional moral paradigms (also referred to as justice ethics) difficult to apply because mothers must deal with the particular challenges involved with each child and raising that child into a community. Like Noddings, Ruddick sees the caring relationship (here embodied specifically in mothers and children) as focusing on meeting the needs of an other, who "demands" our "protection, nurturance, and training," an individual who is vulnerable in a relationship in which power is vastly unequal. Maternal thinking inherently seeks to avoid violent responses to needs and shuns an attitude of indifference to the other (xi).

Since Ruddick is primarily seeking a foundation for a politics of peace, she narrows the scope of her ethical model and does not put it forward as a broad-based alternative to rule-based moral systems the way Noddings does. Ruddick sees herself as both a pragmatist and a theoretical pluralist (127). She acknowledges that maternal thinking is not a theoretical foundation for all human relationships. Nonetheless, since mothering requires responding to specific situations, weighing particular concrete instances of competing demands, maternal thinking offers a new way to conceptualize morality.

Several other ethicists responding to Ruddick's work argued that maternal behavior could not adequately respond to any number of interpersonal conflicts in need of moral resolution (for instance, stranger rape or breach of contract).[15] Like Noddings's notion of caring, Ruddick's maternal thinking is an attempt to export a model of domestic interaction to the public sphere. This problematizes her theory, since so many relationships in the public sphere do not at all resemble that of a mother to her child. Ruddick herself appears at times to realize this. She discusses extensively the constraints mothers face in pursuing the three goals mentioned above, and acknowledges that her work pertains less to real mothers than to the ideals of motherhood (161). Despite such caveats and an unwillingness to let go of her conceptualization of maternal thinking as a foundation for peacemaking, she admits that "for [her] purpose, it is sufficient that there are *some* maternal practices actually governed by the ideals I articulate" (163). Ruddick's work led to further feminist scholarship on ethics that acknowledges the need to recognize the complexity of moral dilemmas in all of their situational varieties. It brought some feminist philosophers and ethicists to question the moral centrality of maternal behavior and others to push for another foundational category other than motherhood — or even care itself — for ethical systems.

## Challenging Moral and Gendered Boundaries

While feminist ethicists such as Sara Ruddick and Nel Noddings readily admitted that in reality mothers are, in fact, often grumpy, frustrated, angry and even cruel, they still saw in an idealized bourgeois version of the mother the seeds for an alternative approach to social interaction.[16] Cautiously acknowledging that men can act maternally too, Ruddick nonetheless attempted to formulate a limited ethics based on what she considered to be the three foundational aspects of maternal caring. Ruddick's and Noddings's work ushered in the possibility of looking at ethics through an entirely new frame. It also seems intuitively sound that feminists like Noddings and Ruddick writing in the eighties should look to their experiences as women to counter what they experienced as an overemphasis on rule-based, acontextual ethical systems that the male-dominated discipline of philosophy had propagated.

And yet, in their own reasoning lay the seeds for the future directions that feminist ethics would take — directions that shift the parameters of these early paradigms and that are mirrored in the works of the three literary writers discussed in this book. In response to these revolutionary new theories, other feminist ethicists insisted that making the mother-child relationship the basis of reflection on moral theory not only perpetuated the patriarchally sanctioned definition of woman as mother, but also tended to exclude from consideration relationships that do not conform to that model. Joan Tronto, for instance, has worked to revise care ethics in order to eliminate the essentialist tendencies critics saw in it and to expand the contexts in which we can employ it. Margaret Urban Walker, on the other hand, has rethought the concept of responsibility as the fundamental aspect of moral behavior, exploring a geography of morals on a much broader terrain.

My purpose here is to explore how feminist ethics can help us understand the dynamics of interpersonal relationships and the political and historical realities that our three authors depict in their novels. Although their work either predated or appeared at the same time as early articulations of feminist ethics, it shared the focus on care and maternal ethics and anticipated much of the frustration and dissatisfaction that developed with care ethics among later feminist ethicists. It would go beyond the scope of this chapter to lay out in detail how feminist ethics as a discipline has developed since Noddings's and Ruddick's pathbreaking work; however, it is worth highlighting the moments in feminist ethics that articulate well the ethical questions at the heart of the literary works examined in this book as Drewitz's, Wolf's, and Weil's literary projects evolve over time.

Early feminist ethics tried to build on the roles that women had traditionally played in the private sphere and believed that insights gleaned from mothering practices would help us to overcome the constraints of moral theories that assumed the primacy of the autonomous moral agent in the public sphere. Often these early efforts were criticized by both feminist and non-feminist ethicists for applying solely to relationships in the private sphere. Later feminist ethicists, however, came to question the boundaries that such traditional divisions had erected. Joan Tronto, for instance, asks us to rethink the implication that the mother/child relationship should be the model for ethical behavior in the private sphere and the relationship of autonomous individuals the model in the public sphere. Tronto's *Moral Boundaries: A Political Argument for an Ethic of Care*, published in 1993,[17] is one of the most influential studies of how best to expand the concept of care to make its application to moral dilemmas in the public sphere more apparent.

Tronto approaches this project in two ways. First, she historicizes the origins of our philosophical propensity to see these two spheres as distinct from each other, locating it in the move from a moral system of context and community to one based on autonomous individuals who can — should they wish to do so — enter into contracts (relationships) with other autonomous individuals. Tronto argues persuasively that this notion of the moral agent arose in the eighteenth century as the European economy responded to the increasingly impersonal character of commerce and trade. As human interaction in the marketplace became ever more abstract, an ethical system guided by the application of reason and rules permitted people to interact and trade who did not know each other at all. This required, however, a conceptualization of individuals as homogeneous beings that could be counted on to leave issues of personal context and attachment out of negotiations in the public sphere. Tronto maintains that this shift also resulted in a clearer division between what gradually became labeled as feminine (private) traits of drawing on emotion and context to respond to other human beings and the reason-driven moral calculus of public man (52–56). Her purpose is to reveal as historical that which we have come to see as a "natural" human order. This should enable us to recognize that the apparently distinct division of human life into public and private spheres is artificial.

Tronto also indicates how this division has been detrimental to our own welfare. One of her most important aims is to reveal that the moral boundaries we have erected mask privilege and power and exclude issues of care and the complexity of human relationships from public discussion. They also exclude from the discussion those in our society who are most closely associated with caregiving, the ones with the greatest insights into the actual practice of care (96, 112, 114, 117). Tronto concludes that socioeconomic and political changes of the late twentieth and early twenty-first centuries are again forcing us to reconsider how care is distributed and delivered as a public good. As women have increasingly taken on full-time occupations in the public sphere, society has had to address issues of caregiving that used to be private, familial matters (151). In contrast to Noddings, who links care ethics to the adjective "feminine" and thus ties it implicitly if not explicitly as a moral perspective to gender and gendered hierarchies, Tronto insists on explicitly moving beyond thinking of care as something that pertains only to the private or domestic sphere of human interaction and, thus, to women.

She argues that ethicists must work to illustrate the many ways that care is both a private and public concern, indeed, that care is an integral aspect of all human existence. She and one of her collaborators, Berenice Fisher, offer the following, deliberately broad definition of care:

> On the most general level, we suggest that caring be viewed as a *species activity that includes everything that we do to maintain, continue, and repair our "world" so that we can live in it as well as possible.* That world includes our bodies, our selves, and our environment, all of which we seek to interweave in a complex, life-sustaining web. (103; emphasis in original)

Acccording to Tronto and Fisher, this definition of care would avoid creating social hierarchies that relegate both those who need care and those who actually give the care to the margins of public discourse. For, if the autonomous, independent male is considered to be the norm for human existence, then anyone who requires or gives care — either temporarily or over the long term — must, by definition, be abnormal or deviant (102). This might seem like an extreme representation of traditional moral philosophy that emphasizes the autonomous individual as the moral subject. However, both Tronto and Selma Sevenhuijsen assert that it is the logical ramification of such an exclusionary perspective.[18]

Furthermore, Tronto and Fisher's definition makes it possible to use care as a tool to think about relationships that extend beyond our immediate personal spaces (family, community, and nation). Attentiveness to the needs of others is one of the foundational elements of care ethics, but generally the implied other is someone close to us. Tronto, however, engages this specific aspect of caring to enlarge the boundaries of care into the international realm. She asks, for instance, whether it is a moral failing that people in the developed world do not notice that the global capitalist system in which they are complicit results in "the starvation of thousands, or in sexual slavery in Thailand" (128–29). She concludes that it is a moral failing, albeit on a social or collective level rather than on an individual level. Feminist scholars continue to explore how care applies to issues of responsibility and political action in international contexts.[19]

This brief introduction to Tronto cannot possibly do her work justice. Instead its purpose is to call attention to issues that Tronto raises and that pertain to the directions Drewitz, Wolf, and Weil go in their own texts. First, Tronto calls into question the idea that care — as an ethical paradigm — may help us to understand human relations in the private sphere, but cannot adequately respond to issues facing us in the public sphere. Then she shows how a broader definition of care can apply to questions of individual and collective responsibility. Indeed, her definition of care would include such diverse things as environmental politics, gardening, and personal physical fitness. However, when the boundaries of caring are extended this far, one could question whether one is not, in fact, moving into a different ethical model altogether.

Margaret Urban Walker's *Moral Understandings: A Feminist Study in Ethics* (1998) provides a new map to understanding the geography of moralities by bringing both the justice (rule-based ethical paradigms) and care perspectives into a discussion of how we negotiate questions of responsibility generally. Walker's work reveals clear links to Tronto's, but changes the parameters of ethics and resonates closely with Drewitz's, Wolf's, and Weil's literary struggles with the concept of responsibility.

Walker offers what she calls a study of ethics as opposed to a study of specific moral practices. The distinction she makes is one between practice and epistemology: in her definition, morality concerns the ways people behave and the choices they make in any given situation; ethics looks at the way theories represent and articulate morality. Thus, her book intends not to tell us how well or badly we behave, or even to show us how to behave better. Its purpose rather is to look at the "nature, sources, and justification of moral knowledge" (3).[20] Nonetheless, Walker does present a very clear picture of what she thinks morality consists and lays out how societies conceive of and create community-specific practices of responsibility.

Right from the beginning of *Moral Understandings*, Walker tells us that she opposes "theoretical-juridical models" of ethics, by which she means approaches based on relationships between autonomous agents and consisting of universal codes of behavior that can be applied regardless of the specific sociohistorical situation. As she puts it, a theoretical-juridical model "prescribes the representation of morality as a compact, propositionally codifiable, impersonally action-guiding code within an agent, or as a compact set of law-like propositions that 'explain' the moral behavior of a well-formed moral agent" (7–8). It is an impersonal model not grounded in particular situations nor linked to particular individuals.

In opposition to the theoretical-juridical model, Walker proposes an "expressive-collaborative model of morality." Since she casts her book as a research project into moral paradigms, she calls the basic components of her theory hypotheses and lays out the following four as central to her model: First, morality itself — as opposed to ethics — consists in practices, not theories (15). Rather than being a set of abstract principles, morality is an interpersonal practice, one that is negotiated, reproduced, and modified in the ways human beings deal with one another. Walker cautions, however, that morality may be socially negotiated, but that not all of the actors engage in such negotiations from equitable or voluntary positions (10). The second hypothesis is that moral practices are "practices of responsibility" (16). The fundamental concern for morality is how a society decides who is responsible for what or whom and to whom. Responsibilities are not, however, simply assigned by society. Practices of morality must also include the fact that people accept, refuse, and negotiate specific responsibilities (94). They are thus neither entirely set by individual agents, nor imposed on individuals by more powerful instances. Walker's third hypothesis is that "morality is not socially modular" (17). Since moral understandings are shared communal ways of looking at who is responsible to whom for what, they cannot be independent of the specific society in which they are formed. They cannot be transplanted simply from one society or social group to another. Walker's fourth and final hypothesis is that in order to understand moral values in society we must be able to look at the ways in which any number of different individuals bear and fulfill any number of different responsibilities, rather than comparing individual behavior to a list of ahistorical ideal categories and declaring some individuals to be moral and others to be moral failures (18).

Two aspects of Walker's work make it particularly relevant to how the literary texts of Wolf, Weil, and Drewitz examine moral issues. The first is her emphasis on the role of extended narrative contextualization in understanding moral problems, which she shares with care ethics more broadly. The second has to do with her privileging of responsibility as the foundational term for moral practices. Walker notes that human beings accept and fulfill numerous responsibilities in their lives, the scope of which also change over time or in new circumstances. They do not remain fixed as would a list of obligations generated by a specific moral code. The flexibility with which she construes the term makes it possible to apply it to relationships that go beyond the scope of geographically localized social groups and communities to cross over community boundaries. "Care" is generally seen as applying to proximate personal relationships. At least potentially, this narrows its scope to individuals in one's immediate environment. In contrast, the concept of responsibility can address issues that include the individual, but exceed his or her immediate sphere of influence. Both of these aspects of Walker's work (the emphasis on the role of narrative in understanding moral dilemmas and ourselves and responsibility as the fundamental category of moral deliberation) are central to the literary works that the succeeding chapters will examine.

Walker is not alone in representing narrative as one of the primary ways in which human beings represent moral dilemmas to themselves. A hallmark of care ethics is its insistence on understanding the contexts in which individuals make moral decisions. Such understanding requires, in turn, extensive narrative contextualization. Walker insists that we use stories not only to think through moral problems, but also to think of ourselves as moral beings. She argues that there are three kinds of narratives we construct about ourselves in this context: "identity" narratives that describe who we see ourselves as; "relationship" narratives that detail how and as whom we portray ourselves to others; and "value" narratives that map out what we place emphasis on and what we care about (111).

The stories we tell are both personal and social: they cannot be one without being the other as well. Our understandings of the ways in which we impact other people and the ways in which they constrain our behavior or expand the choices we have available for action are central to the stories we tell of ourselves as individuals (112). In other words, there is simply no way to tell the stories of ourselves without including the stories of our relationships to others. Furthermore, in telling those stories we also express the things we value most. However, once we admit the role others play in our self-narratives, we must also recognize that these stories are highly situational and very much "works in progress." Because we have multiple relationships with varying degrees of connection and responsibility, we must recognize that the stories we tell ourselves and others are not representations of a fixed identity but rather change to address different situations. Walker argues that our lives entail multiple and competing responsibilities and that we often cannot control which responsibilities become dominant at any point. For this reason, she rejects narratives of the self that assume that one's life is a coherent and consistent narrative from birth to death, a conception that ultimately rests on a teleological model of human development (146).

Nonetheless, although our narratives are in some sense fluid and change to respond to different situations and relationships, we are constrained both socially and historically in the kinds of narratives we can tell of ourselves. Factors governing these constraints include race, gender, and class, but also the broader histories of which our lives are part. Walker stresses that our individual narratives overlap both with other people's stories and — over time — with different ways of contextualizing historical experience. She also points out that the multiple narratives that we tell of ourselves "coexist in various states of stratification or alternation" over the course of our lives (119). Of particular significance here is that this conception of self-narrative manages not only to acknowledge fully the constraints on the process of narration (e.g., historical events, race, class, gender, sex, and age), but also at the same time to leave ample room for individual agency and intervention in our constructions of self.

Walker's concept of responsibility recognizes not only the fact that our relationships with others entail certain responsibilities to them, but also that we choose whether or not to accept those responsibilities. Additionally, her focus on responsibilities allows for numerous interpretive emphases for both the individual fulfilling those responsibilities as well as for the ethicist who looks more broadly at how society values and distributes responsibilities among its members. For Walker, feminist ethics analyzes the way society has distributed responsibility and how these responsibilities are reflexively coded by gender (73). It allows for varied analyses of responsibilities across numerous cultures. Not only that, but Walker's notion of responsibility acknowledges a broader differentiation of responsibilities from care to non-interference and does not require us to focus on one particular kind of responsibility (78).[21] This becomes particularly important for the discussion of the literary writers that will follow because they too search for answers about how certain people and certain groups of people come to assume (or not) the responsibility for others. They too ask these questions across community boundaries.

Walker's notion of responsibility allows sufficient flexibility to address such relationships between different moral communities and across community boundaries without falling back on abstract principles (or rules) that fail to accommodate their complexity. Just as we have differing degrees of responsibilities to members of our own communities, responsibilities that change in response to heightened need or developing capabilities, our responsibilities to individuals and groups beyond our own moral communities vary in situations where the power balance among actors is changing or in which one actor has disproportionate power over the other. Walker writes that "an ethic of responsibility within an expressive-collaborative framework can acknowledge a moving horizon of commitments and adjustments, allowing individual distinctiveness of situation and commitment. It preserves livable flexibility in tandem with reasonable reliability" (109). The boundaries of our various moral communities remain neither clear nor constant, since such communities often "nest within each other and overlap each other, and so do people's senses of their own and others' identities and responsibilities" (202).

The evaluation of responsibilities within extended communities or to those outside our own communities requires a great deal of critical self-reflection. The third hypothesis of Walker's work is that morality is not socially modular. Therefore, one group cannot simply impose its moral assumptions and agreements on another group. Along with other critics of universalist ethical paradigms Walker insists that we must reflect on our own moral understandings and how we should conceive of our responsibilities to other groups given the differences between our moral practices and beliefs and the differing levels of interaction between groups. We can attempt to persuade them, but we cannot justify compelling others to believe as we do (209).

In conclusion, Walker turns to the concept of integrity, proposing a definition of it as "a kind of reliable accountability" (106). Such a concept maps well onto the novels discussed later. It does not look for individuals who have remained rigidly consistent in their relationships with others, since such a concept of integrity takes into account neither the "deeply relational character of human lives" nor the ways in which our lives and our responses to conflict or need are dependent on the behaviors of others. Walker instead suggests a concept of integrity that would demonstrate a resilient reliability in our responsibilities to others. As Walker phrases it:

> This view of integrity takes utterly seriously to what and to whom a person is true, but looks with suspicion upon true selves. It features the role of stories in making sense of lives, but is skeptical about certain overly ambitious or monopolistic narrative demands on selves. It links our senses of meaning and responsibility to the stories we can tell, but notices that "we" are not all in the same discursive positions any more than we are all in the same social ones, and that these are importantly linked. (106–7)

Walker refocuses the discussion of integrity, moving from a view of the individual alone to the individual within any number of different relationships with other individuals. Because we do not live in a vacuum, but are rather affected by numerous intersecting relationships and areas of responsibility, her approach allows us to see that "a life fully shared with others will often be taken up, or taken along, by those others as much as undertaken by the one whose life it is" (42). While such an acknowledgement does not exculpate us when we fail to fulfill responsibilities we have accepted, it lowers the threshold of what counts as a well-lived, legitimate, or moral life.

In sum, Walker reconceives morality as a socially negotiated fabric of relationship and responsibility, a collective work "of many hands down generations meeting different strains and circumstances" (203). Moral understandings are not unique to individuals or universal in nature. They are not the product of "concerted effort or design," but are rather "sustained by their reproduction in many activities of many people who are only sometimes aware that they are sustaining something at the level of 'society' or 'morality.'" Indeed, Walker argues that individuals are generally aware that they accept certain responsibilities in order to maintain relationships they consider valuable, but that their efforts to explain their actions in a way that makes sense to them and to the community in which they act is a collective product: "a specific form of moral-social life" (203). Furthermore, because we cannot really step completely outside the spaces we occupy socially to get an overview of the moral-social order in which we form and maintain relationships, none of us can judge an entire moral system. Since we cannot stand outside or above our own moral community or view another moral community from a reliably neutral perspective, we cannot formulate or hold others to uniform crosscultural moral standards of responsibility. Walker maintains that we can argue that certain acts are immoral. We can also attempt to demonstrate that many of the claims that cultures draw on to justify horrendous practices are manifestly erroneous (205). She agrees that "there are cases in which we are obliged to assist and protect people from the aggression of those who live very differently from us, but who do so at the expense of some among them who do not want to live that way with them" (210). However, forcing or attempting to force entire cultures to adopt our moral perspectives can lead, indeed has led to many situations in history in which one culture brutalizes another on the basis of the supposed moral superiority of its beliefs.[22] Thus, she insists that judgments across cultural groups "with significantly different moral ways of life" require us to reflect extensively on our own vantage point and our actual motives in a far deeper way than the application of purportedly universal moral principles does (210).

## Feminist Ethics as a Tool and Literature as a Moral Laboratory

Feminist ethics proves useful to analyzing the literary works that are the primary focus of the book both as an analytical tool for understanding the moral narratives that Drewitz, Wolf, and Weil present and as a way to explain how the literary works function as moral laboratories, expansive narrative spaces in which to think through the implications of ethical theories and the questions that they leave open.

### Ingeborg Drewitz

As the quote from her novel *Gestern war heute* at the opening of this chapter revealed, the question of women's specific, indeed unique perspective on human relationships interested Ingeborg Drewitz at a very early point in her career. Drewitz wrote a number of novels that focus on the lives of women — almost to the exclusion of male characters. This series begins with *Wer verteidigt Katrin Lambert?* in 1974 and continues through *Eis auf der Elbe,* which was published in 1982. In the former, Drewitz tries out a model of female moral agency that resembles very closely one of the earliest articulations of care ethics — namely Noddings's *Caring*. Ultimately, Drewitz seems to reject the implications of an ethical theory similar to Noddings's and pushes forward to experiment further.

Her next novel, *Gestern war heute,* centers on Gabriele, who as a daughter and mother responds to the world around her in a very different way than her emotionally remote husband, Jörg. She is the emotional, attentive one and he the distant breadwinner. Feminist ethicists like Sara Ruddick and, later, Virginia Held can help us to analyze the parameters of Drewitz's moral paradigm in this work, which examine how women and mothers approach the question of responsibility. However, already in this novel, Drewitz herself starts to point in entirely different directions. We can see these new directions clearly in *Eis auf der Elbe,* one of Drewitz's last novels. In this work, she has moved away from a selective emphasis on the particular characteristics of women's moral responses to the communities in which they live. This novel, much more so than the earlier ones, addresses the question of individual and collective responsibility in a world in which we exist in numerous intersecting communities. Both Joan

Tronto's insistence on making visible the artificial moral boundaries that prevent us from thinking about care beyond the confines of immediate personal relationships and Walker's approach to the geography of morals via the social negotiation of responsibility significantly clarify Drewitz's ethical arguments.

## Christa Wolf

In Drewitz one can see a developing insight into the limitations of an ethics based on a narrowly-focused concept of care or maternal socialization. There is no similar emphasis in Wolf's writing. Her approach to motherhood differs greatly from Drewitz's and — in many ways — from the theoretical perspectives of early care ethics. Nonetheless, Wolf's protagonists are almost always women, and Wolf stresses their roles as both mothers and daughters. However, she brings to the topic a less romanticized notion of motherhood, which in itself opens new perspectives on mothering. Undoubtedly, this stems from personal experiences, but also arguably from Wolf's living in a culture that moved away from idealizing the role of women solely as mothers — namely that of East Germany.

Despite the arguments of some critics, such as Bella Brodzki, that Wolf's work is staked upon the relationship between daughter and mother,[23] Wolf never comes anywhere near portraying "the mother" as the locus of a special ideological significance. In fact, she never invests mothers with as much hope as do Ruddick in her theoretical work and Drewitz in her fiction simply because they are mothers. It is true that in *Kindheitsmuster* Charlotte Jordan plays a far greater role in the upbringing and psychological development of Nelly than does Bruno Jordan, but there is little in the text to suggest that this owes to something special about Charlotte as mother. There is nothing in the novel that would lead us to believe that "maternal thinking" would provide a firmer foundation for peace than "paternal thinking," indeed nothing to suggest that "maternalism" and the relationship between mother and child would serve as a better foundation for social ethics. Wolf's narrator admits that Charlotte was the person in the family who came closest to being able to develop something like a social conscience (327), and yet this doesn't seem to attach in any particular way to her being a mother. In fact, one could argue that Charlotte blatantly refuses to fulfill her caring obligations as a mother, because she chooses to stay behind in the family's hometown as the battlefront nears. She leaves her children's future in the hands of others and is not at all sure she will ever find them again.

However, Wolf's work — particularly *Kindheitsmuster* — consistently examines the questions of personal and collective responsibility that arise in her interrogation of Germany's troubled past. Like Drewitz, however, she refuses to pose these questions either in regard to the limited domestic spaces of families (both nuclear and extended) or even the broader collective spaces of national or ethnic communities. Instead, she consistently interrogates the ways that questions of responsibility transcend the boundaries in which we would like to keep them. Her work prefigures in many ways the later directions that care ethics and feminist ethics more generally took. Again, Walker's geography of morals allows us to articulate the ways in which Wolf envisions the moving horizon of commitments and adjustments that Walker discusses and that permit us to look at responsibility across vast social and geographical spaces while at the same time problematizing and interrogating responsibility in such situations. Furthermore, Wolf's literary work repeatedly shows us how porous are the boundaries between public and private spheres, and she does so while consistently drawing together chronologically and geographically separate events.

**Grete Weil**

Weil's examination of the scope of personal responsibility begins from a standpoint that is diametrically opposite to that of either Drewitz or Wolf: namely from the perspective of Germany's victims during the Holocaust. And yet, Weil's strong — if uneasy — identification first as German and then as Jewish gives her an entry into the topic of responsibility that travels over different conceptual paths. Her attempts to (re)connect to different cultural heritages (the Germany of the educated bourgeoisie on one hand and the beginnings of Jewish history on the other) lead her to comparable moments of systemic oppression and violence in both cultural traditions. Her efforts to find the morally "right" way to respond to such violence reveal a conflict between personal responsibilities and abstract moral dictates.

This clash results in a personal if reluctant rejection of moral systems that require an individual to respond to a moral dilemma according to universally valid moral precepts — systems such as those repeatedly criticized by feminist ethicists from Noddings to Walker. In Weil's *Meine Schwester Antigone*, the narrator explores at length Antigone's refusal to follow what she perceives to be an unjust law. In her own eyes, the narrator fails morally because in key situations she did not refuse to obey unjust orders, and she tries again and again to imagine what ramifications applying that principle of refusal would have had in her own life as well as how such a refusal competed with her responsibilities for keeping her mother alive. She recognizes that the rigid adherence to such abstract principles inevitably runs afoul of our commitments to other people.

Weil's work illustrates the feminist critique of moral theories that assume the autonomous moral agent as the bearer of moral rectitude. Furthermore, the narrator's struggle with the sense of failure she feels for not having been able to apply one particular — but in her mind unchallenged — moral dictum allows us to see the impact such moral theories have on individual lives.[24] A discussion of the relationship between mothers and children as well as Walker's critique of moral theories that rest on "whole life projects" will play a significant role in the analysis of Weil's work.

So far, I have primarily talked about how we can use the work of feminist ethicists to analyze and articulate the ethical reasoning Drewitz, Wolf, and Weil offer us in their literary texts. As I mentioned above, however, the analysis of the works of our three literary writers can also help us to understand the breaking points and new directions that feminist ethics has taken in the roughly thirty years since its beginnings. By viewing theoretical work in ethics and the literary treatment of material rife with moral implications side by side and interrelating them, we can attain a clearer articulation of the ethical perspectives that come out in the novels and see how these literary texts have contributed to a much broader international feminist discourse on ethics.

# Notes

[1] At the outset of this section, I should clarify that I have abstracted the theoretical points that feminists ethicists have made in their critiques of Euro-American ethical traditions from their very extensive and detailed engagements with other ethicists. In their own work, they focus on specific examples of such traditions that include many philosophers of the neo-Kantian, utilitarian, and contractarian approaches to morality. Margaret Urban Walker, for instance, scrutinizes Anglo-American ethical traditions that have their origins in the work of Henry Sidgwick and his foundational *Methods of Ethics* (1874). Although she acknowledges that the different approaches generated by Sidgwick's work have fundamental differences, she argues that they all see morality as a corpus of universalizable judgments or rules. Joan Tronto, on the other hand, centers her examination of the historical origins underlying ethical models that focus on the notion of an autonomous moral agent and a set of codifiable precepts for public behavior primarily on the Scottish Enlightenment philosophers Frances Hutcheson, David Hume, and Adam Smith. Other feminist ethicists concentrate their critical attention on yet other philosophers. I cannot possibly do justice in this book either to their complex treatment of these other traditions in ethics or to the philosophers whose work they critique. Since I am primarily interested in what feminist ethicists themselves have to say about the kinds of relationships that are fundamental to morality and how societies establish the parameters of socially acceptable behaviors, I will not try here to weigh in on whether their analyses of the individual philosophers or ethical theories are accurate. Nor will I deal with non-feminist philosophy that shares certain elements with feminist critiques of traditional philosophy, such as communitarian ethics. Instead, my aim is to see how feminists use their critique to formulate an alternative vision of ethics. Margaret Urban Walker, *Moral Understandings: A Feminist Study in Ethics* (New York: Routledge, 1998). Joan Tronto, *Moral Boundaries: A Political Argument for an Ethic of Care* (New York: Routledge, 1993). All quotations from these works will be cited with page number in parentheses.

[2] Virgina Held, *Feminist Morality: Transforming Culture, Society, and Politics* (Chicago: U of Chicago P, 1993), 203. See also 168, 183. In a similar vein, see also Margaret Urban Walker *Moral Understandings*, 51.

[3] See e.g., Laurie Shrage, *Moral Dilemmas of Feminism: Prostitution, Adultery, and Abortion* (New York: Routledge, 1994), 5; Jane Flax, "Displacing Woman. Toward an Ethics of Multiplicity," in *Daring to Be Good: Essays in Feminist Ethico-Politics*, ed. Bat-Ami Bar On and Ann Ferguson (New York: Routledge, 1998), 144; Virginia Held, *Feminist Morality*, 68–69; and Margaret Urban Walker, *Moral Understandings*, 52.

[4] See Immanuel Kant, *Werke*, vol. 7, ed. Wilhelm Weischedel (Frankfurt am Main: Suhrkamp, 1968).

[5] See John Stuart Mill, *Utilitarianism* (Oxford: Oxford UP, 1998) and John Rawls, *A Theory of Justice* (Cambridge: Harvard UP, 1971).

[6] To quote Virginia Held once more: "The conception of freedom as the absence of interference has been a central aspect of the liberal democratic tradition. Underlying this conception has been the assumption that a man could fend for himself if he were not assaulted or interfered with. He could make a living by growing produce or he could develop a trade, and if he had not land or skill, he could move to some unoccupied land and put his labor to use; he could, Locke suggested, go to America. He would be able to earn a living, acquire some property, and live his life, if only others would leave him alone and not force him to do what he did not want to do" (*Feminist Morality*, 162).

[7] See e.g., Walker, *Moral Understandings*, 54.

[8] In a chapter entitled "Career Selves," Walker looks at this particular aspect of certain moral philosophies through the work of Charles Taylor, John Rawls, and Bernard Williams. Walker, *Moral Understandings*, 131–52.

[9] Selma Sevenhuijsen, *Citizenship and the Ethics of Care: Feminist Considerations on Justice, Morality and Politics* (London: Routledge, 1998).

[10] Claudia Card, "The Feistiness of Feminism," in *Feminist Ethics*, ed. Claudia Card (Lawrence: U of Kansas P, 1991), 3–34.

[11] Carol Gilligan, *In a Different Voice* (Cambridge, MA: Harvard UP, 1982).

[12] Nel Noddings, *Caring: A Feminine Approach to Ethics and Moral Education* (Berkeley: U of California P, 1984, 2003).

[13] Sara Ruddick, *Maternal Thinking: Toward a Politics of Peace* (Boston: Beacon Press, 1989).

[14] Essentialist thinking marks at least one of the authors in this study too, as Ingeborg Drewitz occasionally falls prey to the trap of biological essentialism in her early work. She once commented, for instance, that women are less likely to pursue and succeed in academic study because university studies usually coincide with a period in a woman's life during which her body urges her to become a mother. See her essay from 1971 entitled "Gespaltenes oder doppeltes Leben? Gedanken über die Frau als Künstlerin" (150). Some scholars have gone so far as to insist that German culture as a whole has erred in defining woman as mother. See e.g., Barbara Vinken, *Die deutsche Mutter: der lange Schatten eines Mythos* (Munich: Piper, 2001). A good example of a feminist study that challenges such essential-

ist understandings of gender is Judith Butler's *Gender Trouble* (New York: Routledge, 1990).

[15] See for instance, Sarah Hoagland, "Some Thoughts about 'Caring,'" in *Feminist Ethics*, ed. Claudia Card (Lawrence: U of Kansas P, 1991), 246–63, Michelle Moody-Adams, "Gender and the Complexity of Moral Voices," in *Feminist Ethics*, 195–212, Laurie Shrage, *Moral Dilemmas of Feminism*, and Walker, *Moral Understanding*, 54, 57.

[16] See here also e.g., Virginia Held, *Feminist Morality*.

[17] Subsequent references to this source will be referred to using page numbers in parentheses.

[18] In a chapter on feminist ethics and public health-care policies, Selma Sevenhuijsen argues that particularly neo-liberal conceptions of personhood and citizenship relegate those individuals who are not autonomous to second-class status: "The idea of the independent individual fits into a neo-liberal conception of citizenship, where it figures as the central normative ideal for human personhood. In the neo-liberal view, normality is constructed as self-sufficiency or the ability to lead an independent life in economic, social and political respects. This self-sufficient individual is someone who has no need of care during his or her 'normal social participation.'" (130) Earlier in her book, she makes a broader argument that moral theories that posit sameness or equality as a primary assumption of moral human relations implicitly see "differences, whether speculative in nature or accompanied by convincing evidence, [as] . . . deviant and negative in relation to a universal norm" (45). Similarly, she maintains that "vulnerability and dependency easily become separated from the ideal self and localized in, or projected onto others: weak or 'needy' people" (57). Sevenhuijsen's work is deeply influnced by Joan Tronto. Citing Tronto, Sevenhuijsen asserts that an overemphasis on the "the autonomous, rational, life-project choosing vision of the (male) individual, who perceives illness as a 'foreign invasion'" leads to seeing illness "as a deviation from normal social functioning, rather than as an inherent, even if often disturbing, part of human life" (131).

[19] For just two examples, see Fiona Robinson, *Globalizing Care: Ethics, Feminist Theory, and International Relations* (Boulder, CO: Westview, 1999) and Maurice Hamington and Dorothy Miller, eds., *Socializing Care* (Lanham, MD: Rowan and Littlefield, 2006).

[20] Subsequent references to this source will be referred to using page numbers in parentheses.

[21] The way Walker talks about moral practices and their social negotiation is not restricted to an audience of feminists — it allows any number of groups to look at their moral assumptions more critically. Her work gets around the dilemmas of care ethics, which tends to reinforce current distributions of social responsibility along gendered lines. See, e.g., 51. Walker also notes that feminists can fall prey to general abstractions in ways very similar to more traditional moral theorists. Once this happens — whether within or outside of a feminist framework, individuals whose experiences do not fall within the given parameters are often characterized as "different" or "problematic."

[22] Walker gives several specific examples here including Christian missionaries forcing indigenous population groups in the "new" world to alter their way of

living, leave their "savagery" behind them and enjoy the "enlightenment" that the missionaries brought to them and British colonial officers trying to change the cultures under their dominion that granted their women greater social and economic freedoms than British society did. Other examples readily come to mind, like the Crusades and the Inquisition. Her argument in this area is extensive, but she realizes that there are many ethicists whom she will not persuade. I cannot replicate here the complexity of her argument, but would refer interested readers to the chapter "Peripheral Visions, Critical Practice." See Walker, *Moral Understandings*, 201–23.

[23] Brodzki's argument refers specifically to *Kindheitsmuster*. Bella Brodzki, "Mothers, Displacement, and Language in the Autobiographies of Nathalie Sarraute and Christa Wolf," in *Life/Lines: Theorizing Women's Autobiography*, ed. Bella Brodzki and Celeste Schenck (Ithaca: Cornell UP, 1988), 245.

[24] Of course, people who have faced tragic situations that involve the loss of loved ones are very likely to second-guess their own choices in the events that occurred and experience extreme sadness and regret. However, Weil's fixation on what she sees as the moral principle governing Antigone's choices lead me to conclude that there is more to her examination of the Antigone story than just an exploration of personal bewilderment and grief.

# 3: Ingeborg Drewitz: Families, Historical Conflict, and Moral Mapping

THE CENTRAL QUESTIONS OF THIS STUDY deal with the individual's relationship to or impact on political, social, and economic history and the concomitant ethical implications of individual and collective responsibility. This chapter examines Ingeborg Drewitz's development as a novelist in terms of the ethical constructs she explores and how they relate to her characters' attempts to understand their place within any number of historical narratives. Two of her novels in particular, *Gestern war heute* (1978) and *Eis auf der Elbe* (1982), examine the positioning and self-positioning of individuals within their historical present with a consistency and intensity not found in her earlier or later novels. Beginning with *Oktoberlicht* (October Light)[1] in 1969, Drewitz wrote four novels that concentrated specifically on female characters and their experiences, but it was not until *Gestern war heute* that she systematically and thoroughly began to treat her characters' perception of their historical present.

Drewitz attempts in her novels to illustrate how individuals are placed and place themselves in history and how we use these understandings to map what Margaret Urban Walker has called a "geography of responsibility."[2] In particular, they show how we do so in a world in which the boundaries of the communities in which we live — through two world wars, several other global conflicts (such as the Vietnam War, armed conflicts in the Middle East, the coup in Chile, etc.), and the broad expansion of the mass media — have become unclear and beyond the ability of most individuals to grasp. Of central concern to the analysis of these works is how Drewitz fleshes out the intricate relationships between personal and national history, between local and national politics, and between society and the individual. As she lays out the connections between these various spheres, she begins to fashion a concept of political agency that can respond to the particular texture of historical and political experience at the beginning of the twenty-first century. It is a form of agency that allows us to see both our own imbrication in history and politics and the limits to individual activism on many levels. Put simply, this chapter argues that in these two novels Drewitz offers a model of how individuals can understand their places within history and decide how to act from within those positions. The two issues intersect with the discussions of collective memory and feminist ethics contained in the preceding two chapters, from which my analysis here will draw.

As mentioned above, both *Gestern war heute* and *Eis auf der Elbe* focus on the lives of female narrators. There is little actual plot in either novel. Instead, they concentrate on depicting the everyday lives and struggles of their female protagonists, Gabriele in *Gestern war heute* and the unnamed narrator in *Eis auf der Elbe*. *Gestern war heute* begins formally in 1923, the year of the main character's birth. However, it also reaches back in history by including the reflections of members of her extended family on their own history. It proceeds chronologically with the occasional insert of what the author called "Aus dem Arbeitsbuch zum Roman" (From the Notebook to the Novel) up to the end of the 1970s. *Eis auf der Elbe*, on the other hand, is structured loosely as a diary, and covers formally roughly five weeks in 1981. As in *Gestern war heute*, however, the narrator reflects on historical developments that begin much earlier than the novel's narrative present with the Second World War. Although there is little plot, the novels explore the relationship of the individual to broader historical developments through the characters' own reflections on the history that preceded them and the political events going on in their own lives.

Since this study concerns individuals' perceptions of their historical present and their place within it, a good first question is what kind of individuals Drewitz writes into these two works. As mentioned above, both novels deal with the lives of women born around the same time as Drewitz herself: 1923. They represent intelligent, self-assured women. The main character of *Gestern war heute* eventually becomes a successful journalist, and the narrator of *Eis auf der Elbe* is a lawyer. The professional and personal engagement of women like Drewitz's characters helped pave the way for the incipient women's movement of the 1960s and '70s in Germany.[3] As pathbreakers, however, they also come into conflict with the gender expectations of their immediate environment — at times with some people pushing them toward and some warning them away from traditional gender roles. Gabriele, for instance, the central character of *Gestern war heute*, finds herself in 1945 at odds with a professor who is trying to foster her academic future. He urges her to leave Berlin for more stable territories in the West. He suggests that her refusal to leave will prevent her from ever overcoming the educational restrictions of wartime Germany and the physical limitations of a city trying to rebuild itself from the ground up. Part of their conversation draws attention to the way in which the various segments of Drewitz's narrative become inseparable:

> Es ist schade um Sie! Sie reden sich über etwas hinweg! Warum gehen Sie nicht nach Westen? Sie hören doch BBC. Die Stadt, dieses Berlin wird nie mehr hochkommen. Das können Sie sich doch ausrechnen, oder?
> Meine Eltern sind hier, die Familie.

Eine Frauenantwort! Er nimmt jetzt den Stuhl und stukt ihn auf, da müssen Sie drüber hinwegkommen, rücksichtsloser werden, sich durchsetzen wollen.
Ich bin nicht sicher, ob wir noch das Recht haben, an uns zu denken. (147)

[It's a pity about you! You're talking yourself out of a future! Why don't you go to the West? You listen to the BBC. The city, this Berlin, will never rise again. You can calculate that, can't you?
My parents are here, the family.
A woman's answer! He takes the chair and rights it, you must get over this kind of thinking, become more inconsiderate to get what you want.
I am not sure that we still have the right to think just about ourselves.]

Whereas the professor implies that Gabriele's reaction is driven by some woefully inappropriate feminine solidarity, her response is really much more complicated. Gabriele is willing to recognize how interwoven her own life has become with those of her family and friends in Berlin, so interwoven in fact that a physical separation would bear serious consequences for many more people than just herself; her response is an acknowledgment of perceived mutual responsibilities.

The collective fate of these individuals depends, however, on the ways in which Berlin progresses, which — in turn — responds to the decisions and policies of governments, of particular groups, and of individuals.[4] As the entanglement of individual and collective decision-making takes shape, the reader becomes unable to distinguish clearly between the various spheres of human existence. Where does the private world of individuals begin, and just what is their relationship to public life and to the process of history in which they are enmeshed? How do the actions of governments and institutions affect the lives of individuals, and how do those individuals ultimately influence the choices governments and institutions make? What moments of history transcend such concepts as "choice"?

Nowhere in these two novels can one locate a narrative hierarchy that would stratify human life in such a way as to pinpoint the culprits or heroes of history. The professor interprets Gabriele's reference to family as typically female, because she allies herself with concerns we have largely considered to be part of the private sphere, beyond the concerns of politics and the grand path of human history. When second-wave feminists sought to reveal the interconnectedness of the public and private spheres with the slogan "the personal is political," they too underscored the fact that women had largely been restricted to operating within the confines of a domestic space, and one can certainly read Drewitz's novels as exploring the ways in which the slogan holds true. However, Drewitz's literary project goes beyond an exploration of how women's position within history has developed. She also goes further than the Marxist tenet that being determines consciousness. Drewitz's novels reveal how subtle the connections are between mind and body, between individuals and individuals, between individual subjects and collective subjects, and between personal and political history.

Drewitz shapes characters who are not powerful members of society, unusually gifted or intelligent, or even particularly exceptional. One can almost hear Pierre Nora's dismissal of such characters and their attempts to place themselves in history. Nora comments in his introduction to *Realms of Memory* about what he sees as the late twentieth-century tendency to "archive" historically inconsequential material in the hopes of preserving traces of individual history. He writes: "Everyone has gotten into the act: not just people whose role in history was minor at best, but also the relatives of such people and their doctors and lawyers and anyone else who happened to be standing about. The less extraordinary the testimony, the more aptly it is taken to illustrate the average mentality."[5] And yet, Nora also acknowledges that attempts to uncover the histories of marginalized and minority groups (in Drewitz's case women and some immigrants) led to a radical revision of history as a discipline. One must admit that although the two central women characters of *Gestern war heute* and *Eis auf der Elbe* aspire to exceed the traditional limitations society has placed on women, neither of them has pretensions of greatness or of extraordinary service to the communities in which they live. The other individuals in their lives (children, husbands, friends, employers, clients, etc.) stand out only for their apparent historical insignificance.

That is to say, if we look among Drewitz's characters for people with immediate, self-evident connections to postwar politics and history, we will not find them.[6] Some are criminals, but their crimes are localized and personal. Some are political activists, but their involvement in the political realm is circumscribed. Some of her characters play important community roles in helping the underprivileged, but they are not engaged in electoral politics or government organizations. How then does Drewitz manage to create with them a literary account of one century's history? In order to answer this question, this chapter first returns to Margaret Urban Walker's theory of a "geography of responsibility." Her approach will allow us to move beyond the realm of historiography and memory to the question of their function in our lives as members of communities.

As we have seen, Walker settles on the notion of responsibility as a "conceptual framework" for ethics.[7] Moral responsibilities, she argues, are both socially construed and distributed among any given community's members. Responsibilities are multiply defined, re-defined, and negotiated as the sociohistorical terrain on which they are mapped changes. Walker tells us that "patterns of ascribing and deflecting responsibility are socially shaped and differently shapeable. The point of seeing this is not just better descriptions, however; it is to be able to appreciate what is gotten and what is lost, what is secured and what left to chance, when responsibilities are shaped in one way rather than another" (99).[8]

When Drewitz's two female protagonists in these novels look back on their lives, they seek to account for their choices, and for the unexpected paths their lives have taken. Toward the end of *Gestern war heute*, Gabriele's daughter grills her about why she never amounted to much, in other words, why she never became the star journalist she could have become. Gabriele tries to explain this to her daughter and to herself by talking about the relative gains ("what is gotten and what is lost") when we choose to define our responsibilities in certain ways. She says:

> Aber das Wort taugt nicht: Ich. Der Satz taugt nicht: Sich selbst verwirklichen. Denn er setzte voraus, daß uns das Leben eigen wäre, Substanz, an der wir, jeder nach seinem Entwurf, modeln könnte. Wer kann das noch, Renate? Wie wenige haben je ihr Leben zu eigen gehabt? Und auf wessen Kosten? (376)
>
> [But the word is no good: I. The sentence is no good: to realize oneself. Because it assumes that our lives are a substance we are each free to mold according to our own design. But who can still do this, Renate? How few have ever had their lives to themselves? And at whose expense?]

The scholar Katharina Aulls has emphasized the fatalistic tone of this statement, but what I find implied in it is that to have "realized her full potential" would have meant not fulfilling her responsibilities to those dependent on her.[9] It acknowledges that our lives as individuals are embedded in contexts that exceed the boundaries of the individual self, and that to act as if one were autonomous (as the professor suggests) would entail not living up to the responsibilities given to us and chosen by us. Gabriele knows that she consciously accepted a level of responsibility toward those near to her. She realizes that the people around her will all continue to re-examine the level of responsibilities they bear, but she recognizes that she has chosen to accept certain responsibilities and intends to fulfill them.

Both Walker's feminist conceptual framework for morality and Drewitz's attempts to discern the responsibilities individuals strive to fulfill in life have arisen from within women's sociohistorical roles as caregivers and nurturers. While Walker's study shies away from any essentialist attribution of moral behavior, Drewitz clearly links the perspectives of Gabriele and the narrator in *Eis* to their roles as women, wives, and mothers.[10] In this regard, her novels echo the work of early feminist ethicists like Carol Gilligan, Sara Ruddick, and Nel Noddings, who explored basing ethics on the fundamental concept of caring, as well as the work of Virginia Held, who uses the concept of mothering in an abstract form to move beyond the essentialist concerns critics raised about care ethics.[11] In order to clarify how Drewitz's position on women and responsibility changed over time, a brief excursus into the ethical questions she raises in an earlier novel, *Wer verteidigt Katrin Lambert?*, will be helpful.

This novel resonates much more closely with Nel Noddings's early text on care ethics than with either Drewitz's own later work or Walker's study of ethics. Indeed, the basic premise of *Wer verteidigt Katrin Lambert?* offers a virtually ideal narrative for thinking through a model such as Noddings's *Caring*. The novel, which takes place in the period immediately preceding its publication in 1974, centers on the narrator's investigation of the title character's death: Katrin Lambert, a social worker, drowned after venturing too far out onto thin ice for no apparent reason. The narrator is a female journalist who had known Katrin when they were both in school. She comes across the notice of Katrin's death in the newspaper and decides to find out more about it.[12] Only through the narrator's interviews with Katrin's many friends, relatives, clients, and colleagues do we get some sense of who she was. In other words, her character takes literary form only through the eyes of those for whom she cared — either professionally or personally.

Drewitz embodies the impetus of care in Katrin, a person entirely committed to caring for others. In addition to her own children, Monika and Knut, Katrin strives to care for her friends, her ex-husband, and of course, as a social worker, her clients. Yet already in this work, Drewitz explores the possible detrimental ramifications of care ethics for women's psychological and social development. Katrin's approach to the people around her is to offer unequivocal support. In the process, she suppresses her own needs, which are in turn ignored by those around her. Katrin's children never manage to get beyond the uni-directional care model of mother as caregiver and child as cared-for: only after her death do they begin to realize that their mother might have needed them as much as they needed her. When considering her relationship to her own children, Monika regrets the distance that grew between her mother and herself. She says, "Vielleicht hat sie mich (endlich einmal) gebraucht, und ich war nicht bereit" (Maybe she finally needed me, and I wasn't ready; 53). Knut, too, eventually considers that his mother was not there simply to respond to him (173). Robby, a troubled young man and one of Katrin's clients, provides another kind of example of how Katrin's version of care ethics fails to foster and nurture the cared-for as she hoped. Although he acknowledges that Katrin cared for him — one of Noddings's requirements for the reciprocity of care — he rebels against his subordinate position both in their relationship and in society. First he sets the group home in which he lives on fire, then he tries to rape Katrin the night before she dies.

One could summarize Katrin's life philosophy as follows: "Wenn Menschen in Bedrängnis sind, zählt das eigene Gesicht überhaupt nicht" (When someone is in trouble, one's own self doesn't count at all; 147). It's as if the entire identity of the caregiver — metonymically represented here by the face — vanishes into meeting the needs of the cared-for. She exemplifies the self-sacrifice of an *unreflected* ethics of care. Both Noddings and, later, Sara Ruddick underscore the importance of critical self-reflection on the part of the caregiver or the one mothering. Katrin's unnecessary death, however, does draw attention to the tensions inherent in early articulations of care ethics.

Drewitz herself claimed that we should not see Katrin's death as a premeditated suicide, but rather as an attempt to test whether the ground beneath her would hold, or to establish whether her approach to others was sufficient to sustain her emotionally. Although Noddings takes it for granted that, in order to care, the caregiver must devote similar energy and creativity to maintaining her own self (99 and 105), she maintains that the efforts of the caregiver depend completely on the reaction of the cared-for for confirmation and completion (4). Drewitz's novel asks what happens to the caregiver when such receptivity is either denied her or when the response is limited to the mere acknowledgment of the caregiver's service to the cared-for. Noddings argues that the caregiver can decide not to care any longer in such a situation, but the lack of reciprocity in all of Katrin's relationships critiques the very nature of her approach to other people. In this regard Katrin's death represents a fairly negative answer to such a question on Drewitz's part. It foregrounds the pitfalls of locating self-worth too extensively in an unbalanced care relationship: Katrin's other-orientation and the uni-directional nature of her sense of care, which is similar to Noddings's care ethics, ultimately lead to Katrin's emotional exhaustion and probable suicide.

Drewitz's own narrative experiment with an ethics based on unequal relationships of caring from 1974 led her to push on in her attempts to understand the nature of personal and, ultimately, collective responsibility. She continued to explore the relationship women have to their children and, beyond that, to the world around them. Her subsequent novels reflect the understanding that one cannot adequately fulfill one's moral responsibilities while denying one's own needs. In a very real sense, *Wer verteidigt Katrin Lambert?* questions the effort to export domestic models of behavior into the public sphere and challenges the benefits of such a caregiver model to self-development. However, in her next two novels Drewitz comes to revise this position both by questioning the boundaries that separate private and public lives and by integrating more thoroughly questions of historical and contemporary political relevance.

In *Gestern war heute*, which appeared four years after *Wer verteidigt Katrin Lambert?*, Drewitz shifts her emphasis to the role of women as social caregivers through their position as mothers. In this sense, the novel echoes Sara Ruddick's thematization of maternal practices as a philosophical foundation for particular social and political agendas. Ruddick specifically seeks a way of approaching ethics that will lead to global peace. Drewitz, too, queries the mother as a locus for implementing an ethics of caring or a politics of peace. Her protagonist in the novel, Gabriele, reflects Drewitz's changing conception of a woman's relationship to her children and to the other people with whom she interacts.

Gabriele struggles intensely with what she feels is a woman's intrinsic approach to others. While dining with a male acquaintance who has asked her to leave her family and explore the world with him, Gabriele makes the statement, already cited in chapter 2, that women experience the world with arms open to care for others (298). Gabriele is, nonetheless, torn between this understanding of what it means to be a woman and her thirst to find her own place in the wider world, one she can claim solely for herself. While she does not give in to her acquaintance's proposition to leave her family, she is frustrated by how constrained she feels in her personal development. Ultimately, she acquiesces partially to the traditional demands on women to stick by their husbands and care for their children. She cannot free herself entirely from a model of caring that locates in the mother the fundamental human gesture of caring. As such, she offers the reader a transitional figure in the development of Drewitz's understanding of ethics. We see in Drewitz's novels the struggle to reevaluate critically the idea that mothers have a special capacity to care and the ramifications of such an understanding of motherhood.

In *Gestern war heute*, Drewitz's main character Gabriele marries Jörg, a man who cannot respond to her emotional and professional needs. While they have a mutually satisfying sexual relationship, they have little else in common. For a while, Gabriele even manages to break free of the relationship, moving away and launching her own career as a journalist. She tries repeatedly during the separation to explain her motives to Jörg, to get him to respond to anything other than financial needs, but he cannot. Only the death of her second daughter and the impending birth of her third disrupt her confidence enough to send her back into this strained partnership.

In the earlier novel, the author never identifies the father of Katrin Lambert's children, and she lives alone. In *Gestern war heute*, Gabriele breaks free initially from a loveless relationship, returning later only under extremely stressful conditions. Although Jörg, the male partner in this relationship, is not only identified but also plays a role in the novel, he remains a rather pale figure. Indeed the author seems little interested in the representation of male characters or in exploring how male-female relationships might take a different form. Instead, she focuses exclusively on the relationship of Gabriele to the broader world around her, primarily, as the novel progresses, to the increasingly complicated and problematic lives of her daughters. One daughter goes into the political underground and begins to reconcile with her family only when her fellow protester and boyfriend is arrested and incarcerated. Another daughter becomes pregnant and marries before she even finishes high school. None of the female characters in the novel manage to break away from destructive and constraining relationships with men. Drewitz's emphasis on the mother figure and her struggles to protect, nurture, and assist her daughters socially, not only resonate with the ideas in Ruddick's *Maternal Thinking* but also problematize them.

*Gestern war heute* explores the possibilities for maternal thinking to shape the world for the better, but arrives only at tentative conclusions. Drewitz never really uses her female characters to propose that women — because of their experiences as mothers — might be uniquely in a position to contribute to a project as large as the one Sara Ruddick proposes in *Maternal Thinking* — namely "imagining or creating peace."[13] Nonetheless, she explores how women's historical conditioning within families has led them to be more attuned to the needs and emotions of those around them than men are. Indeed, she sees women as recognizing much more acutely than men to what extent the existence of each of us is interwoven with the lives of others. This recognition, however, does not seem to contribute to a viable ethical framework.

Yet in the space of the few years separating the publication of these two novels, Drewitz begins to shift her focus from thinking about women's responsibilities, particularly as driven largely by their roles as mothers and wives, to a model of responsibility in which we are all imbricated equally — if not in exactly the same ways — in the social construction and distribution of responsibilities. We can see this progression in the character constellations themselves. In *Wer verteidigt Katrin Lambert?* the central character is both a mother and a social worker. Her entire being is devoted to caring for others. Furthermore, although her ex-husband is one of the sources for the narrator's efforts to piece together Katrin's life, her children have no known father. Thus, the role a father might be expected to play in caring for his children is completely absent in the novel.

In *Gestern war heute* only Gabriele comes over the course of the book to understand her life choices as responding to particular networks of responsibilities. The reader never sees her uncommunicative and emotionally distant husband Jörg go through this process as well. He recognizes his financial obligations to his family, but none of the emotional or nurturing responsibilities that need to be involved in such personal relationships. Gabriele cries out repeatedly in frustration about missed and missing opportunities for self-fulfillment, seeking in vain some concrete sense of her own self-worth distinct from her role within her own family, while Jörg exists independently and unquestioningly outside of the family. For him there is both a "we" and an "I." For Gabriele, there is really only the "we."

By the time Drewitz wrote *Eis auf der Elbe* another four years later, she had moved away from her almost exclusive focus in *Gestern war heute* on the figure of the mother and her quest for an independent self and a better understanding of her own responsibilities toward her children and others. Instead, *Eis* portrays a more mutually shared quest between husband and wife. The novel depicts the narrator's husband Heinrich as plagued by similar self-questioning as the narrator. Both are unsure exactly why they have come to be who they are but they explore the web of interconnections within which they made all of their choices and grapple with their multiple and sometimes competing responsibilities, the fulfillment of which had mutually significant ramifications. Thus, the narrator in *Eis auf der Elbe* displaces the self-denial or self-repression displayed by Gabriele in *Gestern war heute* onto both marriage partners. She says of her husband: "Wir haben Verantwortung zu übernehmen, war seine Redensart. Verantwortung für unsere Kinder, die Schüler, die jüngeren und älteren Kollegen. Wir. Wir. Das Wort Ich hat er nicht gekannt. Ich. Und du" (We have to take the responsibility, was the way he talked. Responsibility for our children, the students, the younger and older colleagues. We. We. He didn't know the word I. I. And you; 17). This last passage demonstrates how different the character of Heinrich is from Jörg. Indeed, in a certain sense, Heinrich represents an inversion of the gender roles that one sees in either *Wer verteidigt Katrin Lambert?* or *Gestern war heute*. The reader learns that this character is equally invested in caregiving, almost to a fault. Virginia Held, in her work in feminist ethics, makes a similar developmental gesture when she abstracts the characteristics of mothering from the gendered and sexed "mother" and attempts to shift the foundation of ethics to "mothering" as an activity divorced from specific familial roles.[14]

Drewitz's characters, however, also demonstrate how the traditional underpinnings of Western morality, which is founded on the concept of the autonomous moral agent and the centrality of non-interference and contractual obligation, have led people to ignore whole aspects of human life as integral to our social responsibilities. Teaching, socializing, and caring for children, for instance, or tending the sick and the elderly become, as a result, peripheral activities. In such a view of human morality, people who dedicate themselves to such activities can see themselves as not measuring up to society's moral expectations. In both *Eis* and *Gestern war heute*, Drewitz's female protagonists grapple with a definition of the self that would leave them believing their lives to be failures.

This insight applies as well to other characters in the two novels under discussion. In *Gestern war heute* both the professor, who urges Gabriele to leave Berlin, and Gabriele's daughter, who wonders why her mother did not become an important journalist, have internalized a concept of the self that ignores or rejects the centrality of interdependence and responsibility to human identity. While *Gestern war heute* does begin to question the losses involved in looking at individual success in this way, it is in *Eis auf der Elbe* where Drewitz explores most thoroughly the role of the individual within the historical present and — as part and parcel of that process — attempts to chart the ways we acknowledge, struggle against, and assume our positions as responsible individuals within multiple and shifting communities.

Drewitz integrates history and the historical awareness of individuals into her narrative of their lives on the personal level and into the context of national — and even at times world — history.[15] She consciously and consistently positions her characters within specific historical moments. One key to understanding the significance of Drewitz's characters, even those who are apparently secondary figures is recognizing how all of them both respond to and affect the way society develops, that is, present history. Furthermore, this is true whether they do so intentionally or unintentionally, acting after rational reflection or based on irrational, spontaneous decisions.

One of Drewitz's chief accomplishments is that she consistently and thoroughly charted the ways in which individual life stories coincide or intersect with local, regional, national, and — in a limited sense — international history. At the same time she created a very concrete picture for the reader of what she perceives to be the historical present of her characters. Gerhild Brüggemann Rogers, who has written a comprehensive study of Drewitz's novels, acknowledges this feature of the novelist's work. Brüggemann Rogers notes how Drewitz has woven ("geflochten") political events into her narratives, but also suggests that Drewitz shies away from incorporating monumental historical events into her characters' conscious reflections.[16] Brüggemann Rogers's choice of the word "woven" is very apt. However, when she adds that Drewitz avoided letting her characters reflect on the monumental events at the center of her novels, she chooses not to explore the implications that Drewitz's choice has for the structure of individual historical consciousness or for how we internalize "monumental" events. Brüggemann Rogers argues at a later point that Drewitz's portrayal of historical developments functions solely as a backdrop, as quasi-historical color. Compared either to the work of her contemporary Heinrich Böll or to documentary literature of the 1960s and '70s, Drewitz's work fails, she argues, to connect for the reader the lines between personal and political praxis, leaving instead only a watery and obscure political-historical landscape so inscrutable that her characters acquiesce to a sense of helplessness and frustration.[17]

In contrast to Brüggemann Rogers, I see Drewitz's uncanny ability to weave monumental historical events into the day-to-day consciousness of her characters as a reasonably accurate representation of how individuals incorporate, contribute to, and literally embody such monumental events in the course of their lives. It also shows the different paths historical events take to reach our (sub)consciousness. Drewitz does this on several different planes: on the level of individual consciousness and personal history, in the physical surroundings of her characters, and in the broad political history to which they respond.

The subtitle of this novel is "Hundert Jahre Gegenwart" (One Hundred Years of Now), thus announcing already on the book's cover that its chronological parameters are broad. The narrative begins with the birth of Gabriele, the main character. The novel approaches her birth, however, via the individuals most closely touched by the event. Although the novel's narrative present begins in 1923, Drewitz reaches quite a bit further back into history by including the voices of the main character's relatives. First, Drewitz presents the thoughts of Gabriele's great-grandmother, who is eighty years old when Gabriele is born and over 100 years old when she dies at the end of the Second World War. Then Drewitz moves into the thoughts of Gustav, Gabriele's grandfather, the son-in-law of the great-grandmother, He wonders why people keep bringing children into a world full of such misery. He recounts his own family's immigration to Berlin from Silesia, the suffering, poverty, and misery they all endured and how their current cramped quarters merely perpetuate the troubles. The narrative moves from his thoughts to those of his wife, Gabriele's grandmother Alice. She contextualizes the life of the child about to be born within the socioeconomic disaster of an inflation-ridden Weimar Republic. We learn from each subchapter how the family has fought its way up the social ladder, but is perpetually threatened with the slide into unemployment and poverty. Gustav and Alice worked and saved to provide Susanne, their daughter and Gabriele's mother, with an entrance into the social sphere of the German middle class. A pianist of great talent, Susanne showed every sign of becoming a successful musician — until she married a man who struggled against unemployment for most of his adult life. At every turn in the characters' lives, political, economic, and social developments mark the crucial co-determinants of their choices. Gabriele's own voice emerges slowly from this multi-layered reflection on history and politics, and although she remains the central focus of the narrative, her children's voices become part of the historical framework within which her own story unfolds. As the Second World War ends, the characters' horizon gradually widens to take in political and social developments from across the globe.

While *Gestern war heute* provides a rich historical texture, *Eis auf der Elbe* adds more complexity in its depiction of how individuals conceive of their place within history and then actively work to define the spectrum of their own responsibilities. Although the narrative in its diary form covers only one month in 1981, *Eis* incorporates history and contemporary political developments in many different ways: sometimes in the language of dreams, sometimes through disjointed stream-of-consciousness moments, occasionally as fadeaways or the afterthoughts of particular characters, or as punctuation, so to speak, of other narrative developments. Some of these passages represent what we could see as examples of "covert" and "overt" rehearsal. For instance, describing a dream that reorganized elements of a dinner conversation she had had with her children and their spouses and partners, the main character in *Eis* underscores for the reader not only the fact that demonstrations against nuclear power plants were a pressing issue in Germany in the late 1970s and early '80s, but, calling to aid the syntactic lapses of dream imagery, also the connection between nuclear power and German economic interests. She describes what she hears in her dream as follows:

> Die Stimmen der Einsatzleiter über den Polizeifunk: Wie sollen wir sonst konkurrenzfähig bleiben? (So was Unsinniges sagen doch Einsatzleiter nicht, wenn sie Demonstrationen auflösen wollen.) ... Megaphone bellen, der Polizeifunk schnarrt: Und die Erde war wüst und leer, verstehe ich, und die Erde war wüst und leer, und die Erde war wüst und leer. (11)

> [The voices of the commando leaders over the police bullhorn: How else can we stay competitive? (Police commando leaders never say such nonsensical things when they want to break up a demonstration.) ... Megaphones bark, the police radios rasp: and the earth was barren and empty, I hear, and the earth was barren and empty, the earth was barren and empty.]

Although the narrator had remained silent over dinner when the subject of the demonstrations came up, her emotional involvement in the issue of nuclear power and its potential dangers for life on earth reveal themselves clearly enough through the language of the dream, which escalates in intensity literally to biblical proportions by the end of the diary entry. The drastic character of the closing image, "und die Erde war wüst und leer" (Genesis 1:2), belies her apparent indifference to the topic over dinner and demonstrates how viscerally private citizens responded to the attempted expansion of the nuclear power industry, how it strained family relationships, and pervaded individual perceptions of environmental concerns. The dream gives us an example of how our conscious selves often do not explicitly take stock of pressing issues in contemporary political reality and often do not recognize just how great an impact it has on our daily interactions with the people around us — visible in this scene in the tensions that arise among family members over dinner. It also represents the narrator's covert rehearsal of an event that was overtly rehearsed by the others over dinner. The tensions in the dinner conversation resulting from the different political perspectives of the individuals around the table, led her to block herself out of an open discussion, but this in turn forced her confrontation with the issue into the less public realm of dreams. One should add, however, that the narrator stages the events in her dream in an even more public arena than the initial discussion itself: a demonstration complete with police presence, megaphones, and arrests.

Occasional interruptions in the mundane patterns and flow of individual consciousness also open up a view into the web of relationships that lie embedded in our subconscious just below our awareness of them. Christine, one of the narrator's daughters, had been deeply involved in the extra-parliamentary movement in Germany, had married a protest singer-songwriter, gone off to Spain to wait for the political promises that Franco's death might entail, and had then returned to Germany and a dreary job as a chemist to support her child and now disillusioned, abusive husband. In one moment of the text, the reader sees Christine drive off after leaving her son at school, mulling over the traffic, the weather, and her life choices: "Sie raucht die fünfte Zigarette, als sie aus der Parklücke ausschert (wozu lebe ich eigentlich?), Chemikerin, was produziert die Firma? Sie muß auf den Verkehr achten . . ." (She smokes the fifth cigarette as she tears out of the parking space (why am I actually alive?), a chemist, what does the company produce? She must pay attention to the traffic . . .; 12). In the midst of the activities of smoking, driving, dropping children off at school, a character suddenly reviews her past and what it means that someone of her politically activist background should find herself working in an industry whose business practices she surely would have bitterly protested a few years ago. Giving in to what she perceives as the needs of her family, she suppresses her political and philosophical beliefs, generally even refusing to think about them. She cannot, however, make them go away, and so they become part of the bitterness and struggle of her life.

At the same time, Christine's personal history connects more broadly to the social and political developments in 1960s and 1970s Europe and allows Drewitz to comment on differing understandings of individual involvement in political developments. The character of Christine, for instance, illustrates well how Drewitz's thinking about the particular kind of political activism that characterized the student movement develops between the two novels. Renate, Gabriele's daughter in *Gestern war heute*, serves as something of a prototype for Christine. *Gestern war heute* captures this character still caught up in the heady climate of political activism in Germany of the late 1960s and early 1970s. Written only four years later, *Eis* already reflects the disillusioned exhaustion that characterized many former activists like Renate and Christine, and in it, Drewitz explores the possible reasons for such exhaustion.

History, however, intervenes in our daily lives through more than our own past and the choices we have made as individuals. Drewitz's narrator repeatedly uses German and world historical events to punctuate or to locate chronologically and geographically the course of her character's life. In one passage the narrator talks about how the stories in the news either affected her and her husband directly or they overlooked them: "Nachrichten gingen uns etwas an, oder wir übergingen sie" (Either the news affected us, or we ignored it). But what follows reveals that statement to be untrue:

> Weltkriegsgefahr wegen Kuba, die Raketen schon auf der Abschußrampe; oder in Hamburg die Spiegelaffäre; oder der tägliche Donner, wenn die Düsenjäger über West-Berlin die Schallmauer durchbrachen; oder, oder. Wir richten nach dem Bau der Berliner Mauer unsere erste Wohnung ein, haben drei Kinder, haben Einschulungsfeiern hinter uns, schleifen Parkettfußböden, legen Kabel unter Putz, die Hände sind rauh und geschunden, die Augen tränen von Staub und Müdigkeit. (43)[18]

> [Danger of a world war over Cuba, the missiles are already on the launching pad; or in Hamburg the Spiegel Affair; or the daily thunder when the jet fighters flying over West Berlin break the sound barrier; or, or. After the construction of the Berlin wall we furnish our first apartment, have three children, get the children started in school, sand wooden floors, lay cables under plaster, hands raw and chafed, eyes teary from the dust and the exhaustion.]

Moving from a region as remote as Cuba and a potentially global conflict ever closer until we hear the jets thundering over the divided city of Berlin, the narrator draws in the international and national crises that have an impact on them just as does the physical and domestic activity that rounds out the scene. What was happening in Cuba could, of course, have had an impact on the lives of Drewitz's postwar German characters, but the degrees of connection also differ considerably as she makes her way from Cuba, to Germany, to West Berlin.

Margaret Urban Walker's "geographies of responsibility" can help us to understand how varying degrees of connection between people and groups of people manifest themselves in the perspectives of the individuals. Drewitz structurally engages in traversing what Walker would call "a moving horizon of commitments and adjustments." She localizes or ties her narrative travels to all sorts of different places by drawing them into the consciousness of the characters who remain in a specific place, Berlin. This further enables Drewitz to explore that moving horizon while still "allowing individual distinctiveness of situation and commitment" (Walker, 117). The ever-shifting horizon permits us to approach the question of responsibility within a flexible structure, revealing to us that moral communities often "nest within each other and overlap each other," as well as intersect and crisscross each other (Walker, 202). In order, however, to situate ourselves vis-à-vis our contemporary realities, we must also attempt to find ourselves in history, consciously to link our individual experiences to broader historical developments.

Perhaps nowhere in this novel do the different layers of history — personal, national, international, familial — show their mutual implications as well as the moment when the narrator describes how she and Heinrich first became a couple:

> Wir gingen im Schloßpark Charlottenburg spazieren, saßen auf dem Trümmerfeld am Spreebogen . . ., sahen Kindern zu und wie traurig sie waren, weil ihnen ein Luftballon davongeflogen war und langsam über die Spree hintrieb. Unsere Gedanken damals: Wie Kinder leben konnten ohne Erinnerung an alles, was auf uns lastete. Kinder in Deutschland. Unsere Fragen: Haben Sie das gewußt: Vergasungen, Erschießungen, Massengräber, gelöschter Kalk, die Berge von Schuhen . . ., und der süßliche Rauch aus den Verbrennungsöfen. (41)

> [We walked in the garden of the Charlottenburg Palace, sat among the ruins in the field by the Spree . . ., watched children who were sad because a balloon had gotten away from them and was slowly floating over the Spree. Our thoughts were then: How can children live without a memory of all the things that weigh on us. Children in Germany. Our questions: Did you know? Gassings, shootings, mass graves, water-slaked lime, the mountains of shoes . . ., and the sweet-smelling smoke from the crematoria.]

The walk through the palace gardens recalls the glory days of Prussian dominance, now lying in ruins, upon which they sit and among which children play their games. The ruins, which become a physical historical experience, and the children remind the narrator and her husband of the recent past and its unbelievable horrors. However, when they ask how children can possibly live without the memories that haunt the adults, they miss the significance for these children of the ruins and of their parents' burdensome memories, which will become — albeit through multiple mediations — part of the children's historical present too.

As if to underscore that our queries of how history shapes us in our present also determine how we try to respond to the present, the characters broaden the scope of their questions about their immediate past:

> Und Hiroshima? Und Nagasaki?
> . . . Paris ist stehen geblieben, weil ein deutscher General einen Befehl verweigert hat, sagte ich. Und was ist mit dem Algerienkrieg, dem Krieg in Indochina? Wie war das in Korea?

...
Und die Kinder hier bekommen Schulspeisung aus amerikanischen Spenden.
So einen Luftballon muß es doch zu kaufen geben. . . .
Wir hatten keine Antworten auf unsere Fragen. An dem Tag sind wir zum Du übergegangen. (40–41)

[And Hiroshima? And Nagasaki?
. . . Paris remained standing because a German general refused to carry out an order — I said. And what about the war in Algeria, in Indochina? What happened in Korea?
. . .
And the children here get school rations from American donations.
One ought to be able to buy such a balloon . . .
We didn't have any answers to our questions. On that day our relationship really began.]

The narrator and her husband pursue the questions of how Hiroshima, Paris, the war in Algeria, the conflicts in Indochina and Korea relate to their own situation. What is it about these remote sites that captures their thoughts repeatedly? Or rather how do these characters attempt to relate these conflicts to the ones in the divided city of Berlin? To answer these questions we can draw again on both Walker's concept of the geography of responsibilities and Halbwachs's theory of collective consciousness.

As noted already in chapter 1, Halbwachs uses the example of his own parents to discuss how each generation's response to the events unfolding around it creates response registers that they pass on to successive generations. Collective responses to such events are structured by the patterns of socialization and the collective social values of the preceding generations. For this reason, the specific significance of the ruins within the series of events that comprise the Second World War and the fall of Berlin may not be apparent to the children who grow up among the ruins, but the way their parents respond to developments in postwar Berlin, the kinds of questions they ask of those events, and the very physical reality of the ruins themselves will create the new social and perspectival structures within which the children confront the realities of their own times.

The narrator and her husband struggle to connect in their own minds the major historical conflicts of their times to their daily lives. As they do so, we see the fragmented, fragile lines they use to delineate their own position vis-à-vis the war in Algeria or in Indochina become ever clearer as they move in toward the space of their own lives. The lines are more tenuous and blurred the further away geographically such conflicts are, despite the characters' efforts to find their way in such a large political, geographic space. Unsure how to make the extended, more remote lines clearer, they concentrate on the closer, clearer, more tangible lines before them and go off to find the children another balloon. Their inability to map accurately and convincingly the topographies of connection and responsibility does not mean they do not acknowledge either that responsibility or the fact that they live their lives within communal spaces whose boundaries shift depending on the perspective from which they approach them. Furthermore, their hesitant attempts to explore the connections between geographically and socially remote happenings pave the way for the much more vigorous efforts of their children's generation to confront injustice across the globe. Drewitz's narrator and her husband felt compelled to address issues of personal and collective guilt in the aftermath of the Second World War and the Holocaust. Their efforts to do so were still largely local and personal, but the questions they asked themselves were taken up and expanded by the student movement and the global justice initiatives that followed it.

In the information age of the late twentieth and early twenty-first centuries, the proliferation of access to global information often confronts us with world events that make little sense to us or to which we cannot personally relate, and yet, they enter our field of vision; they become part of our understanding of the spaces in which we act.[19] We may intellectually be able — as Drewitz's characters surely are — to explain the various different political, ideological, and economic factors that lead to different situations and crises in the world, but we often cannot determine how the events are linked to our individual lives. Nonetheless, we know on some level that what happens in Algeria or in Korea happens in our space.

Drewitz expresses this challenge in the way she constructs the sentences that draw geographically remote events into her narrative. She often inserts them into the narrative flow as solitary questions or simply as a string of references with arbitrary punctuation: "Ein neuer Präsident in Argentinien, wieder ein Militär. Hausbesetzerkongreß in Münster. Zwei weitere Häuser in Berlin besetzt. Estnischer Bürgerrechtler mutmaßlich nach Hungerstreik gestorben" (A new president in Argentina, another military man. Squatters' conference in Münster. Two more houses occupied in Berlin. Estonian civil rights activist purportedly dead after a hunger strike; 173–74). As remote or indeed irrelevant as many of these international events may seem to the situation in Germany in the period of time the novel covers, Drewitz's protagonists refuse to allow the events simply to recede in their consciousness into a world-historical vacuum. The more remote physically or systemically national or international conflicts appear, the more the sentences that describe them resemble the dotted lines of unfinished mappings. The disconnected strings of "headlines" or events that she inserts into her narrative repeatedly, have the rhythmic feel of distinct pulses rather than complete thoughts. Similarly, we know there are or will be "roads" connecting two places on a map where currently there are only dotted lines that often mark unfinished roads or highways, but we are not yet ready or able to see them drawn in fully. However, it is through the characters' understanding and especially their questioning of history and world politics that they come to understand (or frankly — not to understand) themselves. They literally find their way to each other through their experience of the historical present: "An dem Tag sind wir zum Du übergegangen" (On that day our relationship really began).[20]

It is not that history, both recent and more removed, makes them what they are, but that they make themselves in and through their particular confrontation with history. Echoing what Halbwachs would say, David Carr, in *Time, Narrative, and History*, explains this distinction as follows:

> We can sum up this notion of historicity by saying that what the individual is is thus a function of his or her place in a historical setting. This is not a "straightforward" affirmation of the sort that might be made by a historical determinist, who calls the individual a "product" of history or the inevitable result of historical forces. Instead it is a phenomenological assertion about what the individual is "for himself." It means that the individual's self-understanding of himself passes through history.[21]

For Halbwachs the individual's self-understanding would pass through collective consciousness. And although Carr uses the expression "passes through," he (and Drewitz for that matter) do not see this passing through as a passive activity, but rather as an active, selective, and creative self-narrative. One example of how Drewitz illustrates this process is a scene from *Gestern war heute* previously discussed in chapter 1, in which Gabriele, her daughter, and Gabriele's sister Ulrike look through and select items they wish to keep from Gabriele's deceased father's apartment. From among seemingly immaterial and largely inconsequential items — at least Pierre Nora would presumably find them so — Gabriele and her daughter both respond to one particular item, namely a letter written by Gabriele's uncle (305–7) about his experiences of the January 1905 massacre in St. Petersburg, Russia, known as Bloody Sunday.[22] For a historian, the item could at best be supporting evidence of the social and political climate surrounding the massacre in St. Petersburg. For Gabriele and Renate, however, the item establishes different kinds of historical narratives into which they each individually and differently insert themselves.

As mentioned earlier, the two characters respond to the historical legacy of Gabriele's uncle Paul differently — Gabriele as the sympathetic but largely passive reporter of social injustice and Renate as the political activist of the 1970s.[23] In such scenes, history is shown to be a constitutive moment in the formation of an individual's identity — be that individual a disillusioned adult, a fervently activist student, or a small child wandering through a city's ruins in search of a balloon. Nonetheless, history is constitutive only as we selectively appropriate it. Neither completely constrained by some ill-defined, perhaps even non-existent historical reality, nor completely free of it, we shape and form history in our attempts to make sense of it.[24]

Although our historicity does not derive from a logically ordered, chronologically structured set of perceptions, individuals gather disparate moments and elements into manageable life stories. Carr formulates this process as follows: "Narrative coherence is what we find or effect in much of our experience and action, and to the extent that we do not, we aim for it, try to produce it, and try to restore it when it goes missing for whatever reason."[25] The narrator in *Eis* addresses her own largely unsuccessful efforts to make sense of what often seem disparate and unrelated events when she reflects on her autobiographical project: "Erinnerungen aufeinanderschichten, zusammenhanglose Erfahrungen sammeln: Und dabei doch *Mein Leben* denken. Die Zeitung von der ersten bis zur letzten Seite lesen. Was wird aus Polen? Eine Flugzeugentführung in Südostasien" (Layering memories on top of each other, collecting unconnected experiences: and still thinking *My Life*. Reading the newspaper from the first to the last page. What will become of Poland? An airplane hijacking in Southeast Asia; 173).[26] She goes on with a long string of seemingly unrelated world events that intersect with the day-to-day lives of people like her. But by including them, she shows how even such remote and often unintelligible occurrences become part of our life stories and leave each of us with an individual as well as a collective history, a collective history that goes well beyond the scope of our families or our specific communities. Additionally, this perception of our historical present demands of us critical reflection on individual and collective relationships and our responsibility for other communities that intersect with ours.

Both *Eis auf der Elbe* and *Gestern war heute* are narrative histories of particular individuals and families, but they are also chronicles of twentieth-century Germany. This is especially true of *Gestern war heute*, which covers roughly one hundred years of German history. If Drewitz's literary and historicist project were limited to the impact of the Third Reich and the Second World War on her German characters, one could simply group her work with the many literary texts that thematize the relationship of Germans to their past, and thus restrict its scope to one of *Vergangenheitsbewältigung*. What makes her work so intriguing and so much richer is that she insists on the role of history in identity-formation for everyone — and tries out various different ways to illustrate this within a spatially and temporally limited context: Berlin in the second half of the twentieth century. Furthermore, by constantly drawing international developments and conflicts into her narrative, she works toward revealing gradually the relevance of those events, many of which seem so remote, and explores the connections between communal, national, and international history. As mentioned above, the more spatially remote certain events are from her characters, the harder it is for them to conceptualize or visualize the relationships underlying historical processes. Yet Drewitz manages, by exploring the increasingly heterogeneous character of the German population, to sketch some initial mappings of how the histories of very diverse groups of people become intertwined with one another.

For instance, Drewitz was an early proponent of the rights of *Gastarbeiter* (guest workers) in Germany and an active participant in efforts to highlight for a German audience the literary and cultural tradition of their homelands. She draws them into her literary world already in *Gestern war heute*, but in *Eis* she portrays a whole array of Turkish characters, not limiting her view to the caricature of the essentially illiterate factory worker so familiar from other literary or cinematic efforts of the 1970s and early '80s,[27] but also including Turkish intellectuals, social activists, teachers, and children. Through these figures she demonstrates how the personal, political, and national histories of separate population groups intersect and grow together (however slow and painful that process may be). She writes not only of the problems her Turkish characters have because of Turkey's history and political situation, but also how Germany's national past and Turkish history come together in the lives of Berliners of the '70s and '80s. The narrator speaks of a Turkish client she has, Feride, and the part of Kreuzberg in which she lived before her incarceration:

> Feride hat in der Waldemarstraße gewohnt, hat nichts vom Prinzen Waldemar gewußt, nach dem die Straße benannt ist, hat die Graffiti an den grauweißen Flächen nicht entziffern können, auch die Zeichen nicht, das A für Anarchisten, das V für Neonazis. Hat sicher auch nicht darüber nachgedacht, warum diese Mauer mitten in der Stadt errichtet wurde. (20)

> [Feride lived in Waldemar Street, didn't know a thing about Prince Waldemar, after whom the street is named, didn't understand the graffiti on the greyish-white surfaces around her, nor the symbols — the A for anarchists, the V for the neo-Nazis. Surely didn't even think about why this wall was built through the middle of the city.]

Feride, as a recent immigrant, may not be able to decode the historical markers and boundaries of the world she has entered. To her, the embodied history of the city in which she lives is as unintelligible as the coded graffiti spread out on the wall before her. In fact, they must function textually for her much like the distant global events, the reality of which the narrator herself feels, but cannot bring together into a personally meaningful context. While Feride may not be able to read sense into the walls around her, the many children of foreign descent who play soccer in Kreuzberg's streets and guide the lawyer to Feride's old apartment house will certainly be able to do so, even as they leave their own impressions on these old *German* streets.[28]

The idea of these children growing into their own history allows us to acknowledge the awareness most of us have on some level that it is not simply famous men who make history, but indeed the entire myriad of individuals who respond to and then act upon the history which has taken shape within them. Given their knowledge of the city in which they are growing up and the fact that they will learn the language formally in school and informally on the city's streets, the Turkish-German children already provide us a good example of how this happens. However, Drewitz's narrator herself also offers us other opportunities to view the complex process that is history through historical developments that cross numerous national boundaries.

Another example is the fact that the narrator at one point mentions (rather obliquely as it happens) that when she became pregnant for the last time she had an abortion. She tells us,

> Heinrich und ich haben bis zuletzt zusammen geschlafen, auch in der Nacht vor der Geburt und dem Tod unseres vierten Kindes, auch in den Nächten, bevor ich in die Privatklinik von Dr. F. ging, der schon die Absaugmethode praktizierte, als darüber noch nicht gesprochen werden durfte. (15)

> [Heinrich and I slept together until the very end, even in the night before the birth and death of our fourth child, even in those nights before I went to Dr. F's private clinic, who practiced the suction method even before one was allowed to speak of it.]

The seemingly innocuous phrase "even before one was allowed to speak of it" evokes the many stories that women in Europe and the United States began to tell publicly in the early 1970s about abortions they had had before abortion became legal. Telling such stories contributed to a change in public consciousness about this issue and represented both a covert and an overt rehearsal of a series of personal traumas. While the political and social developments surrounding the issue of abortion vary from country to country, the passage reveals to the reader how the narrator's story, although a story of one individual, combines with the stories of thousands of others, generally of individuals who did not intend to make a contribution to the political history of the industrialized world, but who did so nonetheless. The public rehearsal of these private traumas allows individuals who have not lived through such experiences to participate in a collective social narrative.

Many of the characters and events in Drewitz's novels serve a similar function, whether it is the Turkish immigrant incarcerated for shoplifting, or the young lovers, who, seeking adventure, drop their university studies to join squatters who have occupied empty apartment houses in Berlin, or the husband and wife who wonder why they turned out to be so insignificant. In one scene, the narrator walks with her husband, who is dying of cancer. While they walk, they question directly why they did not do more to combat injustice in the world:

> Hätten wir nicht auf Marktplätzen reden müssen, um uns die Bettler, die Obdachlosen, die Mütter und die Kinder mit den vorquellenden Bäuchen? Hätten wir uns in Wüstengebirgen verstecken müssen, roter, gelber, grauer Sand, alte Gewehre im Anschlag, auf die gerichtet, die mit Maschinenpistolen eine Grenze verteidigen, die wir nicht anerkannten? . . . Hätten wir nicht Streikposten sein müssen, wo immer die Arbeit niedergelegt wurde? Hätten wir nicht Schulen und Krankenstationen entlang der verkarsteten Flußbetten in Afrika, in den Urwäldern Braziliens bauen müssen? . . . Wir waren wieder stehengeblieben. Hundebesitzer, Liebespaare hatten uns zugehört, Leute, die ihr Auto einparkten, ein Betrunkener, der in weitem Bogen auf den Fahrdamm pißte.
> . . . Es war Zeit, nach oben zu gehen, Zeit für die abendlichen Medikamente. Heinrich war müde. Und ich?
> Ich wagte nicht weiterzudenken. . . . In diesen letzten Wochen musste ich seine Bettwäsche täglich wechseln. (185–86)
>
> [Shouldn't we have spoken on the market squares, around us the beggars, the homeless, the mothers, and the children with their protruding bellies? Shouldn't we have hidden ourselves in mountains of sand — red, yellow, gray sand, old weapons aimed and ready to fire on those with the automatic weapons who guarded the borders we did not recognize? . . . Shouldn't we have gone out with the strikers wherever they were laying down their work? Shouldn't we have built schools and first-aid stations along the karstified river beds in Africa, in the rain forests of Brazil? . . . We had stopped again. Dog owners, couples had listened to us, people who were parking their cars, a drunk who was pissing a broad arc onto the roadway.
> . . . It was time to go upstairs, time for his evening medications. Heinrich was tired. And I?
> I didn't dare think any further. . . . In these last weeks I had to change his bedding every day.]

In this passage, the narrator and her husband both show the reader that they are fully aware of having responsibilities within larger communities than their own immediate ones, but they are not sure exactly what those responsibilities are and how they can fulfill some responsibilities without neglecting others. The text does not offer or pretend to make excuses for them, nor does it answer the questions they ask. It simply acknowledges what they did not do and hints repeatedly as to why they did not.

Feminist ethicists such as Joan Tronto and Selma Sevenhuijsen push us to think of the responsibilities we have to care for those beyond our families and people with whom we have personal relationships. Tronto, for example, connects these responsibilities to the concept of attentiveness: our awareness of our own implication in situations that impact others' need for care makes it imperative that we seek to address those needs. Not doing so in her eyes makes us morally culpable. However, in contrast to Drewitz's characters in *Eis*, who are struggling to understand the scope of personal responsibility, Tronto and Sevenhuijsen also clearly see it as both an individual and a collective phenomenon, one that — as Margaret Urban Walker argues — must be established collectively. Sevenhuijsen stresses that this cannot be accomplished if we continue to think of caring and responsibility as domestic or private matters.

One way to understand how Drewitz attempts to think through the complexities of individual and collective responsibility is to look at the disappointment and confusions with which the narrator of *Eis auf der Elbe* views her own daughters' life choices. In her article about mothers and daughters in German literature of the 1970s and 1980s, Helga Kraft addresses the narrator's sadness at not having been a positive role model for her children. Kraft attributes this failure in some measure to the narrator's implicit message to her daughters that they should stick to their men no matter the consequences for themselves.[29] Monika Shafi offers a slightly different assessment of both Gabriele in *Gestern war heute* and the narrator in *Eis auf der Elbe*. She argues that they are seeking and modeling for their daughters a new, more political form of the self, but that what they are seeking and what they are modeling for their daughters is not yet possible in society.[30] In other words, the mothers fail because they are ahead of their time. Nonetheless, Drewitz's texts seem to suggest that it is misleading to think that the necessary conditions for a conflict-free existence will ever be achieved. In contrast to the revolutionary political philosophy of the student movement activists, who had recently dominated public discussion of social change (and whom Drewitz embodies in such characters as Christine and Renate), Drewitz's work suggests that as human beings act, react, and reflect on their actions, they gradually come to change what they see as the social distribution of power and responsibility. Her novels stress that the process is an ongoing and slow one. As Margaret Urban Walker writes, our narrative accounts to ourselves of what we believe are our responsibilities link "past moral lives (individual, interpersonal, and collective) to future ones in a way not completely determined by where things started, and open to different continuations that may yet affect what the resolution means" (69). The process of historical change does not allow us to turn insight into the nature and causes of oppression into an immediate remedy, nor can we always predict what the outcomes of actions will be — on both the collective and the individual level.

Drewitz also gives us a real sense of why this is true. It may strike the reader as odd that a work encompassing roughly sixty years of German, European, and world history — as *Eis* does — should begin in the drudgery of the kitchen: "Es ist wie jedesmal, wenn sie gegangen sind. Ich lasse Wasser ins Spülbecken, spritze Spülmittel hinein, reguliere die Wassertemperatur (der Boiler ist alt, die Wassertemperatur läßt sich nicht anders als mit der Hand kontrollieren)" (It's like this every time when they have left. I let water run in the sink, squirt in the soap, set the water temperature [the boiler is old, the water temperature can only be controlled manually]; 5). The text goes on like this for several pages. In fact, Drewitz consistently drags world history and politics down to the level of the mundane. With varying degrees of detail, she integrates into the narrative flow a local or national historical-political problem, expands her gaze to the level of global politics, but never strays far from the kitchen — or the daily tasks and drudgeries that it represents.[31]

While this narrative practice could become increasingly irritating if it were merely an attempt to aestheticize domestic life, Drewitz's repeated incorporation of the physical regimen of our lives, the demands involved in raising children, putting food on the table, and creating a space in which to live is telling. School celebrations, worn-out boilers, cases of the measles, burned dinners, recitals, etc. are not metaphors for anything else, nor are they an ersatz source for personal fulfillment.[32] They simply underscore the limitations within which human history and society progresses — and not only women's history. I argue, however, that this insight into the significant role that mundane tasks and the fulfillment of basic human needs in human life play begins in both the particular forms of women's socialization in twentieth-century Europe and in early feminist theory.

This last point leads to what I see in Drewitz's work as a protofeminist conceptualization of moral responsibility and political action. Her emphasis on the multiple ways in which individuals act in and react to history reveals as untenable arrogance a notion of history and social progress that assumes that certain individuals can act autonomously and turn insight into instant equality. Our roles as moral agents in society are much more complex than that, determined within a web of relationships that do not simply go away when we act as if we were responsible only to ourselves or, obversely, only to the world. In other words, our roles within the private and public spheres are neither distinct nor separately manageable. Both the narrator of *Eis* and Gabriele in *Gestern war heute* come to learn that an insistence on the pivotal role of the individual in historical change is bound to lead to frustration and hopelessness. Indeed, that underlying such a concept of political agency is a streak of arrogance that assumes that an individual agent can act outside of both an immediate as well as a mediated network of responsibilities. In response to her daughter's accusation that she failed to fulfill her professional potential as a star journalist, Gabriele muses:

> Sie kann ihr nicht sagen, daß das ihre eigenen Fragen sind, daß ihr das ICH als Ziel abhanden gekommen ist, weil sich das ICH nicht behaupten kann ohne Hochmut. Daß sich das ICH nicht nur am Erfolg messen läßt, am Platz in der Gesellschaft, sondern auch im Zuhören, im Bereitsein für andere erfahren werden kann. (315)

> [She cannot say to her that those are her own questions, that she has lost sight of the "I" as a goal, because one cannot insist on the "I" without arrogance. That this "I" need not measure itself solely according to its success or its status in society, but also in listening, in being ready to help others.]

Gabriele and the lawyer in *Eis* may both be saddened and frustrated by the suffering they see in their daughters, but they also acknowledge that they are not the sole influence in their children's lives and that success is a nebulous term. It has been defined historically by social structures that fail to recognize the demands of both sustaining life and maintaining interpersonal relationships that are of value to us.

Nonetheless, it would be a misreading of these characters to assert that they give up when faced with the seeming inefficacy of individual political or social activism aimed at systemic revolution, or that they have retreated from social engagement because it seldom yields discernible changes quickly. Drewitz's protagonists participate actively in the struggle for social equality and human rights, but they also recognize that the revolutionary optimism that characterized the student movement's activists, and the very notion of revolution itself, was bound to result in exhaustion and cynicism. Repeatedly in both novels, the characters vent their frustration at how little they seem to effect change through their struggles to lighten the load for the poor, to protect the environment from overly profit-hungry industries, to help others in their struggle with impersonal and often cruel courts. Christine, for instance, talks about her early activism and her decision to work with the chemical manufacturer that represents so much of what she despises: "Wahrscheinlich gehen die Revolution und die Revolutionäre am Jedenmorgen kaputt" (Revolutions and revolutionaries probably all flounder in day-to-day existence; 132). On the other hand, Drewitz herself suggested in her own statements that there are successes in the face of failures. In an interview with Ekkehart Rudolph, she said, "Aber . . . etwas an zwischenmenschlicher Substanz [ist] noch nicht ausgelöscht, [ist] nicht verdorrt, daß *ein* Mensch, auch im Scheitern, noch etwas bewirken kann." (But there is still some substance in interpersonal relationships that hasn't been exhausted, that isn't dried up, that a human being — even in failure — can still change something).[33] Ultimately, her protagonists suggest implicitly that we must rethink our concepts of political agency and historical change in order to avoid the brick wall of disappointment that we run into when revolutions fail to succeed or even to occur.

Leslie Adelson argues in her book *Making Bodies, Making History* that "feminist writing strategies are necessarily bound to the extra literary struggle for social and cultural self-determination, a struggle that requires some working notion of historical agency for women."[34] Drewitz's novels demonstrate how women have been, can be, and surely always will be historical agents, but she also consistently contextualizes individual actions within the specific constraints of human existence. I do not, on the other hand, see in her work a quietistic satisfaction with the way things are — or with our individual efforts to act responsibly. Instead the two novels offer a version of social activism that entails a recognition of one's own imbrication in several layers of history. It pushes us to act where we see injustice, but also to protect ourselves in a sense from larger-than-life expectations that do not take into account the drudgeries and complexities of human life. In one scene from *Eis*, the narrator comments on the apparently isolated and lonely death of the old man in the building across from her. Thinking about him allows her to relate the importance of her reflections on her life in her narrative:

> SEIT DIE WOHNUNG DES ALTEN MANNES GEGENÜBER NICHT MEHR BEWOHNT IST, NICHT MEHR BEWOHNT ZU SEIN SCHEINT, weiß ich warum ich das Tagebuch führe. Sie könnten mich auch so finden, allein in der Wohnung. Ob sie dann in der Kladde auf dem Schreibtisch blättern würden über den Einzelheiten, begreifen würden, daß ich versucht habe, ein gewöhnliches Leben zu leben, und daß es mir nicht leicht gefallen ist? (111)

> [SINCE THE APARTMENT OF THE OLD MAN ACROSS FROM ME IS NO LONGER OCCUPIED, OR AT LEAST APPEARS TO BE EMPTY, I KNOW WHY I'M WRITING THIS DIARY. They could find me like that too in this apartment. Would they then page through the notebook on the desk, understand through the details that I have tried to live a normal life and that it has not been easy for me?]

In other words, we must always see that being involved in one's community, working toward social equality on a daily basis, is embedded within the context of life as a struggle for balance between the emotional, the physical, the ideological, the social, and the political. Rather than being a frustrating and depressing trudge through our collective political and historical failures, Drewitz's novels help to re-orient a concept of political agency within a larger framework. A framework that includes global history, international politics, parent-teacher conferences, and doing the dishes.

The aesthetic-structural choices Drewitz made that allowed her to combine so seamlessly the political and the personal, the individual and the communal, still require some clarification. In this section I am particularly interested in exploring narrative — as David Carr formulates it — as "our primary (though not our only) way of organizing our experience of time."[35] Margaret Urban Walker would add that narrative is also the way in which we try to understand our own moral framework. In other words, the stories we tell ourselves about our past function not only to "make sense" of that past, but also to help us figure out how to be in the present and, protensively, in the future. The extended narratives of fiction help us to think through or to experiment with specific ethical frameworks because they allow us to emplot such frameworks first in fictional relationships either to see how well they correspond to how we believe individuals interact or to push our thinking about ethics in new directions.

Although we experience the world through our bodies and our minds, and time is literally inscribed on our bodies, we nonetheless explain these inscriptions to ourselves at some point in narrative form, even if that narrative is not a chronologically ordered one.[36] As mentioned above, Carr argues that we need to tell ourselves stories in order to create sense in our lives, to gather together the disparate elements of experience into something that we can recognize:

> At no level, and certainly not at the scale of the life-story itself, is the narrative coherence of events and actions simply a "given" for us. Rather it is a constant task, sometimes a struggle, and when it succeeds it is an achievement. As a struggle it has an adversary, which is, described in the most general way, temporal disorder, confusions, incoherence, chaos. To experience, to act, to live, in a most general sense, is to maintain and if necessary to restore the narrative coherence of time itself, to preserve it against this internal dissolution into its component parts.[37]

The narratives we write for ourselves allow us to act. Both Carr and Walker suggest that we must first remember and structure our memories before we can decide which course of present action seems the most promising.[38] We selectively appropriate elements from our experience and from our historical present in order to understand both ourselves and the people around us.

Generally, such narratives do not attempt to include what is happening or has happened in the past but in some area of the world that is remote from us. However, the implicit attempt in Drewitz's novels to map a geography of responsibility and to create sense out of the chaos of experience makes such an expansive narrative necessary. For Drewitz this takes shape as the narrative of an individual positioned within multiply intersecting communities. This story then becomes a shared story, not shared equally by all members of the community, but recognizable to all. Carr argues that the story-teller can be an individual who speaks on behalf of the community, but the other members of the community must "believe or accept [the story] as the genuine account of what the group is and what it is doing."[39] There can be conflicting interpretations, but the general parameters of the story must be acceptable to the members of the community. As we will see in the next chapter, Christa Wolf incorporates the process of generating public dialogue and — at least to a limited extent — consensus on her historical narrative in *Kindheitsmuster* by including in the book the responses of audience members who attended public readings of the book at various stages in its creation. Drewitz's narrative style, primarily a straightforward realist approach, is not as complex as Wolf's, but the inclusion of several generational perspectives works toward establishing a minimal common ground.

In telling the life histories of her two female protagonists, Drewitz brings in not only what the two women experience or feel individually, but also the experiences and events that intersect with their lives. Because the two stories are told from the perspective of the protagonist, they show how two individuals try to make sense of the very disparate events and developments that enter their consciousness. They do not attempt rigorously to integrate the experiences of all of the other characters, but rather — and this is particularly true in the diary form of *Eis* — only speculate on how the others create sense out of their lives. The immediate community whose narrative Drewitz relates is specific to her generation of Germans. Elements of that narrative are shared by minorities living in Germany, by younger Germans, and by communities that share significant aspects of their historical present. While the narrative is thus historically specific, the process it illustrates of how individuals grapple with their position within history and their responsibilities to history goes beyond that very circumscribed community.

Gerhild Brüggemann Rogers suggests that the narrative perspective in these novels permits Drewitz to connect world historical events and social conflict to and through the consciousness of the individual. The perspective of the authorial narrator, she argues, is not consistently clear in Drewitz's work. Rather the personal perspectives of the characters on the historical events happening around them dominate, giving the reader a more limited but more personal access to their significance.[40] The advantage to such a narrative strategy in this context is that we as readers can watch how someone else, namely Drewitz's protagonists, try to create a story out of their lives — much as in a kind of laboratory space. We see how, in the case of these two novels, two women pick and choose from the experiences of their lives, their knowledge of history, and what happens in the world beyond their immediate environment to fashion a more comprehensive narrative of their time. Of primary importance to the narrator in *Eis* and Gabriele in *Gestern war heute* is the experience of growing up during the Third Reich and having to spend the rest of their lives coming to terms with that past. But since they do not live in a community consisting only of Germans born in the 1920s, they must also attempt to understand the sociopolitical and emotional forces that influence the actions of those around them. Again, Margaret Urban Walker can add to our understanding of how individually specific understandings of values intersect with and must be intelligible to the broader community or communities with which they intersect:

> Responsibility ethics clarifies the structure of the moral accounts people actually tend to keep and give. It sees these accounts as individual and individuating narratives of lives that are particularly our own. But these narratives, even if individuating, cannot be private or idiosyncratic. They serve purposes of *shared* understanding, not only of self-guidance but of justification and criticism. We are neither unfortunate enough to have to go it all alone in trying to find an acceptable and vital moral order in our lives nor lucky enough to have the last word on whether we have succeeded. (106)

In order to function, in order to act, the narrator in *Eis* often finds herself compelled to create provisional life stories for her clients and acquaintances. In one such instance she tries to imagine a life story for one of her clients, because she realizes that she does not, and probably will never know the *real* story: "Ich muss einen Menschen erfinden, wenn ich ihn nicht finden kann" (I have to invent a person if I cannot actually find him; 14).[41] There is, however, always an underlying recognition on the part of the narrator that such stories are at best only our rather weak attempts to stave off the real chaos of experience, of life: necessary, but never more than provisional, never more than tentative. As chronicles of individual lives, both novels show us how many and varied are the ways we incorporate our historical present into the narratives that we tell ourselves in order to function: narratives we also need to tell in order to understand how we decide which actions we consider best.

Clearly, we are neither able nor willing completely to invent the historical present in and through which we live. We are constrained in our narratives by so many intervening factors that, as Alasdair MacIntyre formulates it, "We are never more (and sometimes less) than the co-authors of our own narratives."[42] But it is neither the accuracy of our accounts nor the content of those accounts that is most interesting in Drewitz's work. What she does most effectively is to show us *how* we relate to or construct our historical present as individuals. She does so in a way, furthermore, that makes us aware that we are capable of effecting change within that structure as individuals on multiple levels — intentionally, unintentionally, and often both.[43] Her aesthetic strategy is well suited for revealing the web in which all aspects of our lives as individuals are caught up: family and community as local, national, and international factors in the life of the individual. Drewitz's novels offer readers models of how we try to make sense of our own position within the historical present and to interrogate and negotiate our individual and collective responsibilities on the basis of that understanding.

## Notes

[1] Ingeborg Drewitz, *Oktoberlicht* (Düsseldorf: Claassen Verlag, 1969).

[2] Margaret Urban Walker, *Moral Understandings* (New York: Routledge, 1998). All quotations from this work will be cited by page number in parentheses.

[3] Barbara Becker-Cantarino describes Drewitz's female protagonists broadly in the following passage, but what she says also applies to the protagonists of the two novels at the center of this analysis. "Ihre Frauenfiguren sind realistisch, experimentell, suchen neue Wege aus den Zwängen des Alltags, ohne Heroinen zu werden und scheitern zumeist. Als solche waren sie Vor- oder Leitbilder für Leserinnen, mögliche Identifikations- oder bessere Figuren, die zur Selbstreflexion anregen (sollen)." Becker-Cantarino, "Zum Frauenpolitischen Engagement von Ingeborg Drewitz," in *"Von der Unzerstörbarkeit des Menschen": Ingeborg Drewitz im literarischen und politischen Feld der 50er und 80er Jahre*, ed. Barbara Becker-Cantarino and Inge Stephan (New York: Peter Lang, 2005), 34. I'm not sure why Becker-Cantarino sees these figures as failures. Seeing them as such would require a particular definition of "success" that seems unwarranted in this case. See also Monika Shafi, "Die überforderte Generation: Mutterfiguren in Romanen von Ingeborg Drewitz," *Women in German Yearbook* 7 (1991), 26.

[4] Berlin was Drewitz's home base. Her novelistic work rests heavily on the geographical and political realities of the city. For more information on this aspect of her work, see Hannelore Scholz, "Gedächtnis Berlin: Anmerkungen zum Verhältnis von Individual- und Zeitgeschichte in Texten von Ingeborg Drewitz," in *"Von der Unzerstörbarkeit des Menschen,"* ed. Becker-Cantarino and Stephan, 379–99.

[5] Pierre Nora, ed., *Realms of Memory: Rethinking the French Past*, vol. 1, trans. Arthur Goldhammer (New York: Columbia UP, 1996), 9. All citations of this work will be cited by the page number in parentheses.

[6] This holds true not only for Drewitz's characters, but also for the figures that inhabit and enliven the works of Christa Wolf and Grete Weil.

[7] See particularly, chapter 4, 77–100.

[8] See also 78, 94, 96.

[9] Katharina Aulls, *Verbunden und gebunden: Mutter-Tochter-Beziehungen in sechs Romanen der siebziger und achtziger Jahre* (Frankfurt am Main: Peter Lang, 1993), 132.

[10] Drewitz expressed an opinion about women's needs and desires that tended toward essentializing biological functions and gender roles. ("To essentialize" in this context refers to the tendency to see gender characteristics that are socialized

and learned behavior as the essential characteristics of biological sexes.) See in particular her essay from 1971 entitled "Gespaltenes oder doppeltes Leben? Gedanken über die Frau als Künstlerin" Gedanken über die Frau als Künstlerin" in *"Die ganze Welt umwenden": Ein engagiertes Leben*, ed. Uwe Schweikert (Düsseldorf: Claassen, 1987), 150. However, such an essentializing gesture gives way in the novels to a more historicized view of socially constructed gender roles. On this topic, see also Yvonne-Christiane Fischer-Lüder, *An den Rand gedrückt — zum Opfer gemacht — Subjekt geworden: die Entwicklung der Frauenfiguren in den Romanen von Ingeborg Drewitz* (Frankfurt am Main: Peter Lang, 1990), 260–78, and Katharine Aulls, *Verbunden und gebunden*, 134–36.

[11] See Carol Gilligan, *In a Different Voice* (Cambridge, MA: Harvard UP, 1982) and Virgina Held, *Feminist Morality: Transforming Culture, Society, and Politics* (Chicago: U of Chicago P, 1993).

[12] The narrator is at least partially motivated by guilt: Katrin's family had been political outcasts during the Third Reich, and the narrator once pretended not to know her so that she would not fall under similar social suspicions. Katrin herself had lived in America after the war and then moved back to Germany, where she earned a living as a social worker.

[13] Sarah Ruddick, *Maternal Thinking: Towards a Politics of Peace* (Boston: Beacon Press, 1989), 6.

[14] Virginia Held, *Feminist Morality*, 80.

[15] Hans-Gerd Winter argues that political events play an important role in the perception of certain figures and that such moments are expressed generally either in stream of consciousness or reported speech, sometimes as an internal monologue. Winter, "Ingeborg Drewitz' Bild der frühen Nachkriegszeit," in *"Von der Unzerstörbarkeit des Menschen,"* ed. Becker-Cantarino and Stephan, 165.

[16] Gerhild Brüggemann Rogers, *Das Romanwerk von Ingeborg Drewitz* (New York: Peter Lang, 1989), 15.

[17] Brüggemann Rogers, *Das Romanwerk von Ingeborg Drewitz*, 221–22.

[18] This passage echoes several in Christa Wolf's *Kindheitsmuster* and carries similar implications about both how important the news becomes in our lives as well as how we assimilate this information.

[19] In many ways, of course, this has been true for much of human history. However, the access to information about events happening in places geographically distant from us and the pace and detail of this information have expanded exponentially — first through television and then through the internet. Often, media outlets present information from regions remote from us in the same way that they present stories about events that happen literally in our own backyards, which makes it difficult to understand the connection of the event to one's own life or community. This doesn't even touch on the impact that the enormous increase in global migration waves in the last two to three decades has had on the way local communities define themselves and the spectrum of their responsibilities.

[20] It is for this reason that I cannot accept Helga Kraft's assertion that there is no bond between the narrator and her husband other than sex. Helga Kraft, "Seiltanz der Mütter und Töchter in der Männerwelt. Schweigen und Sprechversuche,"

in *Mütter — Töchter — Frauen: Weiblichkeitsbilder in der Literatur*, ed. Helga Kraft and Elke Liebs (Stuttgart: Metzler, 1993), 272. The common experience of history proves to be a bond much stronger than any other bond between individuals.

[21] David Carr, *Time, Narrative, and History* (Bloomington: Indiana UP, 1986), 115.

[22] Bloody Sunday occurred in January of 1905 in St. Petersburg. Peaceful demonstrators gathered in the city to deliver a petition to Tsar Nicholas II with the hope of creating better conditions for workers. They were met by armed resistance from the Imperial Guard and hundreds of people were killed or wounded.

[23] See Gudrun Loster-Schneider's similar reading of Paul and the various characters' responses to him in her "'Du darfst nie wieder so reden!' GeNarrations-Risiken in Ingeborg Drewitz' Roman *Gestern war Heute. Hundert Jahre Gegenwart*," in *"Von der Unzerstörbarkeit des Menschen,"* ed. Becker-Cantarino and Stephan, 323–28.

[24] See also Carr, *Time, Narrative, and History*, 88–89.

[25] Carr, *Time, Narrative, and History*, 90. His argument here echoes what Margaret Urban Walker says about identity narratives.

[26] The motif of the newspaper reader/media consumer is central to all three authors examined in this book. Needless to say, Wolf, Drewitz, and Weil are not the only authors who use newspapers to draw in events external to their characters' lives, although, of course, they do not do so in exactly the same way.

[27] See for example, Franz Xaver Kroetz *Furcht und Hoffnung der BRD* (Frankfurt am Main: 1984), *Angst Essen Seele auf*, dir. Rainer Werner Fassbinder, Filmverlag der Autoren, 1974, and Günter Wallraff, *Ganz unten* (Cologne: Kiepenheuer & Witsch, 1985).

[28] My analysis of Drewitz's commitment to acknowledging and calling attention to international struggles runs the risk of making Drewitz herself seem a paragon of political and cultural sensitivity. Of course, she was committed to fighting injustice and inequity in many places, but she was also burdened by contemporary ideologies that still rested — for instance — quite substantially on colonialist and racist legacies. See here for instance, Monika Shafi, "Entdeckung und Entfremdung. Ingeborg Drewitz: *Mein indisches Tagebuch*," in *Schriftsteller und "Dritte Welt,"* ed. Paul Michael Lützeler (Tübingen: Stauffenberg Verlag, 1998), 243–62, as well as Renate Bürner-Kotzam, "'Mein Fragen ist von Mitleid aufgesogen.' Indien im respektlosen Blick des Mitgefühls. Ingeborg Drewitz: 'Mein indisches Tagebuch,'" in *"Von der Unzerstörbarkeit des Menschen,"* ed. Becker-Cantarino and Stephan, 269–81.

[29] Kraft, "Seiltanz der Mutter und Tochter in der Männerwelt," 270, 272. I would argue that this is not the only interpretation of the message these two mothers send to their daughters about male-female relationships. In the case of the youngest daughter, Almuth, in *Eis*, for example, the narrator repeatedly wonders what keeps her daughter with the man she joins in the squatter's apartment and questions whether young women still feel compelled to seek recognition from their male partners. In *Gestern war heute* the main character leaves her husband because

she feels she cannot develop as a person within the constraints of the relationship he wants to have. In sum, I believe that Drewitz's emphasis on partnerships and relationships has far more significance than Kraft would grant it. It pertains implicitly at the very least to the concept of human existence in history that takes shape in her work. There is in any case enough material in Drewitz's depiction of relationships in general to warrant a separate study.

[30] Monika Shafi, "Die überforderte Generation: Mutterfiguren in Romanen von Ingeborg Drewitz," *WIG Yearbook 7* (1991): 35.

[31] For an interesting treatment of this aspect of Drewitz's work, see Monika Shafi, "'Montagdienstagmittwochdonnerstagfreitag . . .' Zur Darstellung des Alltags in Ingeborg Drewitz's Romanprosa," in *"Von der Unzerstörbarkeit des Menschen,"* ed. Becker-Cantarino and Stephan, 297–314. Drewitz's insistence on emphasizing the routine drudgeries — both physical and mental — of daily existence has echoes also in Wolf's work, although there it is not as extensive.

[32] Helga Kraft argues that Drewitz's characters experience the act of caring for others — particularly children — never as a source of joy, but rather mostly as a kind of duty to fulfill. One need not, I believe, be this pessimistic about her characters' relationship to the ones in their care. I see her portrayal of these moments instead as an attempt to avoid sentimentalism. See Helga Kraft, "Zwischen Traditionalismus und Fortschritt: Frauengenerationen im Werk Ingeborg Drewitz,'" in *"Von der Unzerstörbarkeit des Menschen,"* ed. Becker-Cantarino and Stephan, 340. Although Kraft reads the narrator's attitude twoard raising children as quite negative, it could also be simply realistic. Readers can find similar language in Sara Ruddick's *Maternal Thinking* (88), a book that is intent on using mothering as a foundation for ethics.

[33] Reprinted in *Ingeborg Drewitz: Materialien zu Werk und Wirken*, ed. Titus Häussermann (Stuttgart: Radius-Bücher, 1988), 73.

[34] Leslie Adelson, *Making Bodies, Making History: Feminism and German Identity* (Lincoln: U of Nebraska P, 1993), 43.

[35] Carr, *Time, Narrative, and History*, 4–5.

[36] I agree with Leslie Adelson's objection to an overemphasis on the importance of narrative in the experience of history, if it implies overlooking the importance of the body for historical experience. She writes: "Without taking issue with the notion that history requires narrativity to be perceived as such (and hence does not exist outside of narrative), I would like to point out that the emphasis on narrativity as a grounding or as a function of historical consciousness tends to displace or render of somehow peripheral interest the fact that historical consciousness is perforce mediated first and foremost through sentient bodies" (23). While a thorough analysis of the way Drewitz consistently thematizes the role of our physical, bodily selves in our perceptions of our selves and others would give us a more thorough understanding of the concept of self underlying Drewitz's characters, it would exceed the parameters of this study.

[37] Carr, *Time, Narrative, and History*, 96.

[38] Carr, *Time, Narrative, and History*, 57, 61.

[39] Carr, *Time, Narrative, and History*, 156, 158.

[40] Brüggemann Rogers, *Das Romanwerk von Ingeborg Drewitz*, 165.

[41] See also 21, 23–24, and 142. The author plays here with the shared root in German between "erfinden" — to invent — and "finden" — to find. The wordplay is lost in English.

[42] Alasdair MacIntyre, *After Virtue* (Notre Dame: U of Notre Dame P, 1981), 199.

[43] Drewitz's largely realist aesthetic paradigm may not serve well to approach more abstract or symbolic dissections of history, to create models of the individual in conflict with history, or to analyze the ways in which individuals are destroyed in the confrontation with institutions or collective agents. Gisela Ullrich and Monika Shafi both suggest that the reception of Drewitz's work has suffered because of her realist style, but both agree that a rejection of her work on that basis alone would be unfortunate. See Gisela Ullrich, "Ingeborg Drewitz," *Kritisches Lexikon der deutschsprachen Gegenwartsliteratur*, 1978 ed. and Monika Shafi, "Die überforderte Generation," 28.

# 4: Christa Wolf: Rehearsing Individual and Collective Responsibility

CHRISTA WOLF OCCUPIES A SPECIAL SPACE within the landscape of post–Second World War German literature. Legions of scholars have analyzed, interpreted, contextualized, and historicized her work. So much so that it makes one question just how much more insight we can squeeze out of her substantial body of work. Nevertheless, within the context of postwar German women writers, a book that examines how individuals look at history and how they then conceive of their own social responsibilities would be incomplete without attention to Wolf's treatment of these issues. Her 1976 novel *Kindheitsmuster*, a quintessential example of how Wolf's particular generation struggled to confront its own national and individual pasts, created reverberations not only in East Germany, where it was written, and in German-speaking Europe, where it was widely received and intensely scrutinized, but also in many non-German-speaking countries.

For this reason, this chapter focuses primarily on *Kindheitsmuster* with the occasional forward and backward glances at earlier and later works by Wolf.[1] The approach is threefold. Beginning with a discussion of how we remember the past, the chapter then unfolds Wolf's sense of remembering as a moral activity. The conclusion analyzes the importance she sees in the relational character of identity, the interconnection of world events (both synchronically and diachronically), and the ethical implications of this realization. At different points in the chapter, the issues raised in chapters 1 and 2 factor into the analysis. From chapter 1, I am particularly interested in testing the arguments of Halbwachs, Nora, and Pennebaker and Banasik. Specifically, Wolf illustrates well Halbwachs's idea that individual memories remain embedded in collective historical experience. On a limited scale, I look at Nora's complaints about late twentieth-century trends to archivize everything without a concomitant sense of what really bears historical significance. Finally, the concept of "rehearsal" to which Pennebaker and Banasik refer proves useful when describing the memory project of a novel such as *Kindheitsmuster*. The discussion of feminist ethics in chapter 2, on the other hand, builds the conceptual parameters of the discussion about Wolf's understanding of relational identity and its implications for her questioning of individual and collective responsibilities. As in chapter 3, Margaret Urban Walker's ideas about a geography of morals will be central in the analysis of Wolf's work.[2]

In the years preceding and following the publication of *Kindheitsmuster*, Wolf's thoughts revolved often around the nature of memory as a process, the function of memory, and what we then subsequently make of memories — both individually and collectively. During a 1983 conversation with Jacqueline Grenz, Wolf talked about the role of narrative and narrators in this activity:

> Erinnern, Sich-Erinnern und Erzählen sind eng miteinander verknüpft. Ein Motiv für das Entstehen des Erzählens ist, wenn wir es historisch betrachten, dass die Mitglieder einer Gesellschaft — ich denke z.B. hier wieder an die Homeriden — es brauchten, sich erinnert zu fühlen oder erinnert zu werden an ihre lange vergangene Geschichte. An Geschichte und an Geschichten erinnern, damit der Dorf-, der Stammes-, der Volksgemeinschaft ihre eigene Herkunft und Entwicklung vor Augen zu führen, ist schon immer eine Funktion des Erzählens gewesen.[3]
>
> [Reminding, remembering and narrating are closely bound together. One reason for the emergence of narration, if we look at it historically, is that the members of society — I am thinking again here of the Homeridae, for example — needed to feel remembered, or to be reminded of their long past history. The recalling of history and stories in order to make the village, tribal, or national community aware of its own origin and development has always been a function of narration.]

Wolf emphasizes here the collective nature of memory, declaring the process of telling our memories to be quite clearly aimed at reintroducing a society to its history and keeping its connections to its past fresh. Thus, although *Kindheitsmuster* nominally tells the story of one girl and her family during the Third Reich, the novel never strays from the broader social context in which individuals experience and come to understand their environment. Halbwachs's theory of collective memory supports Wolf's assertion through the novel that while individuals have distinct personal memories, experience itself takes place in a specific social context that shapes the way individuals perceive what happens to them and around them. Wolf herself talks about the many voices that flood her mind when she thinks about the past: "Solche Stimmen nun, haufenweise. Als hätte jemand eine Schleuse hochgezogen, hinter der die Stimmen eingesperrt waren" (46; These, then, are the voices that come streaming in. As if someone had opened the sluice gates: 32).[4]

Partially because of the collective filters we acquire through socialization, we cannot strictly speak of remembering the past "as it was." As we saw in chapter 1, we process our memories of the past at moments in the present when we need to draw comparisons between "then" and "now" in order to act today. Numerous passages from *Kindheitsmuster* echo this assertion, but I will take one in which the narrator talks explicitly about how the narrative of our pasts represents an act of mediation, of drawing two realities together — not presenting them as distinct units that one can clearly delineate:

> Die Beschreibung der Vergangenheit — was immer das sein mag, dieser noch anwachsende Haufen von Erinnerungen — in objektivem Stil wird nicht gelingen. Der Doppelsinn des Wortes "vermitteln." Schreibend zwischen der Gegenwart und der Vergangenheit vermitteln, sich ins Mittel legen. Heißt das: versöhnen? Mildern? Glätten? Oder: Eins dem anderen näherbringen? (215)
>
> [The past — whatever the continuously accumulating stack of memories may be — cannot be described objectively. The two-fold meaning of the word "to mediate." To be the mediator between past and present — the medium of a communication between the two. In the sense of reconciliation? appeasement? smoothing out? Or a rapprochement of the two? (164)]

Owing both to the specific needs of the present and to the selective capacity of memory, what we conjure up when we set out to remember the past alters, embellishes, and reconfigures that past. Wolf's narrators talk about these alterations, embellishments, and reconfigurations explicitly not only in *Kindheitsmuster* but also in *Nachdenken über Christa T.* (1968), and in *Kassandra* (1983). They set out consciously and critically to monitor these shifts and their own role in them, as we will see in more detail further along. Ultimately, *Kindheitsmuster* becomes an extended examination — via a specific case study — of how individuals are socialized into a collective, learn to experience their realities through that collective's lenses, and subsequently revisit those experiences with the lenses they acquire through socialization.

On the other hand, Wolf's interest in memory goes well beyond what memory "is" or how we remember. From the perspective presented in *Kindheitsmuster*, the whole point of telling history and of situating ourselves within that history is to examine our social roles and our moral obligations to those around us, both in our immediate vicinity (i.e. our family and our local community) and in broader social contexts. Wolf refers to this as our "moralisches Gedächtnis" (53; moral memory: 36). Although Wolf plays with various different definitions of memory, it is this latter concept of moral memory that links the discussion of memory and history to the discussion of ethics and responsibility.

Wolf's narrator in *Kindheitsmuster* comments frequently on both linguistic definitions of and scientific (that is, bio-chemical) characteristics of memory. She cites lexicographical sources such as *Meyers Neues Lexikon*

(49–50) and scientific studies (66, 197–98). She mentions, too, categorizations of memory into subgroups like mechanical, logical, and semantic memory (49), but she also notes at this point, "Heftig vermißt wird die Gattung: moralisches Gedächtnis" (The absence of one category is acutely felt: moral memory: 36). *Kindheitsmuster* represents the attempt to study just that — moral memory. Several scholars have written about Wolf's view of memory, her theory of medallions,[5] and the similarity of her thought to certain philosophers, such as Walter Benjamin.[6] While it will be necessary to review some of this material, my major concern is not with further specifying the mechanics of memory, but with fleshing out the importance of memory in the discussion of moral responsibility. Through her interrogation of the past, Wolf queries the extent of individuals' responsibility for what happened during the Third Reich. Of course, she doesn't leave it at that, since her interest lies not exclusively in answering questions about Germany's Nazi past, but rather also in mapping out the various levels of interconnection (locally, nationally, and internationally) between individuals and between communities. This aspect of her work resonates most intensively with developments in feminist ethics from the early 1980s into the present.

Because of the implications that the deliberate and active process of remembering can have for our own self-evaluation, memory as a process in *Kindheitsmuster* takes on a rather threatening character. What will we find out about ourselves when we probe our own past (both individual and collective)? How well will we stand up before our own scrutiny? Chapter 4, for instance, opens with the question: "Brauchen wir Schutz vor den Abgründen der Erinnerung?" (95; Do we need protection from the abysses of memory?)[7] Wolf's narrator acknowledges the prevailing human instinct to expend energy in order to preserve our distance from our memories. Encapsulating them in manageable bits (medallions), we work actively — although not necessarily consciously — to protect ourselves from confronting the past deliberatively (94–95).[8]

Wolf also scrutinizes exhaustively the question of what we remember versus what we forget. For instance, the narrator ponders in chapter 12 why she remembers how the girls in her confirmation class mocked the confirmation ceremony when they passed behind the church altar, but she does not remember the battle of Stalingrad.[9] While social psychology could provide some answers to that question, Wolf's interest lies in probing the individual's ranking of memories, hoping to determine the social values that lead us to prioritize certain experiences over others. For instance (in the same passage), the narrator clearly remembers the voice of Joseph Goebbels screaming from the family radio "Nun Volk, steht auf! Nun, Sturm, brich los!" (335; Now, my people, rise! Now, storm, break loose!: 257). But she critically notes the absence in her memory of the Scholl siblings or the resistance of the Jews in the Warsaw ghetto.

Analyzing this question in a similar vein to Halbwachs, Wolf's narrator notes that neither the Scholls nor the Warsaw ghetto uprising were ever mentioned in her presence as a child — despite their co-occurrence with the main character's (Nelly Jordan's) confirmation. In this way, Wolf can demonstrate how what we perceive and remember comes to us through a series of social filters (parents, school, church, etc.). What we remember depends not only on what we are told, but on what the dominant influences in our lives emphasize or de-emphasize as part of a collective value structure. Ultimately, Wolf doesn't use this as an argument to exempt her generation from moral responsibility — *Kindheitsmuster* is less about assigning blame than about understanding the genesis and ramifications of the Third Reich's brutalization and extermination of Europe's Jews. Her analysis — through its concerted attempts to establish connections to the international conflict areas contemporaneous with either the narrated time or the narrative present of the book — becomes a model for how to question collective and personal responsibility.

It is worth reiterating that Wolf's project is not historiographical in the sense that her intent does not lie in creating an accurate or minutely detailed account of actual events and the people involved in them.[10] Instead *Kindheitsmuster* becomes a kind of "mnemonography" (the writing of memory) that scrutinizes not only *what* we remember, but also *how* we remember. The novel's plot illustrates the actual process of remembering in a self-critical and reflective manner, a project Wolf admits resembles a kind of reconstruction. The next section clarifies the extent to which this project differs from attempts to present an objective or disinterested chronicle of past events.

## "Mnemonography"

Wolf began to question the ability of a narrator (individual or collective) to capture objective truth long before she wrote *Kindheitsmuster*. *Nachdenken über Christa T.* already highlights the subjectivity involved in trying to recount events of the past — either those from our own lives or from the lives of others. Not only does the narrator admit her "power" over her subject (that is, Christa T., in death, certainly cannot contest any claims the book's narrator makes), but she also unabashedly states that she has constructed some scenes that she knows did not happen in order to tell the kind of story she wishes to tell. The narrator states of Christa T., "Ich aber sehe sie noch. Schlimmer: Ich verfüge über sie. Ganz leicht kann ich sie herbeizitieren wie kaum einen Lebenden. Sie bewegt sich, wenn ich will" (9; But I can still see her. Worse, I can do what I like with her. I can summon her up quite easily with a quotation, more than I could do for most living people. She moves, if I want her to: 4).[11]

This technique resurfaces in *Kindheitsmuster* in several different ways. Wolf's narrator addresses not only the difficulties, but also the dangers involved in trying to reconstruct one's past. At the very beginning of the book, that narrator muses on the distance between herself and the child whose life she is trying to recapture. She writes:

> Weil es schwerfällt, zuzugeben, dass jenes Kind da — dreijährig, schutzlos, allein — dir unerreichbar ist. Nicht nur trennen dich von ihm die vierzig Jahre; nicht nur behindert dich die Unzuverlässigkeit deines Gedächtnisses, das nach dem Inselprinzip arbeitet und dessen Auftrag lautet: Vergessen! Verfälschen! Das Kind ist ja auch von dir verlassen worden. Zuerst von den anderen, gut. Dann aber auch von dem Erwachsenen, der aus ihm ausschlüpfte und es fertigbrachte, ihm nach und nach alles anzutun, was Erwachsene Kindern anzutun pflegen: Er hat es hinter sich gelassen, beiseite geschoben, hat es vergessen, verdrängt, verleugnet, umgemodelt, verfälscht, verzärtelt und vernachlässigt, hat sich seiner geschämt und hat sich seiner gerühmt, hat es falsch geliebt und hat es falsch gehaßt. (14)

> [Because it hurts to admit that the child — aged three, helpless, alone — is inaccessible to you. You're not only separated from her by forty years; you are hampered by your unreliable memory. You abandoned the child, after all. After others abandoned it. All right, but she was also abandoned by the adult who slipped out of her, and who managed to do to her all the things adults usually do to children. The adult left the child behind, pushed her aside, forgot her, suppressed her, denied her, remade, falsified, spoiled and neglected her, was ashamed and proud of her, loved her with the wrong kind of love, and hated her with the wrong kind of hate. (7)]

The years that have passed, the different life contexts, and the narrator's purpose in exploring her own past all contribute to generating a specific image of the child's life. Indeed, the narrator's husband, H., warns her explicitly that the nature of her project may lead her to try too hard to establish connections, embellish meager memories, and force fragments into a coherent story (33). Both manipulation and avoidance constitute traps in our search for memory.

The narrator fears, however, not only our desire to manipulate the past in the memory process, but also our tendency, as mentioned above, to "wall off" portions of our past into "medallions," to manage our unruly memories and protect ourselves from them. In the following passage, she refers to this as a process of encapsulation, one that requires a great deal of energy and investment on our part:

> Du aber, neunundzwanzig Jahre später, wirst dich fragen müssen, wieviel verkapselte Höhlen ein Gedächtnis aufnehmen kann, ehe es

aufhören muß zu funktionieren. Wieviel Energie und welche Art Energie es dauernd aufwendet, die Kapseln, deren Wände mit der Zeit morsch und brüchig werden mögen, immer neu abzudichten. Wirst dich fragen müssen, was aus uns allen würde, wenn wir den verschlossenen Räumen in unseren Gedächtnissen erlauben würden, sich zu öffnen und ihre Inhalte vor uns auszuschütten. Doch ist das Abrufen der Gedächtnisinhalte — die sich übrigens bei verschiedenen Leuten, die akkurat das gleiche erlebt zu haben scheinen, bemerkenswert unterscheiden — wohl keine Sache der Biochemie und scheint uns nicht immer und überall freizustehen. (94-95)

[But twenty-nine years later you have to ask yourself how many encapsulated vaults a memory can accommodate before it must cease to function. How much energy and what kind of energy is it continually expending in order to seal and to reseal the capsules whose walls may in time rot and crumble. You'll have to ask what would become of all of us if we allowed the locked spaces in our memories to open and spill their contents before us. But memory's recall — which incidentally varies markedly in people who seem to have had the exact same experience — may not be a matter of biochemistry, and may not universally be a matter of choice. (69)]

Owing to the dangers she sees inherent in the writing process, Wolf's narrator seeks a writing strategy that will allow her to face both issues head on. That is to say, Wolf works (largely by experimentation) to find a literary form that will permit her both to comment self-critically on the mnemonographic project, that is, on the possibility that unarticulated agendas drive both the content and the structure of the narrative, and to crack open the memory capsules she comes across in her efforts to investigate the narrator's past. In a 1973 discussion with Hans Kaufmann about "subjektive Authentizität" (subjective authenticity), Wolf described the kind of narrative method she sought:

Wieder geht es darum, eine Schreibweise zu finden, die den höchsten Grad an Realismus für diese spezielle Unternehmung ermöglicht, am besten erzwingt: dass Gegenwart und Vergangenheit — wie sie es in uns Menschen ja andauernd tun — auch auf dem Papier sich nicht nur "treffen," sondern aufeinander einwirken, in ihrer Bewegung aneinander gezeigt werden können. Man muss also Schreibtechniken finden . . ., die es fertigbringen, die fast unauflösbaren Verschränkungen, Verbindungen und Verfestigungen, die verschiedenste Elemente unserer Entwicklung miteinander eingegangen sind, doch noch einmal zu lösen, um Verhaltensweisen, auf die wir festgelegt zu sein scheinen, zu erklären und womöglich (und wo nötig) doch noch zu ändern.[12]

[Again, it's a question of finding a style of writing that allows this undertaking a great degree of realism — or even better, imposes that realism upon it — so that past and present can be seen not only to "meet" on the paper, but, as they constantly do in every one of us, to interact and be endlessly rubbing up again each other. In other words, you have to find writing techniques . . . that manage to free up those almost indissoluble bonds and constrictions that hold us in their grip, to unravel that vast range of elements that have become entwined during our development, so that patterns of behaviour in which we thought we were firmly entrenched can be explained, and, where possible (and where necessary), still be changed.]

Specifically, her efforts to historicize in this case seek to bring the past closer to the present, to examine the motives of those living at the time and to specify their level of responsibility (*Verantwortlichkeit*).[13] As Robert Shirer points out, the fragments of experience we have at our disposal can only go so far toward accomplishing this task. Wolf's mnemonographer first groups them together into a kind of mosaic, but must then also generate the interpretive spaces that border and interlock the pieces. At the same time, she holds vigil over herself, wary both of the filters through which she sifts the fragments and of the potential power she wields in her efforts to draw them together.[14]

So, what tools does the narrator have at her disposal when she sits down to draft this mnemonography? As noted in chapter 1, Pierre Nora has complained that people of the late twentieth and early twenty-first centuries archivize everything because they no longer have a meaningful connection to the past.[15] In Nora's view, then, we are amassing mountains of insubstantial material for fear of losing the past altogether.

Christa Wolf shares this perspective — at least partially. In *Nachdenken über Christa T.*, *Kindheitsmuster*, and *Kassandra*, the narrators all talk about the limitations of factual material. Kassandra ridicules the information the palace scribes have to offer, suggesting that the endless lists of ships, sailors, casks, baskets, spears, etc. will do little to explain what motivated the Greeks and the Trojans to go to war or how the people in the city experienced this war emotionally.[16]

Similarly, Wolf's narrator in *Kindheitsmuster* pours over newspaper clippings in the library and scans photographs and books for information on events that occurred during her childhood, but finds herself dissatisfied with what the information tells her. The following passage begins by speculating about when Nelly's mother Charlotte first began to realize the problems inherent in Nazi ideology and state practices, an entirely subjective and individual realization:

Ob die Nacht des 17. März auch die Nacht war, in der Charlotte zum erstenmal mit Schrecken dachte — oder träumte —: Alles ist verkehrt!, das wird niemand je erfahren. Aber gerade diese Art Tatsachen, die keine Zeitung berichtet und keine Statistik erfaßt hat, sind es, die dich heute interessieren könnten. . . . Das Hochreißen der Arme. Bekannte, allzu bekannte Gesten. Was man da gedacht und gefühlt haben mag, ohne selbst davon wissen zu wollen: Dies wäre es, was du gerne wüßtest. (73)

[Nobody will ever know if the night of March 17 was the night when Charlotte thought — or dreamed — for the first time, with a shock: It's all wrong. It is precisely this kind of unreported, statistically unrecorded fact which would interest you today. . . . The upward thrust of hands. Known gestures, known all too well. What were the thoughts that went through people's heads, that they preferred not to know about: that's what you'd like to know. (53)]

Although the narrator uses newspaper accounts, city records, information from television and old books to piece together the structure on which she hangs her memories, the statistics and archives cannot help her to explain the events; they cannot give her access to the individual consciousness of people — like the narrator's mother — who lived during the time. They can prove that people must have known about the concentration camps, the pogroms, the deportations, but they cannot tell her how people can both be and not be in the same place at one time — to paraphrase a comment made by the narrator's daughter Lenka in chapter 2 (57). Confronted with such inexplicable contradictions, the narrator confesses, "du bist gehalten, die Fakten zu verwirren, um den Tatsachen näherzukommen" (77; For you are forced to shuffle the details in order to get closer to the facts: 56). Whereas her motivation for fudging the facts varies, the goal of the project is to put together — much as a paleontologist does — a legible image (both intellectual and emotional) of the past.

Although Nora rejects the obsessively archivist tendencies of people in the late twentieth century, Wolf's narrative makes the point repeatedly that objects (broadly defined) of many different types often unexpectedly reveal glimpses of significance otherwise unavailable to us (195). As Chris Weedon has formulated it, the "newspaper reports enable her to make sense of remembered fragments and to realize how much public knowledge of Nazi practices had been repressed by popular memory."[17] In this way, objects that appear superficially to hold no real significance acquire meaning as we draw them together. However, Wolf works against gluing the various bits of the mnemonographic image into immoveable casts, since only the critical and recurrent effort to remember keeps our memories from freezing into rigid, albeit manageable mnemonographic bits.

Much like Gabriele in Drewitz's *Gestern war heute*, Wolf's narrator consciously picks and chooses from artifacts and memory swatches to construct the historical present from which she has emerged and in which she lives. I would stress the word *construct* here particularly, since there can be no sense that the narrator (either in Drewitz's or Wolf's narratives) actually presents a narrative snapshot of a particular time in history. Instead the past co-mingles with the present on a rather fluid canvas, yielding a story that re-enacts — or as Pennebaker and Banasik have phrased it — "rehearses" the past. David Carr and Margaret Urban Walker suggest that we need such rehearsals in order to understand who we are — or at least believe ourselves to be.

## Rehearsal

Chapter 1 presented the concept of rehearsal and its importance for shaping and strengthening memories of both a personal and a collective sort. It is important to stress that rehearsing an event does not mean that each rehearsal replicates the event itself. Nor is it the mechanistic recitation of lines penned by another. Wolf has spoken of literature's function as creating movement in the inner layers of memory, tossing up memories that have become rigid in order to approach them from new perspectives.[18] We also know that in any given context and at various times in our lives, different aspects of past events become more or less important to us. The facets of the event itself fade in and out of memory, and our ability to explain the connections between events develops both according to need and to critical distance.[19] In *Nachdenken über Christa T.* the narrator notes:

> Aber es wird auch schon schwerer, auseinanderzuhalten: was man mit Sicherheit weiß und seit wann; was sie selbst, was andere einem enthüllten; was ihre Hinterlassenschaft hinzufügt, was auch sie verbirgt; was man erfinden muß, um der Wahrheit willen; jener Gestalt, die mir manchmal schon erscheint und der ich mich mit Vorsicht nähere.
> Da überlagern sich schon die Wege, die wir wirklich gegangen sind, mit ungegangenen. Da höre ich schon Worte, die wir nie gesprochen haben. Schon sehe ich sie, Christa T., wenn sie ohne Zeugen war. Wäre es möglich? (29)
>
> [But it also becomes harder to keep things separate: what one knows with certainty, and since when; what she herself revealed, and what others revealed; what her writings add and what they hide; and what it is that one has to invent, for the truth's sake: the truth of that being who does now appear to me at times and whom I approach with caution. (23)]

Although Wolf's narrators represent unusually self-reflective and self-critical individuals, the narrator in *Christa T.* states explicitly here that her approaches to the past simply cannot separate what *really* happened from what she *needs* to have happened. Every time we seek to retell something from the past, the figurative ground beneath us begins to shift and we must restake the territory on which we tell ourselves every time. The concept of rehearsal, which by definition refers to a work in progress, subject to alteration and refinement, also underscores the provisional character of these mnemonographic exercises, to which Wolf's narrator in *Kindheitsmuster* refers as "Vorarbeiten für künftige Erklärungen" (194; the preliminary work for future explanations: 147). Despite its admittedly provisional character, rehearsal proves quite necessary on an individual and collective level when we try to situate ourselves vis-à-vis the past.

Furthermore, rehearsal necessarily entails either a real or an imagined audience. With a real audience, it becomes *de facto* a social or collective experience. With an implied audience it becomes on an individual level our preliminary screening ground for a collective narrative. For instance, in chapter 4 of *Kindheitsmuster* the narrator creates an imaginary interview with Bruno Jordan, Nelly's father, in which he talks about the upswing in the economy and the consequences of certain government decisions (97). While the interview, of course, did not happen, the narrator's enactment of it works directly to establish a connection between one individual, her father, and events that happen on a much broader social plane. Robert Shirer and Chris Weedon have both noted that Wolf's narrative seeks expressly to "engage" the audience in a dialogue and to expand collective memory.[20] In fact, *Kindheitsmuster* in its entirety functions as a creative dress rehearsal for the interpersonal dialogues the book generated after its publication.[21]

There are different ways to explain this method. Wolf herself described it in a 1989 interview with Therese Hörnigk as the way one processes experiences. It is a deeply personal process (Verarbeitung) in that different events leave substantively different traces in different individuals.[22] Myra Love emphasizes that Wolf's attempts at historicization entail the opposite of working from a critical distance. Instead, she argues, Wolf's work draws the past into the present to give individuals greater and more critical access to the decisions people make.[23] Sabine Wilke compares Wolf's method in *Christa T.* to late-twentieth-century developments in historiography and comes to the conclusion that both are marked by high degrees of self-reflection that go hand in hand with the way one understands and analyzes a text. Such self-reflection leads to the attempt to connect the self-reflecting subject to the material to be studied in order to highlight the importance of the analysis for a contemporary context.[24] Wolf, Love, and Wilke all offer reasonable explanations for Wolf's motivations and methods. My interest is, however, in the public and collective character of this "Verarbeitung," something the concept of rehearsal implies succinctly.

Specifically, rehearsals transmit collective historical experience as well as communicate individual experience to ever larger groups. For example, in chapter 12 the narrator talks about the history books her daughter Lenka's class is reading and their treatment of the Holocaust. The narrator probes the relationship of the students to the material in front of them (that is, how seriously they take what they read, whether they apply any of the material about the Holocaust to their own lives, etc.). Her decision to talk about the history books and what role they play in building the historical consciousness of her daughter's generation presents the reader with an instance in which a society is collectively rehearsing its past. Yet, even in this case, rehearsal doesn't mean that the same information gets transmitted and received every time a new class reads, for instance, the chapter on concentration camps in the Third Reich or the one on European colonialism. Lenka's and her mother's reactions to the material demonstrate not only what their experiential backgrounds have in common but also how they diverge.

A listing of all the vehicles for rehearsing individual and collective memory in *Kindheitsmuster* would grow onerously long, but a few further examples will help to make this concept more comprehensible In addition to the story of Lenka's history books, Wolf's narrator recounts at length and on several occasions her run-ins with Herr Warsinski, a fascist teacher whose approval Nelly strives diligently to secure. Through Nelly's interactions with Warsinski, Wolf explains much about the socialization of children in Nazi Germany — including the way learning a language becomes a disciplinary regime to whose authority Nelly must eventually acquiesce (chapter 5). Warsinski's lessons in German history, his selections of essay topics for his students, and the songs they sing as a class all function to inscribe the school children into a particular rendition of Germany's collective past. Younger school children play an essentially unquestioning dramatic role in a play designed by the adults who socialize them, and as they grow into adults they have either internalized the version of history they enacted as small children or they must begin to renarrate the past, a process Wolf illustrates through Nelly and Lenka as they pass out of adolescence and into adulthood.

In addition to the sometimes viciously antisemitic songs the school children learn, Wolf mentions prominent and influential works of fascist literature, such as Hans Grimm's *Volk ohne Raum* or the periodical "Das schwarze Korps," both of which Nelly reads secretly. These function as moments of rehearsal during which individuals place themselves into a collective historical narrative, and their inclusion in Wolf's narrative — drawn as they are from the stuff of daily life — demonstrates her ability to move from the microcosmic level of the individual enmeshed in a system of relationships to the larger sociopolitical level. Therese Hörnigk describes this process well in a discussion of Wolf's groundbreaking story "Dienstag, der

27. September, 1960" (Tuesday the 27th of September, 1960). Hörnigk argues that Wolf inserts reflection on larger political issues within the spaces surrounding the characters' daily routines. Observations about the everyday are paired with historically important events.[25] Exactly how Wolf lays out those structural connections between the everyday lives of her characters and broader political and/or social events will be discussed later in the chapter.

## Rehearsal and Relational Identity

As noted above, the historical accuracy of the rehearsal is largely irrelevant to the process of rehearsal. Scholars have suggested various motivations behind Wolf's enactment of remembering the past. Sabine Wilke, for instance, argues that Wolf hopes to excavate the reified images from our memories to see how we falsify the past in order to be able to live in the present with relative equanimity.[26] Again, I am more interested in how rehearsal establishes the self within a collective history, and how individuals ask along the way such questions as: "Where was *I*?" "What role did *my* actions play in this theater?" "How do my actions relate to the actions of those around me?" Sandra Frieden formulates this process in different terms as follows:

> The autobiographically historical details are summoned from the childhood memories of the adult, act upon the adult retrieving them, and are commented upon by the reflecting writer, who views their significance within an ever-broadening spectrum of current events and moral values. This expansion of relevance from the specifically autobiographical to the general is rendered formally by the dissection of memory and its application to the present.[27]

Both the narrative itself and the public readings of the partially-completed manuscript upon which the narrator comments as public forms of rehearsal show us some of the spaces in which collective memory is created and recreated on a continuous basis.

Wolf's narrators in both *Christa T.* and *Kindheitsmuster* hope to refashion the narratives' various characters from merely passive role players — as the narrator in the former novel puts it, "wie Figuren in einem gut gebauten Stück" (156; like characters in a well-made play: 157–58) — to active and conscious co-authors of their own narratives. This would constitute a process of assuming responsibility for a common past, a process that is imagined as a highly public performance. Indeed, both the narrator in *Kindheitsmuster* and her daughter have visions of themselves as under a permanent kind of surveillance by an audience that can offer judgment on how well they are fulfilling their responsibilities both to the past and to the present (304).[28]

The purpose of such surveillance is at least partially to ensure that the narrator (and by extension her contemporaries) do not succumb to the temptation to repress memories that would force them to ask about or rehearse their own implication in the events of the past. In one especially poignant passage, the narrator talks about the reason for memory's failures:

> Wo Nelly am tiefsten beteiligt war, Hingabe einsetzte, Selbstaufgabe, sind die Einzelheiten, auf die es ankam, gelöscht. Allmählich, muss man annehmen, und es ist auch nicht schwer zu erraten, wodurch; der Schwund muss einem tief verunsicherten Bewußtsein gelegen gekommen sein, das, wie man weiß, hinter seinem eigenen Rücken dem Gedächtnis wirksame Weisungen erteilen kann, zum Beispiel die: Nicht mehr daran denken. Weisungen, die über Jahre treulich befolgt werden. Bestimmte Erinnerungen meiden. Nicht davon reden. Wörter, Wortreihen, ganze Gedankenketten, die sie auslösen konnten, nicht aufkommen lassen. Bestimmte Fragen unter Altersgenossen nicht stellen. Weil es nämlich unerträglich ist, bei dem Wort "Auschwitz" das kleine Wort "ich" mitdenken zu müssen: "Ich" im Konjunktiv Imperfekt: Ich hätte. Ich könnte. Ich würde. Getan haben. Gehorcht haben. (303)
>
> [Where Nelly's participation was deepest, where she showed devotion, where she gave of herself, all relevant details have been obliterated. Gradually, one might assume. And it isn't difficult to guess the reason: the forgetting must have gratified a deeply insecure awareness which, as we all know, can instruct our memory behind our own backs, such as: Stop thinking about it. Instructions that are faithfully followed through the years. Avoid certain memories. Don't speak about them. Suppress words, sentences, whole chains of thought, that might give rise to remembering. Don't ask your contemporaries certain questions. Because it is unbearable to think the tiny word "I" in connection with the word "Auschwitz." "I" in the past conditional: I would have. I might have. I could have. Done it. Obeyed orders. (229–30)]

Wolf's highly self-reflexive and self-critical narrators continuously problematize the scope of their own projects. The fact that Nelly was a child during the Third Reich exempts her to a certain extent from the guilt of being a complicit bystander. And when Lenka admits that neither she nor the majority of her classmates feel particularly affected by the documents related to Nazi Germany that they are studying in their classes, the narrator at first expresses displeasure, but then gradually begins to wonder to what extent responsibility can be passed on from generation to generation. Is it, she ponders, not better for her daughter's generation to be freed from the enormous burden of guilt she feels that her own generation bears? She concludes, however, that such musings miss the fundamental question, which has to do with querying levels of connection and, therewith, responsibility — both across time and across space.[29]

So far, this chapter has looked at the way rehearsal opens spaces for the intersection of collective and individual memory. At this point, the focus shifts to the many ways Wolf demonstrates how larger political events and decisions impact the individual. Of interest here are not only what kind of individual interests her but also the mechanisms she sketches out that function as transfer points of collective and individual consciousness. The question of personal impact often revolves in the end around the issue of personal responsibility.

In 1983 — eight years after *Kindheitsmuster* and three years after *Kassandra* appeared — Wolf asserted that she was little concerned with the mistakes society ("die Gesellschaft") had made over the years, that she was far more interested in how individuals understood their role in events:

> Mich interessiert: Was habe ich in der oder jener Zeit gewußt, geahnt, gedacht, getan und unterlassen. Was davon habe ich, haben wir "vergessen." Was hat uns von uns selber, unseren früheren Hoffnungen und Vorstellungen entfernt und was taugt, in ein künftiges Zusammenleben von Menschen mitgenommen zu werden: dies ist die eigentliche Frage.[30]

> [I am interested in what I knew, suspected, thought, did or did not do at a particular time. What have I or have we "forgotten" about it? What has distanced us from ourselves, from our earlier hopes and ideas, and what is worth taking with us into a future, more human life together? This is the real question.]

While this claim would seem to belie the importance of collectives as agents, it represents more a question of methodology than anything else. Through her exhaustive examination of individual behavior, individual choices, and individual socialization, Wolf ultimately paints the broader picture that the citation would seem to deny.

From *Moskauer Novelle* through *Kindheitsmuster*, Wolf drew her characters from familiar milieus. She underscored for her readers what she considered to be their relative banality when one considers history writ large. One need only think of the narrator's insistence in *Nachdenken über Christa T.* that the title character represents nothing exemplary, unless one considers her unexemplariness to be exemplary (49). Wolf conceived of Christa T. as an representative figure in the immediate postwar era of the GDR: she is "austauschbar gegen eine Menge Personen ihres Alters" (107; interchangeable with countless other people her age: 107) — not completely interchangeable, of course, but by no means unique. Drewitz, too, draws her characters from a wide swath of society's fabric, but nowhere does she present individuals whom we traditionally think of as history-makers, for example, politicians or military figures. There are even relatively few religious figures. Instead both authors focus on how unexceptional people perceive their places within the historical developments around them.

As they paint their portraits of the various protagonists, they map into those portraits the characters' interpersonal relationships: friendships, professional relationships, and — of course — family relationships. As Robert Shirer writes of Wolf, "A consideration of the individual in the context of this *system* of relationships — especially across several levels of time — can help to portray not only the individual but his or her society as well."[31] Therese Hörnigk also points out that Wolf intentionally draws these relationships across generations in order to give the life of the individual due historical significance and offer as broad a perspective as possible.[32] Although Wolf's characters sometimes struggle to remember the names of decisive battles and the generals who fought them,[33] her description of the trek Nelly and her relatives make from her hometown through one forsaken village after another illustrates well the impact of those battles and the struggles and decisions individuals faced as a result of the war. If Wolf's canvas were limited to the time between 1933 and 1949, then one could question to what extent her insights applied to individuals living in less turbulent times. However, Wolf skillfully interweaves her reflections on the Nazi past with a consideration of the political conflicts happening in the book's narrative present. This feature of the novel creates a broader historical canvas on which to study how rehearsal mediates between individual and collective political and social consciousness.

One particularly important function of rehearsal is to clarify the impact of political events on individuals. Without a sense of how one relates to political decisions, economic developments, military actions, it is impossible for people to question their level of responsibility. Thus, a discussion follows on how Wolf sketches out those connections.

## Individual Imbrication

Many of Wolf's characters reveal attitudes that deny the agency of individuals in the processes of historical change as well as their ability to respond to the impact of political, economic, or military decisions in their lives. Wolf scholars have drawn attention to the apparent lack of connection between individual lives and larger historical developments in *Kindheitsmuster*. Robert Shirer, for instance, suggests that the reason Wolf's narrator in *Kindheitsmuster* is so preoccupied with the past is that she cannot reconcile what seemed to be a largely happy or a harmless childhood with her knowledge of the crimes committed during that period.[34] Much stronger, however, is the collective argument that develops in the novel as a whole about the extent to which larger historical developments and political structures impact individual lives, even lives far from the centers of power.

Wolf herself has spoken about how intensely she feels personally affected by the history of her country and her national community: "Mein Zugang zur Literatur, der Zwang zum Schreiben, ergibt sich daraus, dass ich sehr stark, sehr persönlich betroffen war und bin von der Geschichte, von der Geschichte unseres Volkes, unseres Staates und von allen Ereignissen, die ich seit meiner Kindheit bewußt erlebt habe." (My access to literature, the need to write, stems from the fact that I was and am very much and very personally affected by the history of our people, our country and all of the events that I have experienced consciously since childhood.)[35] Indeed, she was willing to identify this as one of her primary motivations for writing.

When the narrator tries to untangle the weave of Nelly's life story in *Kindheitsmuster*, she finds it virtually impossible to decide what — if anything — does not belong in the story, including contemporary events from around the world. She states, "Nun kannst du nichts mehr sagen, hören, denken, tun oder lassen, das nicht an dieses Geflecht rühren müßte" (125; There no longer is anything you can say, hear, think, do, or not do, that doesn't somehow touch this web: 93). She repeatedly insists on drawing connections from political history to the daily lives of people who are not directly involved. How do events that occur in Germany affect people who live far away — for instance, in the United States or Chile? She tries to envision what a random newspaper reader would have thought upon reading about the mobilization of troops in Germany in 1939, just as she tries to decide what it means to her when she reads about military developments in Israel in October of 1973 (223). Ultimately, she cannot adequately answer such questions. Similar to the situation in Drewitz's work, the extent of the connections remains something of a puzzle. Although the narrator cannot put the pieces together into a coherent picture, each remains a part of the puzzle. As Therese Hörnigk has remarked about *Der geteilte Himmel*, one thing does, however, seem certain: history cannot happen independently from the lives of individuals.[36] Nor do historical developments occur on a plane above or beyond the lives of most individuals. Indeed, as Hörnigk conceives it, for Wolf, literature's task is to reveal history's impact on the lives of those living it.[37]

Wolf illustrates these connections on numerous levels — both chronologically and geographically. Giving examples of how national political events during the Nazi era affected individuals is relatively easy. From the uncle who bought his candy factory at well below market value from a Jewish family hoping to flee Germany, to the aunt whom some acquaintances denounced as being Jewish, to another aunt who fell victim to

Nazi eugenics, to the pride and relief Nelly's parents expressed when Bruno finally joins a Nazi boating club, Wolf lays out instances of how an average ("Aryan") German family both suffered and prospered because of political decisions made by the regime.

In one of the book's key passages, Wolf also depicts how well people like Nelly's family had it during the Nazi years, relatively speaking. At one point, Nelly's family finds itself camping out in the open. Charlotte invites a man who had obviously been imprisoned in a concentration camp to join them for their supper. When it becomes clear to him that none of his dinner companions has any real sense of what the camps were like — or why people ended up there — he comments, "Wo habt ihr bloß alle gelebt" (56; Where on earth have you all been living: 39). Through this solitary figure Wolf can draw in experiences from very different individuals and very different spaces of the Nazi empire and can contextualize the suffering that a family such as the Jordans experienced in their flight from their hometown to where they ultimately settled. They may have lost their business and their home, as well as most of their family possessions, but they had never been beaten, intentionally starved, nor had they watched the rest of their family be murdered by Nazi guards.

Again, with a brutal, repressive regime such as Nazi Germany, such examples are plentiful and easy to find. But how does Wolf draw in similar connections in less turbulent times? Because the historical canvas she paints extends across several decades, she can include both the bitterness and recriminations that formed on both sides of the German-German border between members of Nelly's extended family (42) and events that occur because of continuing tensions in the cold war. Wolf suggests that these global conflicts leave distinct traces in the consciousness of the people living in central Europe and cause noticeable disquiet. Wolf's narrator comments that the sense of peace that people felt after the Nazis' rise to power but before the outbreak of the war never really returned — even years after the Second World War had ended:

> Warum ist dieses Gefühl niemals wiedergekehrt, in achtundzwanzig Friedensjahren nicht? Unterminieren die Kriege in anderen Teilen der Welt, in die der Brennpunkt der Weltgeschichte sich verlagert hat, nun doch die Ruhe der wenig Betroffenen? Das wäre ein Fortschritt. Oder genügten — was wahrscheinlicher ist — die Spannungen auf unserem eigenen Erdteil, auch wenn sie nur zum kalten, nicht zum heißen Krieg führten, ein dauerndes Gefühl von Gefahr in uns wachzuhalten? (162)

> [Why has this feeling never returned during twenty-eight years of peace? Are the wars, which have shifted the focus of world history to other parts of the world, undermining the tranquility of those not involved? That would be a step forward. Or, perhaps more likely,

were the tensions on our own continent strong enough to keep an awareness of danger alive in us, even if these tensions led only to the cold and not the hot war? (121)]

While Wolf seems to reject the idea that wars on distant soil could cause such a pervasive sense of ill-ease in central Europe, she repeatedly attempts to create relationships between those living in central Europe (particularly on the eastern side of the Iron Curtain) and more distant regions of the earth like the Middle East or South America.

Structurally, she often does this through triangulation, a concept the narrator herself introduces in chapter 13 of *Kindheitsmuster* (370). That is to say, she links three different historical spaces together in one passage: a moment in Nelly's life, a moment in the narrator's present, and a reference to a remote conflict in, for instance, Nicaragua, Chile, or Greece. Chapter 8 offers a number of examples of this. The following passage draws lines between a report that the American army was heading to Israel, the putsch in Chile, and the physical traces that the narrator's trek through history has left behind:

> Dein flüchtiges Bedauern über zu früh erzwungene und nun fortschreitende Versteifungen, Schlackeablagerungen in den Muskelpartien, Abfälle heißer und kalter Kriege, an denen man nicht ungestraft teilnimmt, aus denen man nicht ungezeichnet hervorgeht — während die Nachricht dieser Minute aus dem kleinen Transistorradio auf deinem Schreibtisch lautet: Das amerikanische Verteidigungsministerium habe am Abend bekannt gegeben, dass eine begrenzte Zahl amerikanischen Militärpersonals im Zusammenhang mit der amerikanischen Waffenhilfe nach Israel entsandt worden sei.
> Die Meldung wurde später dementiert.
> Selten kennt man das Gewicht der angebrochenen Stunde. Es ist Freitag, der 19. Oktober 1973, ein kühler, regenreicher Tag, 18 Uhr 30 Minuten. In Chile hat die Militärjunta den Gebrauch des Wortes "compañero" verboten. (233)

> [Your fleeting regret about your own prematurely imposed inactivity and now progressive rigidity, slag deposits in the muscles, by-products of hot and cold wars in which one cannot participate without punishment, from which one cannot return without being marked — during the news of the minute from the small transistor radio on your desk you hear: The American Department of Defense let it be known this evening that a small number of American military personnel has been sent to Israel in the context of the American weapons aid program.
> The report was later denied.
> One rarely recognizes the weight of the current moment. It is Friday, the 19th of October 1973, a cool, rainy day, 6:30 pm. In Chile, the military junta has banned the use of the word "compañero."[38]]

Here the flexible bond between the triangle's three sides is both implicitly the costs that individuals bear from international conflicts and explicitly our inability to judge the scope of the events through which we live.

More prevalent are examples in which Wolf questions the relationship between remote spectators and the conflicts they "observe." In the next example (which I had also mentioned above), Wolf links the mobilization of troops in Nazi Germany and the mobilization of troops in the Israeli-Egyptian conflict to one another through dual perspectives, that of a "disinterested" observer and that of the very "interested" children of the soldiers who are departing for war:

> Zu denken, dass an jenem Montag vor vierunddreißig Jahren einer hinter seiner Schreibmaschine gesessen haben mag — einer, der jetzt vielleicht tot ist, von dem du nicht mal den Namen kennst —, irgendwo in der Welt, und mit seiner eigenen Arbeit beschäftigt, kopfschüttelnd die Nachricht von einer Mobilmachung in Deutschland gehört hat. Kein Gedanke an ein zehnjähriges Kind oder einen verzweifelten alten Mann. Und dass jetzt du dieser Jemand bist, im Verhältnis zu den Kindern in Israel und Ägypten, die gestern ihre Väter zu den Sammelplätzen geleiteten (wir haben Sonntag, den 7. Oktober 1973) und denen ein alter Mann — vielleicht hat er das Nazi-KZ überlebt; vielleicht ist er Fellache und kann weder lesen noch schreiben — in hebräisch oder arabisch sagt, dass sie darauf gefaßt sein müssen, ihren Vater nicht wiederzusehen. Und dass du an deiner Schreibmaschine sitzen bleibst, mit eigenen Angelegenheiten beschäftigt, während am Suezkanal "die Kämpfe mit unverminderter Heftigkeit andauern." (223)

> [To think that on Monday, thirty-four years ago, someone may have sat at his typewriter — someone who may be dead by now, whose name you don't know — somewhere in the world, someone who shakes his head at the news of the German mobilization, absorbed as he is in his work. Without a thought for a ten-year-old child or a desperate old man. And to think that you are now that someone, while the children in Israel and in Egypt accompanied their fathers to the rallies yesterday (today is Sunday, October 7, 1973), where an old man — perhaps the survivor of a Nazi concentration camp; perhaps a man who can neither read nor write — says in Hebrew or in Arabic that they should be prepared never to see their father again. You remain seated at your typewriter, absorbed in your own affairs, while "the fighting continues with unabated violence" at the Suez Canal. (169–70)]

The issue that connects the three sides of the triangle in this passage (that is, Nazi Germany, the Israeli-Egyptian conflict, and the narrator's present) is the question of responsibility. What exactly does it mean to me, sitting at my desk, writing this chapter, that American soldiers are fighting in Iraq and Afghanistan? To what extent am I responsible for the fact that they are there? To what extent do I bear responsibility for the abuses of war, the torturing of prisoners, the deaths of civilians? Can I just shake my head, click off the *New York Times* web site and resume work on this book? Just as Weil, Drewitz, and Wolf, I don't really know the answer to those questions, but partially because of them, I keep asking.

## Responsibility

At this point, the focus shifts directly to the question of responsibility. Myra Love maintains that responsibility is central to Wolf's "notions of subjectivity and intersubjectivity" and that "the word *Verantwortung* is indeed one of the most prominently repeated in her essays and literary texts."[39] How precisely does Wolf ask this question? What is her motivation for doing so? Finally, how does the mnemonographic project relate to the question of moral responsibility? Why does this project hold so much importance for the narrative present of *Kindheitsmuster*?

In their article "German-Jewish Memory and National Consciousness" Miriam Hansen and Michael Geyer praise Wolf's ability to paint the past so vividly, but they view her efforts to describe the narrative present in *Kindheitsmuster* as "so far away and so alienated from her own person [that] her remarks on it seem wooden."[40] An alternative interpretation would note that Wolf is attempting to link past historical experience to present-day global crises, establishing connections — however tenuous — between chronologically and geographically remote conflicts. Sabine Wilke has argued that these references form part of a strategy to reveal the relevance of the Nazi past to contemporary political realities in order to speak to generations of Germans, who have no direct personal experience of the Third Reich.[41] Lutz Köpnick, on the other hand, interprets such references as a present legitimation for the exploration of the past.[42] As mentioned above, my reading of the text adds yet another dimension to the function such references have in this novel. Like Weil's self-criticism and Drewitz's hesitant, quasi-stuttering probings of the connections between her characters' lives and distant world conflicts, Wolf's fictional "I" attempts to narrate the multiple layers of relationship and responsibility of which our lives consist. One can label these efforts "wooden," as do Hansen and Geyer, or one can acknowledge that the mapping of moral responsibility across international borders is not exactly an impossible task, but it is rarely a rarely a straightforward one that produces thoroughly convincing results.

In her quest to define the parameters of responsibility, Wolf asks several questions about the level and the extent of personal responsibility. She allows voices of dissent to argue for a very narrow definition. The narrator's brother Lutz, for instance, maintains that important social decisions are structurally beyond the reach of the individual — no matter how much the narrator would wish the opposite — thus also logically beyond our responsibility (439). And she includes the voice of an indefinite "they" to restrict our perceptions of individual responsibility with the explanation that "es ist ja menschenunmöglich, sagen die Leute dass man jeden Krieg der Welt innerlich mitmacht" (499; It is humanly impossible, people say, to become emotionally involved with every war in the world). But the narrator insists that the people who believe this have simply convinced themselves that one can solve all problems with charitable donations. This, she argues, misleads us "zu der Annahme, man bezahle für sein Nichtbetroffensein. Ein Schluss, der wiederum das unsinnige schlechte Gewissen voraussetzt, dass man eigentlich dabeisein müßte" (499; to the assumption that we're paying for not having been hit. A conclusion which once again presupposes an irrationally guilty conscience: that one actually ought to take part in it: 384).[43]

The narrator gives a far more intensive hearing to those who seek to determine the extent of their responsibility As in Drewitz's *Eis auf der Elbe*, several passages in *Kindheitsmuster* position the individual within a wide spectrum of activities and relationships, while at the same time insisting on the more substantial, material experiences of one's immediate environment:

> Vormittags trinkst du ein Gebräu aus warmer Milch, Kakao, Instantkaffee, Zucker und Rum. Du fütterst dich mit Nachrichten, die vergessen sein werden, wenn diese Seite gedruckt ist. In der durch Erdbeben vernichteten Hauptstadt Nicaraguas starben mindestens fünftausend Menschen, die anderen sind von Seuchen bedroht. Auf Hanoi und Haiphong ist in diesem Krieg bis jetzt eine Bombenmenge niedergegangen, die der doppelten Sprengkraft der Hiroshima-Bombe entspricht. Und wir, sagt Lenka, haben den schönsten Weihnachtsbaum, den wir jemals hatten. Der Sturm vom 13. November hat unsere Douglastanne geknickt. (49)

> [Mornings you drink a brew of warm milk, cocoa, instant coffee, sugar and rum. You feed yourself with items from the news that will be forgotten by the time this page is printed. In the capital of Nicaragua, which was destroyed by an earthquake, at least five thousand people have died; the others are threatened by disease. The bombs dropped on Hanoi and Haiphong in this war have twice the destructive power of the bomb dropped on Hiroshima. And we, Lenka says, have the nicest Christmas tree we've ever had. The storm from the 13th of November knocked over our Douglas fir.[44]]

Like Drewitz, Wolf begins at the immediate level of perception — physical reality — then gradually lifts the horizon, only to return at the end to a scene of domestic happiness, albeit one threatened at all times by forces beyond the reach of the individual. Although the narrator believes the items from the news will be forgotten in the near future, Wolf inscribes them into the consciousness of her characters and readers not so much as specific events, but rather as webs of relationships.

She is not content, however, simply to posit such interconnections. Instead, she repeatedly probes the implications it has for personal responsibility. While the Nazi past pursues the narrator, the conflicts of the present haunt virtually all of the characters in the book. For instance, while the family is visiting the narrator's hometown, Lenka can't sleep one afternoon in the hotel because of what Americans are doing to the Vietnamese and how that makes her feel about herself:

> Wenn sie [Lenka] daran denke, daß vielleicht gerade jetzt, während sie gemütlich im Bett liegt, irgendwelche Amis irgendwelche Leute aus einem vietnamesischen Dorf umbringen, dann finde sie sich selbst zum Kotzen. Brauchst nichts zu sagen, sagt sie, ich weiß, daß ich Blödsinn rede, aber vielleicht ist es noch schlimmerer Blödsinn, ruhig zu schlafen, während diese Sachen passieren. (320)

> [When she [Lenka] thinks about the fact that perhaps right now, while she is sleeping soundly in bed, some American soldiers are murdering some people from a Vietnamese village, then she finds herself nauseating. You don't need to say anything, she says, I know that what I'm saying is crazy, but maybe it is even greater craziness to sleep soundly while these things happen.][45]

Both the narrator and the daughter know that they can change nothing about the course of the war in Vietnam by losing sleep over it. The narrator also feebly notes that our ability to focus our energies on our immediate environment has led to the survival of human beings as a species, but that recognition brings neither mother nor daughter much satisfaction. Nonetheless, these concessions leave them feeling — as do Drewitz's and Weil's narrators — that they have somehow failed to fulfill their moral responsibilities.

Furthermore, as Lenka points out, questions about the extent of our personal responsibility prove vexing even when they focus on issues and relationships closer to home. In chapter 13, Lenka describes her experiences during a brief period working in a factory. She talks of how draining and dangerous the work is and whether a society can really ask people to do that kind of work their whole lives. Nonetheless, she concludes that it would make little sense for her to keep working at the factory just to express her solidarity for the people who work there on a long-term basis or to devote her energy to improving the situation in that particular factory:

Dabei wäre es Unsinn, sagt sie, wenn sie selbst, bloß aus schlechtem Gewissen, dasselbe täte. Aber eine Frechheit bleibt es doch, einfach wieder wegzugehen. Dabei wisse sie jetzt schon: Sie werde in ein paar Wochen noch daran denken, aber so schlimm wie heute werde es ihr schon nicht mehr vorkommen. Alles verblaßt, sagt sie. Warum muss das so sein?
Es gibt Sachen, die unlösbar sind. Und das muss nicht mal an dir selber liegen, oder?
So ist es, sagst du. Antagonistische Widersprüche.
Sie sagt: Hör auf. (356–57)

[She'd be crazy, she said, to do the same, just because of a guilty conscience. It would still be impertinent just to quit. She already knew that it would be on her mind for a few weeks, but then it wouldn't look so bad to her any more. Everything fades, she says. Why does it have to be like that?
There are things for which there's just no solution. And it doesn't have to be through any fault of your own, does it?
That's how it is, you say. Antagonistic contradictions.
Stop it, she says. (274)]

Lenka is struggling with what she sees as a moral dilemma in her personal life: to quit a mind-numbing and dangerous job to pursue other goals or stay and work toward improving the conditions of the employees in the plant. Drawing from a great deal more life experience than her daughter, the narrator, on the other hand, hints at the structural issues in the situation that require a more abstract understanding of a society's systemic problems and that even then cannot be easily resolved. Again and again the narrator confronts such antagonistic contradictions. Again and again she can find no convincing answers to these questions. Yet she also ponders repeatedly to what extent these kinds of reservations are simply excuses for inaction or moral paralysis.[46] One of the most powerful lines in *Kindheitsmuster* is one that challenges our propensity to ask unanswerable questions about individual responsibility. When speaking about the futility of some of the questions she is asking, both in her life and in the book, the narrator pauses to consider "Gegenstandslose Fragen, als Vorwand für tatenlose Melancholie" (96; Meaningless questions, as a pretense for inactive melancholy[47]). To what extent does the extensive philosophical reflection about personal and collective responsibility lead to a comfortable excuse for inaction? Anke Pinkert has suggested that Wolf structured her critical dissidence in a way that left the status quo unthreatened. She argues further that it created a "particularly symbiotic, yet contingent and mutable, relationship between dissident writer and state."[48] While Pinkert's arguments are somewhat convincing, there is one element in Wolf's writing that should at least function as a counterbalance: the pervasive self-reflection and self-criticism in her work until *Medea. Stimmen* (1996).[49] Although this characteristic of her work has played a role in the discussions up to this point, a more concentrated look at it will lead into the final section of this chapter, which examines the question of moral responsibility against the backdrop of feminist ethics.

## Self-Criticism and Self-Reflexivity

Several scholars and critics have drawn attention to the self-reflective, self-critical aspect of Wolf's writings from *Nachdenken über Christa T.* to *Kein Ort. Nirgends*, including *Kassandra*, where this is communicated through the voice of Kassandra herself. Her novels are also highly self-reflexive, in the sense that that Wolf engages in a critical, intratextual meditation on their lexical and structural features. Sandra Frieden notes that "Wolf constantly juxtaposes levels, disrupts chronology, and creates a layer of self-reflexivity within the work that insistently interferes with the reader's conventional expectations."[50] Hörnigk argues that Wolf's willingness to bring in her own "Betroffenheit" challenges readers to engage in their own critical, self-reflective practice.[51] Myra Love, on the other hand, defends Wolf against critics' claims that she overvalues herself and her own standards through the constant focus on her own self. Love maintains that "her process of reflection prevents her from elevating her own subjective vision or her personal morality to the status of standard for the world since she treats herself as part of the world upon which she reflects."[52] These scholars and critics each have their own motivation for highlighting this aspect of Wolf's work. My interest lies in linking the act of self-criticism and the processes of self-reflexivity to the discussion of how individuals and societies collectively deliberate moral responsiblity. I see these moments of introspection and critical self-interrogation as evidence of the kind of negotiations over morality to which Margaret Urban Walker refers; the self-reflexive character of the work — rather than being just a "reference to its own artificiality or contrivance" — is the textual method Wolf uses to foster a practice of critical self-reflection.[53]

The author engages in self-criticism in three ways: on a personal/individual level; on a structural level; and in ways that demonstrate how individuals are implicated in social processes, and are — ultimately — held accountable for the outcomes of such processes. There are numerous instances of self-critique that, because of their extreme character, at times take on the tone of self-flagellation. One example can make the point. In chapter 11 of *Kindheitsmuster* Wolf's narrator recalls an episode during which she and her schoolmates worked in a potato field with a group of Ukrainian slave laborers. She begins by describing the reaction she had to the women, a response that she labels "Scheu" (shyness). From the distance of roughly thirty years, the narrator can attribute that sensation to her teacher's indoctrination of her class with the idea that "anders heißt wertvoller" (326; being different made her more valuable: 249). She had learned her lessons well, and yet she does not describe her reaction as one of disdain or of rejection. The narrator goes on to ponder at great length why she did not think to share her ample soup with the women laborers. What the intervening years have taught her to see and what clearly disturbs her the most, however, is the fact that the thought never even occurred to her: "Das schauerliche Geheimnis: Nicht, dass es nicht gewagt, sondern dass es nicht gedacht wurde" (326; The horrible secret: not that one didn't dare, but that the thought didn't occur to one: 249). She did not — at the time — see herself and the Ukranian women as subjects of the same community, something that would have required a more flexible definition of community and interrelation.

As mentioned above, Wolf portrays the kind of memory work that the mnemonographic project of the book represents as potentially threatening. The narrator sees the stressful character of this work as having eventually led to a heart attack and as having taught her to distrust her current perspectives too. Robert Shirer suggests that the narrator fears that the problems and patterns of behavior from her childhood, which she so minutely dissects, "are discernible in her responses to the day-to-day challenges of her own life and work."[54] This last insight is crucial, since I believe, along with Margaret Urban Walker, that morality is not a fixed catalogue of good or bad behaviors, but rather a continual process of negotiation. Since Wolf's narrator can hardly alter the past, her intense scrutiny of her own decisions can really bear fruit only in the narrative present or in the future. Among other things, Wolf's mnemonography maps out this process of negotiation on both an individual and a structural level.

Wolf also, as mentioned previously, builds both reflection on and critique of the narrative's structure into the book itself. The narrator acknowledges often the discomfort she feels at having the power unilaterally to present a particular version of the past. In the following passage, she begins by considering this discomfort more broadly and then settles in on the question of her mother, Charlotte, and how she would have felt about the use of a particular word to describe her reaction to a specific situation: "Warum stört es dich immer mehr, dass all diese Leute dir ausgeliefert sind. Nimm Charlotte. Sie kann keinen Einspruch erheben, nicht klar — oder richtigstellen, das Wort 'Triumph' nicht verbessern, falls sie es unzutreffend fände. Du kannst über sie erzählen, was dir einfällt und was du willst" (264; Why are you more and more disturbed by the fact that all of these people are at your mercy? Take Charlotte. She can't protest, can't rectify or amend anything, can't correct the word 'triumph' if she finds it wrong. You can say what you want about her, whatever comes to mind: 200). In order to insure that the scope of the project and the perspective of the narrator is clear to the readers, the narrator frequently interrupts what could be the linear presentation of Nelly's life from age three to roughly age sixteen to talk about problems in the construction of the narrative, limitations in her own understanding of the subject, and her position of relative power as narrator.[55]

Since Nelly's (and, as an adult, the narrator's) function is to be a model — if not for all children of her generation, then at least for many — the reader often finds the narrator working back and forth between the level of individual and collective responsibility, always calling into question her very personal response. For instance, in chapter 7 she describes how she stumbled across an article in the local newspaper from 1937 that reported Stalin's hanging of eight Soviet generals. Torn between her outrage at the atrocities and her outrage that the smugness of the Nazi state vis-à-vis the early communist regime in Russia should find any justification, she asks:

> Wie es dazu gekommen ist, dass eine solche Meldung in dieser Zeitung dich traf — die Gebeine der Generale sind schon vermodert —, als sei sie neu, vor allem, als ginge sie dich persönlich an, während du von den Zeitungsschreibern des "General-Anzeigers" und von den Leuten, die die Zeitung lasen und unter denen Nelly ja aufwuchs, zu denen sie ja gehörte, "die" und "denen" dachtest, als seien es Fremde. (195)

> [How it came about that you were affected by this report in this newspaper — the generals' remains have long since moldered away — as if it were immediate; above all, as if it concerned you personally, while the newsmen of the *General-Anzeiger* and the people who read the paper, people among whom Nelly grew up, to whom she belonged, were "they" and "them" to her, as if they were strangers.]

She reacts to the news item "als ginge sie dich persönlich an" because it does have to do with her personally. Evidence that calls into question the founding years of the socialist states also calls into question her own involvement in postwar East Germany. It focuses critical attention on both her own willingness to overlook problems as well as that of her contemporaries — people who had emotionally and physically committed themselves to building an antifascist communist state. Concomitantly, however, it also calls into question the adults in Nelly's environment who pointed with critical satisfaction to the horrors of Stalinist Russia while ignoring the horrors occurring in their own state. Thus, this example operates on several levels, demonstrating aptly Wolf's intention of working through the historical period of Nazi Germany from a very personal perspective.

Wolf's narrative also provides a good example of the kind of structural self-reflection on the part of women that Christina Thürmer-Rohr calls for in the introduction to her *Mittäterschaft und Entdeckungslust*, a social-psychological study of issues related to gender and complicity in the Third Reich.[56] Thürmer-Rohr introduces the concept of "Mittäterschaft" to describe more accurately than before the role of women in the Third Reich. In "Mittäter" she sought a term that lies between "perpetrator" ("Täter") and "by-stander" ("Mitläufer"). Thürmer-Rohr sees the term as a "Denkform" (an ideational figure) that looks at the way women's collective behaviors helped to make possible and to maintain the broader culture of violence that was Nazi Germany.[57] She argues that women living in a patriarchal culture internalize the values of that society, begin to accept themselves as they are portrayed by the culture, and forfeit their own self-definition. Thürmer-Rohr argues that this constitutes a kind of moral guilt. She adds that one's moral guilt is subject to judging only by oneself; that no outside body can hand down a moral sentence or punishment.[58] Crucial here is her insistence that the concept has both a personal and a social-structural component. She posits *Mittäterschaft* as an analytical concept that asks about the participation of women on a grander historical scale, as contributors to such a self-aggrandizing male culture.[59] Thürmer-Rohr notes that many women when first confronted with this concept take it personally and begin to analyze their own behavior for their own guilt rather than the social context. This leaves one with an isolated individual's personal guilt instead of the ability to see oneself as part of a social structure.[60] Wolf's *Kindheitsmuster*, however, did in the mid-1970s precisely what I believe Thürmer-Rohr had in mind in the late 1980s when she introduced the concept. Wolf analyzes the socialization of one girl, but embedded within a larger social context. She shows how Nelly struggles against efforts to prescribe certain behaviors and certain attitudes, but also how she eventually acquiesces. Wolf's narrator acknowledges that she personally must complete this process of self-reflection, but never forgets that the concept of guilt — or better yet, responsibility — is a mitigated one.

Thürmer-Rohr speaks from a position informed by feminist debates about ethics that took shape and developed gradually in the eighties and nineties. The early work of writers like Wolf, Drewitz, and Weil in some sense laid the foundation for the critical self-engagement of feminist thinkers with their own presuppositions. Conversely, their reflections in later works on ethics can help us to articulate more thoroughly the ethical questions the authors struggled both to define and to answer.

## Wolf and Feminist Ethics

Clearly, the question of morality and ethics is fundamental to Wolf's writing, particularly *Kindheitsmuster*, but most of her other prose works as well. In *Die Dimension des Autors* (translated as *The Fourth Dimension*), a collection of essays, speeches, and interviews, Wolf states that one of literature's functions is to examine the conditions "in denen sich der Mensch als moralisches Wesen selbst verwirklichen kann" (in which human beings can realize their own potential as moral beings).[61] Of particular importance is the general sense of this comment: She concerned herself not so much with identifying what he/she/we have done wrong in the past, but rather with the kind of social structures and interpersonal relationships that allow us to function as moral beings.

For Wolf, Nazi Germany serves as a starting point or a case study of how morality is the product of collective mediation. As Robert Holub points out, "the key to understanding National Socialism lies in neither the autonomous moral individual nor the social nexus, but rather in the complex interactions that explain and escape these extremes."[62] Holub correctly notes that Wolf does not focus her attention on the subject of traditional moral theories: the autonomous (male) agent. Instead, she examines the parameters of responsibility within numerous overlapping and intersecting relationships that people take on, whether intentionally, by default, or begrudgingly. Working from the case of Nazi Germany outward, Wolf lays out analogies, parallels, and similarities to other situations both contemporaneous with Nelly's childhood and with the book's narrative present. The entire mnemonographic project is inextricably imbricated with Wolf's deliberations on the nature of morality, both collective and individual.

In order to reset the framework in which I will proceed, a brief recapitulation of the major points in feminist ethics as they relate to Wolf's work will be helpful. Specifically, I will draw upon the outline of morality Margaret Urban Walker lays out in *Moral Understandings*. First, rather than a set of abstract principles, morality is an *interpersonal* practice engaged in by individuals with varying degrees of interdependence. As Virginia Held points out, interdependence is not something people choose. Rather it constitutes a fundamental characteristic of human existence. Second, a fundamental concern for morality is the social distribution of who is responsible for what and whom and to whom. Responsibilities are not, however, simply assigned by society, but must also include "accepting or refusing, deflecting or negotiating, specific assignments of responsibility."[63] Finally, understanding moral values in society allows us to look at the ways different individuals bear and fulfill different responsibilities, rather than comparing individual behavior to a list of ahistorical ideal categories and declaring some individuals to be moral models and others to be moral failures.

Wolf shares a number of these assumptions. Morality for Wolf, too, is a continuous process of interpersonal negotiation that does not exist independently of the people who practice it. Wolf wrote in 1972, "Moral ist keine für sich existierende Institution" (Morality does not exist as an autonomous institution).[64] Additionally, neither morality nor history are metaphysical essences independent of human existence. Instead, they are structures and narratives created by human beings, and thus subject to human intervention.[65] Myra Love summarizes this as follows:

> After *Der geteilte Himmel* Wolf begin[s] to define the important questions in the German Democratic Republic as those needing to be addressed through the communicative generation of a social morality and to insist that her role as an author is to be a moralist, an assertion misunderstood by critics who insist that her limitations as a writer are those of a moralist starting from a universalizing and ahistorical standpoint. For Wolf, however, morality is a historical project as well as a historical problem. She defines it in terms of social praxis rather than as a matter of private choices made by individuals. Her concern with morality is how human beings can collectively create the social relations in which it is possible to live as moral beings.[66]

Furthermore, Wolf — like Walker and other ethicists — see narrative as a primary space for human beings to probe the question of responsibility and to question who they are as moral beings — again, not individually, but rather in and through interpersonal relationships. This chapter ends with further discussion of the commonalities Wolf shares with relatively recent feminist ethics. Specifically, the discussion here fleshes out two central components of Wolf's exploration of ethics: first, the importance of relational identity and second, the interconnection of world events between geographically and chronologically distinct communities.

Near the beginning of *Kindheitsmuster* the narrator comments: "Anonym sein, namenlos, ein Alptraum" (40; To be anonymous, nameless, a nightmare: 28). Anonymity strikes the narrator as one of the worst things she can imagine. And yet there is no way for human beings to be entirely unknown. From the moment we enter the world we become part of a tangled mesh of relationships. Wolf expends great literary effort to capture in her narrative a broad spectrum of such relationships. In addition to the familial relationships into which one is born, which Wolf depicts in a complex and pervasive way (including those among and between cousins, siblings, aunts, uncles, nephews, nieces, in-laws, and those of children with their parents), she also details the familial relationships we choose and create ourselves (those of spouses with one another, and parents with their children). These represent, however, only the most obvious relationships of our lives. Wolf also includes encounters with strangers, discussions with friends and colleagues, professional relationships (those of teachers and students, clergy and church members, as well as authors and readers), and remote acquaintances. Such relationships are not merely peripheral to the otherwise exclusive focus on the actions, decisions, and musings of a single character: the relationships become the characters.

I offer here two examples: one that posits the more beneficial impact of relationships and one that illustrates the ways such relationships can negatively shape individual identity. In the first passage, Wolf depicts the complexity of a family scene as all of the different individuals merge into a moment:

> Nach einer Zeit unerquicklicher Mißverständnisse zwischen den Verwandten schien man sich endlich versöhnen zu wollen. Tante Liesbeth lobt die kunstvoll gesteckte Frisur von Tante Lucie, diese kann sich nicht genug wundern, wie sich Klein Manfred ... in jüngster Zeit herausgemacht hat. Und nach dem Abendbrot erheben sich alle drei Schwäger — Bruno Jordan, Walter Menzel, Alfons Radde —, um miteinander anzustoßen, und zwar, was naheliegt, auf das Gedeihen ihrer Familien. Nelly, schweigsam, aber empfindlich für Schwingungen, empfindet Erleichterung, vielleicht "Entzücken," Schnäuzchen-Oma wischt sich die Augen mit dem Schürzenzipfel. Jedermann hat das Gefühl, dass man auf der Welt ist, um ein derart friedvolles und gelassenes Leben miteinander zu führen. Verschämt wird irgendwo der Satz geäußert: Na seht ihr, so geht es auch! — Und ob! sagt Bruno Jordan. (220)

> [After a period of unpleasant misunderstandings among relatives, everyone seemed to wish for a reconciliation. Aunt Liesbeth praises Aunt Lucie's elaborate hairdo, Aunt Lucie can't express enough surprise about how beautifully little Manfred ... has developed lately. And after supper, all three brothers-in-law — Bruno Jordan, Walter Menzel, Alfons Radde — stand up to drink a toast to the prosperity of their families, as seems fitting. Nelly is silent, but she is sensitive to the vibrations; she has a feeling of relief, of "bliss" perhaps. Whiskers Grandma is wiping her eyes with a corner of her apron. Everybody feels that the reason for being alive is to live in peace and harmony with each other. Shyly someone says: Now, isn't that much better. You can say that again, says Bruno Jordan. (167)]

The scene takes place on the seventh birthday of Nelly's younger brother Lutz. Although relationships in the extended Jordan family have historically cemented tensions, one sees in this scene how family members come together in mutual support. Wolf stresses the benefits of such family relationships in the statement that emphasizes that living together is the reason for existence. On the other hand, Nelly, as the somewhat distant observer in the scene, knows that the relief she feels may be short-lived; even the ostensibly hopeful phrase "so geht es auch!" hints at the tensions that are bound to resurface over time.

The second example portrays just such a moment of resurfacing tension, when memories of past injuries that have shaped the relationships of the characters overpower otherwise positive emotions. The passage details the reunion of Nelly's mother Charlotte with the rest of the family after they evacuated from L.:

In der ersten Stunde ihrer Wiedervereinigung, ... nach den ersten tränenreichen Umarmungen, den ersten Kurzberichten hinüber und herüber, begann der große Zank zwischen den beiden Schwestern Charlotte Jordan und Liesbeth Radde. Ein Zank, der von da an tagtäglich aus kleinen Sticheleien und Wortklaubereien bis zur großen Szene sich steigerte und die zweieinhalb Jahre vergiften sollte, die sie gezwungen waren, mit ihren Familien zusammen zu leben. Dutzende von Haßausbrüchen, Schimpftiraden, Weinkrämpfen, stummen, beklommenen Mahlzeiten. Zwei Schwestern, die einander nichts schenken können.

... Dass sie an jedem neuen Tag, den der liebe Gott werden ließ — so sagte es Charlotte —, erneut das Schlachtfeld betreten mußten, weil in der grauen Vorzeit ihrer Kindheit die Frage aller Fragen: Was bist du wert? falsch gestellt worden war: Wer ist mehr wert als der andere? Und weil seitdem der Kampf, ... für immer unentschieden zwischen ihnen hin und her ging. (389)

[In the first hour of the reunion ... after the first tearful embraces, the first short reports back and forth, the great feud began between the two sisters Charlotte Jordan and Liesbeth Radde. A feud that continued from then on, day after day, starting with needling and bickering, and swelling into a grand scene, a feud that was to poison the two and a half years the families were forced to live together. Dozens of eruptions of hate, vituperative tirades, fits of crying, silent meals in an oppressive atmosphere. Two sisters who can't give an inch either way.

... That they had to enter the battlefield anew each day God gave them — that's how Charlotte put it — because in the distant past of their childhood the question of questions: What are you worth? had been asked the wrong way: Which one is worth more than the other? And because since then the battle ... had been waged back and forth between them, forever undecided. (300)]

Wolf does not shy away from portraying the damage that relationships can cause in the formation of individual identity. Here she underscores the scars that even minimal slights from long ago leave in individual psyches causing lasting damage to otherwise close relationships. Thus, her emphasis on identity formation as relational does not yet devolve, as it does in later works, into the kind of rose-tinted utopias that some feminists imagined as the positive alternative that a women's culture could offer humanity.[67] The depiction of complex relationships must include the broad spectrum of human interactions. Who we sense ourselves to be takes shape only in such relationships, for better and for worse.

Similarly to Drewitz's *Gestern war heute*, *Kindheitsmuster* provides portraits of three different generations: the generation of Nelly's parents, Nelly's own generation, and — at least in a rudimentary fashion — the succeeding generation. The narrator repeatedly focuses on Nelly's battles for recognition and acceptance within her own generation, and shows in doing so both how central to identity formation a vast network of relationships is, and how we actively seek to enhance that network. For instance, when the narrator attempts to explain what motivated Nelly to join the Bund deutscher Mädel, all of the reasons she lists have to do with establishing new relationships or managing existing ones. Nelly, she explains, sought a previously unknown intimacy with the other girls, the promise of becoming part of society's elite, an opportunity to separate from her mother, and the hope of finally getting over a sense of not belonging (249–50). Nonetheless, her plan to join the group pits her firmly against Charlotte's wishes, and Nelly senses painfully a case of competing desires and responsibilities.[68]

Wolf does not restrict her portrait of relationships either to one extended family or to Nelly's particular generation. In addition to being, as Robert Shirer formulates it, "both audience and critic for her mother's evolving narrative,"[69] the figure of Lenka functions as something of an antidote to the damaged relationships within Nelly's extended family, characterized by bickering and jealousy. Through Lenka, Wolf can introduce patterns of behavior that offer promise for the future and a way out of the troubled ideologies and common modes of behavior in the narrator's own generation. Additionally, the interactions between Lenka and the narrator move the latter out of the web of relationships into which she was born and introduce her to the kinds of relationships individuals choose — not that they prove to be any less complex.[70]

It is also through Lenka, representative of the younger generation, that Wolf can highlight the topic of responsibility across generations. Frequently, Lenka poses questions about responsibility to her parents, questions to which her parents find it difficult to respond. It is not that the narrator does not wish to respond, but rather that she asks herself the very same things that Lenka does. She admits that one of her motivations for pursuing this mnemonographic project has to do with her desire to stand up and explain her generation to the next. She describes this motivation as, "den Blicken der Kinder nicht ausweichen müssen, die unsere Generation treffen, wenn — selten genug — von 'früher' die Rede ist" (195; not having to evade children's looks that are directed at our generation when — rarely enough — the talk turns to "back when": 148).

Despite my emphasis here on the nature of human identity as emerging from a network of interpersonal relationships, there are different ways to evaluate this fact. German fascist society placed particular emphasis on individuals becoming part of a more meaningful and more forceful social totality. The narrator at one point cites a poem by the nationalist poet Heinrich Anacker that Nelly's group leader in the BDM recited:

> Einst schien das Ich der Angelpunkt der Welt,
> und alles drehte sich um seine Leiden.
> Doch mählich kam erkennendes Bescheiden
> und hat den Blick aufs Ganze umgestellt.
> Nun fügt das Ich dem großen Wir sich ein
> und wird zum kleinen Rad an der Maschine.
> Nicht, ob es lebe — ob es willig *diene*,
> bestimmt den Wert von seinem eignen Sein! (252)
>
> [The me once seemed to be the central pole,
> and all revolved around its woe and weal.
> But growing humbleness helped to reveal
> that you must aim your eyes upon the whole.
> And now the me is part of the great We,
> becomes the great machine's subservient wheel.
> Not if it lives — but if it serves with zeal,
> decides the worth of its own destiny. (191)]

Anacker describes the ideal fascist individual as a cog in a machine, willing to give up his or her self in service to the collective *Volk*. In this model of subjectivity the individual is subsumed into a collective and loses not only any and all sharp contours that would distinguish him or her from an other, but also — at least theoretically — his or her agency and personal responsibility. In an article about *Nachdenken über Christa T.* Sabine Wilke argues that the generation that Wolf portrays has difficulties finding its way back from this dissolution of the self in the chorus of the we that both fascism and bourgeois capitalism require.[71]

The difficulties that some of Wolf's characters have in defining a clearly demarcated sense of "I" may appear to be the same thing as the complete de-emphasis of individuality and individual responsibility that is visible in Anaker's poem, but are not. Although Helen Fehervary asserts of Christa T. that the "difficulty of saying 'I' is ultimately the desire *not* to say 'I,'" this has more to do with Wolf's understanding of individual identity formation through relationships to others than with a desire to subordinate the individual entirely to the collective.[72] Some scholars see Wolf's version of individual development as related closely to early feminist conceptions of the relational self — and I agree that in many ways it is.[73] And yet, feminist theories of subject formation — in particular after Carol Gilligan — stressed the special importance *women* seem to place on relationships in their self-understanding. In contrast, I — along with Myra Love — would emphasize the significance that Wolf sees in the role of such relationality in subject formation generally.[74] Recent feminist efforts to interrogate the essentialist characteristics of early feminist theories of the self have led to the recognition that relationships are central in subject formation for both men and women.[75] In this sense, Wolf's view of how individual identity forms developed in advance of feminist discourse on subject formation.

This conceptualization of identity formation as thoroughly relational leads to a specific kind of moral understanding. If the self is constituted in and through its relations with other selves, then the autonomous agent of traditional moral philosophy cannot be the basis of moral reasoning — as chapter 2 has already discussed. *Kindheitsmuster* repeatedly emphasizes that our own choices are made in relationship to others and that any choice we make has implications for others as well. As one of Nelly's last high school teachers, Maria Kranhold, points out, one must always think through one's own choices with a view to the ramifications they will have in one's various (and often) intersecting communities: "Wenn man 'Freiheit' sage, müsse man wenigstens wissen, dass die Freiheit der einen die Unfreiheit der anderen bedeuten könne" (505; When using the word "freedom," one should at least realize that some people's freedom might mean a lack of freedom for others: 389). While this passage speaks specifically to the question of freedom, it implies the need to conceptualize the various levels of interconnection and responsibility in deliberating behavioral choices.

At this point I am interested in exploring how Wolf attempts to establish the interconnection of world events both across geographic expanses and across time. Recalling the presentation of feminist ethical theories from chapter 2, I begin with Margaret Urban Walker's description of responsibility as a sufficiently flexible foundation from which to explore relationships across the boundaries of different communities. This description permits us to think through interconnection without recourse to excessively abstract principles which in turn can lead us to simplify relationships that are not personal in nature, but represent rather connections between groups or collectives.

Wolf's own method of narration, which was discussed earlier, relies heavily on analogy-building in order to demonstrate levels of connection across space and time. The narrator refers to this as a "Zeitdreieck" (370; time triangle: 284), and she uses this technique to create multiple layers of reader involvement. In addition to the examples given above, Wolf's narrator at one point recalls for Lenka and the reader Nelly's visit to the ruins of the town's synagogue, which the Nazis had burned down in 1938, but as she does so she draws in American military alerts in response to possible Soviet troop movements into the Middle East and events in the aftermath of Pinochet's coup in Chile. She talks about the "progress" made in documenting atrocities: there are no audio tapes from the Gestapo's torture chambers, but such tapes do exist of the grieving wailing of women who must claim the bodies of their dead in the morgues of Santiago (238). Thus, the passage begins with a child witnessing the destruction of Jewish property in Germany and the increasing level of threat to the physical well-being of the members of the Jewish community, and then ties in how the women in Chile mourn the loss of their kin. In chapter 11, Wolf again uses the coup in Chile (a country that under Allende was an ally of the GDR) to talk about the destruction of a regime's political opponents. Here she moves backwards from describing the expressions on the faces of those about to be executed by Pinochet's henchmen to the faces of the witnesses in the Frankfurt Auschwitz trials of the 1960s, drawing a parallel between analogous situations.

Naturally, such analogies do not always convince one of the connection. Wolf's narrator admits as much when she questions repeatedly just how relevant European historical experiences are across oceans and continents. She asks, "Aber darf man seine europäische Erfahrung auf andere Kontinente übertragen? Kennt man in anderen Gegenden der Welt den Folterer noch unter den Alltagsgesichtern heraus? Und wenn, wäre das ein Vorzug zu nennen?" (325; But can one transfer one's European experience to other continents? Can one still recognize the torturer among ordinary faces in other parts of the world? And could one call that an advantage?: 248). Walker insists that the evaluation of responsibilities and connections within extended communities or across the borders of different moral communities necessitates serious and extensive critical self-reflection. My interest lies not so much in whether the analogies Wolf draws are adequate, but rather that she makes such analogies at all. They represent a clear and concerted effort on the author's part to probe questions of connection and responsibility. Gail Finney argues that Wolf's effort in this area "points to the larger significance of what can be called the false dichotonomy between past and present."[76] In other words, Wolf triangulates events that have occurred in different times and in different parts of the world to deconstruct what we see as the boundaries (geographical or chronological) between them. Not in order to deny their differences, but rather to stress their common features. What interests me, however, are the ethical implications of such analogy-building. I will return to this at the conclusion of the chapter, but first I would like to examine other techniques Wolf uses to highlight various levels of responsibility.

One of her preferred ways of querying personal responsibility is to have the characters probe their own behavior through the actions of another. She has characters not only place themselves in the position of the actors in the situations they describe, but also has them link the figures of the "disinterested observer" across time and space. The figure of Lenka often functions this way. In chapter 11, as cited above, she lies sleepless in the hotel room she shares with her mother in G. because she cannot get the image of American soldiers brutalizing Vietnamese civilians out of her head. At another point the narrator relays Lenka's reaction to a photograph of an American soldier holding a gun to the head of an elderly

Vietnamese woman. Lenka is outraged, not so much by what the soldier is doing (which she feels is beyond commentary), but rather by the fact that someone would stop to take the picture instead of intervening:

> Schweine, sagt Lenka. Sie kann nie lange auf Bild- oder Filmdokumente starren, die Folterszenen zeigen oder Sterbende oder Selbstmörderinnen am Dachrand des Hochhauses. Immer muss sie an den Mann denken, der hinter der Kamera steht und dreht oder knipst, anstatt zu helfen. Sie lehnt die gängige Einteilung ab: Einer muss sterben, ein zweiter bringt ihn dazu, der dritte aber steht dabei und beschreibt, was der zweite mit dem ersten tut.
> Sie fordert die bedingungslose Einmischung. (208)
>
> [What beasts, says Lenka. She can't look for long at pictures or documentaries showing torture or death scenes, or would-be suicides on the edges of skyscraper roofs. She always thinks of the man behind the camera who is taking pictures instead of helping. She rejects the common division of roles: the one who must die, the one who will be the cause of the death, but the third person stands by and records what the second does to the first.
> She demands unconditional involvement. (158)]

The narrator, speaking with more historical experience, silently underscores for herself the interchangeability of such scenes ("Tema con variazioni"). Both Lenka's insistence on our responsibility to intervene and the narrator's subsequent assertion of the structural pervasiveness of the inactive spectator in such situations speak to the ambiguity of the moment. This ambiguity gives rise to frustration and ultimately cynicism, but the narrator continues, nonetheless, to pursue rigorously the nature of responsibility in such situations.

In a passage from chapter 8, already cited above, the narrator muses about newspaper readers who shake their heads upon reading of atrocities or troop mobilizations, but then simply lay the newspaper aside and continue with their daily routines (223). This motif of the distanced news consumer reappears frequently in Wolf's narrative. In one such instance, the narrator strings together the names of Chilean opponents of the Pinochet regime with the names of both German communists and German literary figures from the Nazi era who were persecuted because of their opposition to Nazi politics. Just as she reads the names of the Chileans, she speculates about the distant newspaper reader of the thirties and forties:

> In anderen Ländern und Erdteilen haben vor vierzig Jahren die Leute, in deren Zeitungen deutsche Namen standen, das Blatt zusammengefaltet und es neben ihre Frühstückstasse gelegt. Dieser sich wiederholende Vorgang steht dir vor Augen, während du die

Zeitung von gestern zusammenfaltest und sie in den Zeitungständer steckst. (360–61)

[Forty years ago, people in other countries and continents would fold their newspapers and put them down next to their breakfast cups when they read German names in them. You have to think of this action while you're folding yesterday's paper and sticking it in the newspaper rack. (277)]

In this passage there lies an implicit accusation: if all you do is lay the newspaper aside and return to your morning coffee, you are at the very least indifferent to the suffering of those you have just read about. But in what way does one become guilty? Weil's narrator in *Meine Schwester Antigone* argues that we become guilty the moment we do not publicly protest injustice: in other words, stand up in front of others and say "no." The narrator of *Kindheitsmuster*, on the other hand, suggests that individual responsibility must be seen structurally as part of a collective, systemic responsibility.[77] Thus, for instance, in chapter 4, the narrator notes: "Es geht wohl über die Kraft eines Menschen, heute zu leben und nicht mitschuldig zu werden" (224; But it may be impossible to be alive today without becoming implicated in the crime: 171). However, she also notes an inability in society to see the relationship between ourselves and those far away who are caught up in violent conflict.

In order to overcome what the narrator calls our "Ungestörtheitsgrenze" (the boundary of our own calmness), Wolf maintains that we must be able to concretize for ourselves the human connection between us, regardless of the geographic spaces separating afflicted communities. Furthermore, she did note at the time she was writing *Kindheitsmuster* that our sense of the relationships and connections we might have across space was growing:

Wir haben alle nicht verhindern können, was jetzt in Spanien passiert ist zum Beispiel; wir können dieses und jenes auf der Welt, auch bei uns, noch nicht verhindern. Trotzdem habe ich das Gefühl, dass die Bewußtheit zunimmt, auch in dem Sinne, wie ich es meine, nicht nur die rein politische, ideologische Bewußtheit, von der wir als Grundlage ausgehen wollen, sondern auch eine Zunahme von Bewußtheit der eigenen Rolle in diesem Prozeß, daraus folgt eine Zunahme von Aktivität, Aktivität, die sich darin äußert, dass das Bedürfnis wächst, sich mit anderen darüber zu verständigen und darin zu verbinden.[78]

[None of us could have prevented what has just happened in Spain for example; we cannot stop this or that happening in our own country, let alone the world. Nevertheless, I feel that consciousness is growing, also in the sense in which I mean it, not just the purely political, ideological consciousness, which we want to take as foundational, but also an increase in consciousness of one's own role in this process, out of which follows an increase in activity, activity that also expresses itself in a growing need to communicate with others and to unite with them.]

Of course, *Kindheitsmuster* itself provides an example of the kind of activity Wolf refers to here: it seeks to explore connections where they are not yet apparent, to forge bonds that will make more transparent the responsibility we bear across communities.

As we read in chapter 2, Margaret Urban Walker has suggested that our sense of community must have a flexible, moving horizon. In her expressive-collaborative model of morality, we "can acknowledge a moving horizon of commitments and adjustments, allowing individual distinctiveness of situation and commitment."[79] Our responsibilities thus change depending on circumstances and individual capabilities. According to Wolf and Walker, we need to develop strategies to make interdependencies more apparent. In addition to analogies and test cases, Wolf structurally often creates at least a textual proximity between the characters' mundane activities and broader world events. The passage cited earlier in which the narrator recalls her early-morning beverage of choice and her daily consumption of news items provides an excellent example of this. In that passage, she connects her own morning routine with events happening at the time in the near east as well as the atomic bombings of Japan in the Second World War. In an interview with *Sinn und Form* from 1976, Wolf insisted that as the world becomes "smaller" through greater technological progress, we must all find ways to develop our sense of compassion ("Mitgefühl," literally "feeling with") for those who seem foreign or distant to us. She believed at the time that literature could play such a role: "Vorstellungskraft üben, die eigene Phantasie entwickeln" (Practice imagination, develop your own fantasy).[80] And although — as mentioned above — the narrator believes the items from the news will be forgotten in the near future, whether we remember each individual event is not as crucial as being confronted repeatedly with the demand that we consider our mutual interdependence and responsibility.

On the other hand, once we have mapped out the interconnections between communities, we must still define the distribution of responsibility that such interconnections might entail. We must frame our interrogations of personal responsibility with a realistic sense of the limits of individual agency so that people do not establish expectations they cannot meet and ultimately succumb to an overpowering sense of failure. Not only Wolf's characters but also those of Drewitz and Weil struggle with the feeling that they have failed somehow as moral agents. Even though they may acknowledge that their ability to act or to intervene in international conflict areas is limited, they nonetheless carry with themselves the burden of not having done enough. The continuous process of self-scrutiny can — Walker argues — lead to a distorted image of one's own capabilities and a sense of moral failure.[81]

Our ability to recognize various levels of moral interconnection is only part of the process of moral deliberation — a continuous process of negotiation within relationships of all sorts about who is responsible for whom or what. We cannot move from recognition immediately to responsibility without engaging in the process of compromise. Thus, it should not surprise us that none of these authors offers a sense of closure after their explorations into how we are connected to individuals in communities of varying degrees of proximity. Indeed, their explorations of the connections constitute an important part of the deliberative process. And they call on us, the readers, to advance the negotiations further.

## Notes

[1] A novel such as *Kassandra* (1983) could be a second focus for this study. However, it does not deal with the three criteria listed in the introduction in quite the same way or with quite the same analytical acumen. Thus, it will factor into my analysis, but not be at its core.

[2] Margaret Urban Walker, *Moral Understandings* (New York: Routledge, 1998). All quotations from this work will be cited by page number in parentheses.

[3] Christa Wolf, *Die Dimension des Autors: Essays und Aufsätze Reden und Gespräche 1959–1985* (Darmstadt: Luchterhand, 1987), 928. The English translation is from Christa Wolf, *The Fourth Dimension*, trans. Hilary Pilington (London, New York: Verso, 1988), 127.

[4] Drewitz, too, illustrates distinctly the role others have played in shaping our memories and our sense of the past. As mentioned before, *Gestern war heute* begins with a series of different voices from the main character's family, and only with time do her own experiences come to the fore.

[5] The chapter will return to this concept further on with a more detailed description of how Wolf uses this term. In short, she theorizes that human beings attempt to wall off memories into medallions — particularly painful memories — to keep them manageable emotionally.

[6] For discussions of the relationship of Wolf's concept of memory and history to the work of Walter Benjamin, see Sabine Wilke, "'Dieser fatale Hang der Geschichte zu Wiederholungen': Geschichtskonstruktionen in Christa Wolfs *Kindheitsmuster*," *German Studies Review* 13.3 (October 1990): 499–512, and Lutz Köpnick, "Rettung und Destruktion: Erinnerungsverfahren und Geschichtsbewußtsein in Christa Wolfs *Kindheitsmuster* und Walter Benjamins Spätwerk," *Monatshefte* 84.1 (1992): 74–90.

[7] Since this sentence is not in the standard English translation, the translation here is my own.

[8] For an extensive discussion of Wolf's concept of medallions, see Christa Wolf, *Lesen und Schreiben: Aufsätze und Prosastücke* (Darmstadt and Neuwied: Luchterhand,

1972), 195–96. Wolf writes there: "Jedermann führt mit sich eine Kollektion kolorierter Medaillons mit Unterschriften, teils putzig, teils grauslig. Bei Gelegenheiten werden sie hervorgeholt und herumgezeigt, weil wir Bestätigung brauchen für unser eigenes beruhigend eindeutiges Empfinden: schön oder häßlich, gut oder bose. Diese Medaillons sind für die Erinnerung, was die verkalkten Kavernen für den Tuberkulosekranken, was die Vorurteile für die Moral: ehemals aktive, jetzt aber durch Einkapselung stillgelegte Lebensflecken. Einst scheute man die Berührung, man verbrannte sich die Finger daran; nun sind sie kühl und glatt, manche kunstvoll zurechtgeschliffen, manches besonders wertvolle Stück hat die Arbeit von Jahren gekostet, denn man muss viel vergessen und viel umdenken und umdeuten, ehe man sie immer und überall ins rechte Licht gerückt hat: das ist es, wozu wir sie brauchen, die Medaillons. Man wird wissen, was ich meine." (196; We all carry with us a collection of miniatures with captions, some quaint, some gruesome. These we occasionally bring out and show round, because we need confirmation of our own reassuringly clear feelings: beautiful or ugly, good or evil. These miniatures are for the memory what the calcified cavities are for people with tuberculosis, what prejudices are for morals: patches of once active life now shut off. At one time one was afraid to touch them, afraid of burning one's fingers on them; now they are cool and smooth, some of them artistically polished, some especially valuable bits have cost years of work, for one must forget a great deal and re-think and re-interpret a great deal before one can see oneself in the best light everywhere and at all times. That is what we need them for, the miniatures. You will know what I mean. [190–91]). Translation from Wolf, *The Reader and the Writer: Essays, Sketches, Memories*, trans. Joan Becker (New York: International Publishers, 1977). See also Wilke, "'Dieser fatale Hang der Geschichte'" and Köpnick, "Rettung und Destruktion."

[9] See also chapter 15, 394.

[10] Several other scholars have made this point as well. See for instance, Sabine Wilke, "'Dieser fatale Hang der Geschichte . . .'" and Stephanie Bird, *Recasting Historical Women: Female Identity in German Biographical Fiction* (Oxford: Berg Publishers, 1998), 60.

[11] This passage echoes interestingly the relationship Weil's narrator in *Meine Schwester Antigone* sees between herself and the character of Antigone. The narrator says of Antigone, "Wenn ich sie erzähle, ist sie *meine* Antigone" (26, emphasis added; When I tell her story, she is my Antigone: 25).

[12] Christa Wolf, *Die Dimension des Autors*, 786; translation from Wolf, *The Fourth Dimension*, 25.

[13] Wolf, *Die Dimension des Autors*, 793.

[14] See Robert Shirer, *Difficulties of Saying "I": The Narrator as Protagonist in Christa Wolf's* Kindheitsmuster *and Uwe Johnson's* Jahrestage (New York: Peter Lang, 1988), 74–75.

[15] Nora, *Realms of Memory: Rethinking the French Past*, vol. 1, trans. Arthur Goldhammer (New York: Columbia UP, 1996), 11–12.

[16] See for instance, Christa Wolf, *Kassandra* (Darmstadt und Neuwied: Luchterhand Verlag, 1983), 42.

[17] Chris Weedon, "Childhood Memory and Moral Responsibility: Christa Wolf's *Kindheitsmuster*," in *European Memories of the Second World War*, ed. Helmut Peitsch, Charles Burdett, and Claire Gorarra (New York: Berghahn Books, 1999), 245.

[18] Wolf, *Die Dimension des Autors*, 811.

[19] Michael Kinney, an anthropologist, argues that events occur within specific interpretive frameworks that may — or may not — allow for specific analytical approaches. If the framework changes, it often opens up new narrative spaces for the rehearsal of collective and individual memory. Again, rehearsal here is used to mean any conscious attempt on the part of individuals and communities to recall episodes of the past in something akin to narrative format. Examples could be public speeches, visual art, petitions, textbooks, etc. The purpose of such rehearsals is to create a manageable understanding of the past for each contemporary collective. See Kinney, "A Place for Memory: The Interface between Individual and Collective History," *Comparative Studies in Society and History* 41.3 (July 1999): 431.

[20] Shirer, *Difficulties of Saying "I,"* 247 and Weedon, "Childhood Memory and Moral Responsibility," 240.

[21] See, for instance, the narrator's description in chapter 15 of the various reactions she got to her reading of the manuscript to different audiences in Germany and Switzerland, 392–93.

[22] From Therese Hörnigk, *Christa Wolf* (Göttingen: Steidl, 1989), 7–8. I have offered no translation of this passage because Wolf is drawing a distinction between two words here, "'Erlebnis' and 'Erfahrung,' both of which translate into English, however inadequately, as 'experience' but which in German have very different meanings: living through something (*Erlebnis*) and understanding something intellectually (*Erfahrung*)."

[23] Myra Love, *Christa Wolf: Literature and the Conscience of History*, DDR-Studien/East German Studies, vol. 6 (New York: Peter Lang, 1991), 98.

[24] Sabine Wilke, *"Ausgraben und Erinnern": Zur Funktion von Geschichte, Subjekt und geschlechtlicher Identität in den Texten Christa Wolfs* (Würzburg: Königshauen und Neumann, 1993), 36.

[25] Hörnigk, *Christa Wolf,* 111. This method of Wolf's resembles the way Drewitz and Weil handle the relationship between individual lives and larger historical developments.

[26] Sabine Wilke, "'Worüber man nicht sprechen kann, darüber muß man allmählich zu schweigen aufhören': Vergangenheitsbeziehungen in Christa Wolf's *Kindheitsmuster,*" *Germanic Review* 66.4 (1991): 169.

[27] Sandra Frieden, "A Guarded Iconoclasm: The Self as Deconstructing Counterpoint to Documentation" in *Responses to Christa Wolf*, ed. Marilyn Sibley Fries (Detroit: Wayne State UP, 1989), 269.

[28] See my article "Searching for Missing Pieces Around Us: Christa Wolf's *The Quest for Christa T.* and Ingeborg Drewitz's *Who Will Defend Katrin Lambert?*," *Women in German Yearbook* 19 (2003): 159–78.

[29] Drewitz asks similar questions in *Eis auf der Elbe*, for instance the moment at which the narrator and her husband walk through the ruins along the banks of the Spree. While they question each other over how much they knew about the Nazi atrocities, the author draws lines of relationship between them, the children playing among the ruins, and the global crises developing in other parts of the world (41).

[30] Wolf, *Die Dimension des Autors*, 934. See also 811. Translation from *The Fourth Dimension*, 132.

[31] Shirer, *Difficulties of Saying "I,"* 48 — my emphasis. See also Weedon, "Childhood Memory and Moral Responsibility," 239, Wilke, "'Ausgraben und Erinnern,'" 33, and Rainer Nägele, "The Writing on the Wall, or Beyond the Dialectic of Subjectivity (*The Quest for Christa T.*)" in Sibley, ed., *Responses to Christa Wolf*, 250. Wolf herself says something similar in the essay "Abgebrochene Romane": "manchmal hat ein Roman den Mut, all diese abgeschnittenen Fäden aufzunehmen, zu bündeln, miteinander zu verknüpfen und weiterzuführen. Aus dem Autor ist die Bürofrau, der Arbeiter im nächtlichen Zug, der erschrockene Verkäufer, der trotzige Biertrinker geworden." (Sometimes a novel has the courage to take up all these isolated threads, to bundle them, connect them, and spin them further. From within the author emerges the office assistant, the worker in the night train, the surprised salesman, the obstinate drunk.) *Die Dimension des Autors*, 30; my translation.

[32] Hörnigk, *Christa Wolf*, 70. Drewitz and Weil do this as well.

[33] *Kindheitsmuster*, 394.

[34] Shirer, *Difficulties of Saying "I,"* 87.

[35] "Diskussion mit Christa Wolf," *Sinn und Form* 28.4 (July/Aug. 1976): 864. My translation.

[36] Hörnigk, *Christa Wolf*, 91.

[37] Hörnigk, *Christa Wolf*, 100.

[38] I have translated this passage and several others cited in this chapter myself since they were not included at all or not included in their entirety in standard published translations. All future instances will indicate in such cases that they are my translations.

[39] Love, *Christa Wolf: Literature and the Conscience of History*, 77.

[40] Miriam Hansen and Michael Geyer, "German-Jewish Memory and National Consciousness" in *Holocaust Remembrance: The Shapes of Memory*, ed. Geoffrey H. Hartmann (Oxford: Blackwell, 1994), 184.

[41] Sabine Wilke, "'Worüber man nicht sprechen kann,'" 173.

[42] Lutz Köpnick, "Rettung und Destruktion," 81.

[43] This thought echoes the passage in Drewitz' *Eis* in which the narrator and her husband interrogate themselves and the fact that they did not do enough, that they were not on site to fight against injustice in so many different places.

[44] The translation here is my own.

[45] My translation.

⁴⁶ See for instance the following two passages: "Welche Art Pflicht besteht oder soll angeblich bestehen, derartige Einzelheiten anzupacken? Verantwortung — davon könnte reden, wer alles wüßte und imstande wäre, es den Richtigen richtig zu sagen. Verantworten kann zur Formel werden, unverantwortlich zu handeln" (194; Incidentally, what kind of duty, or supposed duty, forces you to spill details of this kind? Responsibility — the only one who could talk about it is the person who knows everything and is able to tell the right thing to the right people. Responsibility can become a formula for acting irresponsibly: 147) and in chapter 16, where she suggests that one's sense of responsibility can become dulled ("abgenutzt," 453) by the number of circumstances one confronts for which one cannot be responsible.

⁴⁷ My translation.

⁴⁸ Anke Pinkert, "Pleasures of Fear: Antifascist Myth, Holocaust, and Soft Dissidence in Christa Wolf's *Kindheitsmuster*," *German Quarterly* 76.1 (Winter 2003): 34.

⁴⁹ Christa Wolf, *Medea. Stimmen* (Darmstadt: Luchterhand, 1996).

⁵⁰ Frieden, "A Guarded Iconoclasm," 271. See also, for example, Stephanie Bird, *Recasting Historical Women*, 78.

⁵¹ Hörnigk, *Christa Wolf*, 62.

⁵² Love, *Christa Wolf: Literature and the Conscience of History*, 22.

⁵³ The Merriam-Webster definition of the term "self-reflexivity" is: "marked by or making reference to its own artificiality or contrivance: self-reflexive fiction." http://www.merriam-webster.com/dictionary/memory (accessed December 2009).

⁵⁴ Shirer, *Difficulties of Saying "I,"* 207.

⁵⁵ See Wolf, *Die Dimension des Autors*, 809–10. Wolf's narrative strategies evolved from an ongoing development within twentieth-century literature toward rupturing the continuous and integral narrative of realist literature. It would be difficult to specify exactly when these developments began, but one could look to Brecht's introduction of alienation strategies to prevent readers from identifying emotionally with literary characters or from responding to the narrative solely on an emotional — rather than rational, critical — level, or to the fragmentation and multiple layering of narratives in such authors as Ingeborg Bachmann, whose work had a significant impact on Wolf. In this stylistic respect, Wolf has much in common with Grete Weil — particularly in *Meine Schwester Antigone* — and less in common with Drewitz's more conventionally realist approach.

⁵⁶ Christina Thürmer-Rohr, *Mittäterschaft und Entdeckungslust* (Berlin: Orlanda Verlag, 1989).

⁵⁷ Thürmer-Rohr, *Mittäterschaft und Entdeckungslust*, 13.

⁵⁸ Thürmer-Rohr, *Mittäterschaft und Entdeckungslust*, 14.

⁵⁹ Thürmer-Rohr, *Mittäterschaft und Entdeckungslust*, 93.

⁶⁰ Thürmer-Rohr, *Mittäterschaft und Entdeckungslust*, 94.

⁶¹ Wolf, *Die Dimension des Autors*, 765; *The Fourth Dimension*, 11.

⁶² Holub, Robert C., "Fact, Fantasy, and Female Subjectivity: *Vergangenheitsbewältigung* in Christa Wolf's *Patterns of Childhood*" in *Facing Fascism and Confronting the Past: German Women Writers from Weimar to the Present*, ed. Elke P. Frederiksen and Martha Kaarsberg Wallach (Albany: SUNY, 2000), 227.

⁶³ Margaret Urban Walker, *Moral Understandings: A Feminist Study in Ethics* (New York: Routledge, 1998), 94.

⁶⁴ Wolf, *Die Dimension des Autors*, 766; *The Fourth Dimension*, 12.

⁶⁵ Wolf, *Die Dimension des Autors*, 804. See also Love, *Christa Wolf: Literature and the Conscience of History*, 53 and 55.

⁶⁶ Love, *Christa Wolf: Literature and the Conscience of History*, 52–53.

⁶⁷ I would emphasize here that Wolf does engage in this type of imagery in *Kassandra* when she experiments with the counterculture the women of the Trojan War construct in the caves along the banks of the Skamander.

⁶⁸ Incidentally, this passage also illustrates the processes of moral negotiation individuals and groups face. From the vantage point of hindsight, the narrator recognizes this situation as one in which Nelly had to choose between two different types of moral perspectives, one that commits the individual to the service of an abstract ideological vision and subordinates all individual desires and choices to the furtherance of that ideology (represented here in the BDM), and one that focuses on the responsibilities we have to each other as human beings (represented in this chapter both in Nelly's reaction to the public humiliation of one of the girls in the group and in Nelly's guilty conscience about abandoning her ill mother to attend BDM events. She consciously takes a middle path that will allow her to keep her mother's approval and still attain the group membership she so ardently seeks.

⁶⁹ Shirer, *Difficulties of Saying "I,"* 212.

⁷⁰ See also Marie-Luise Gättens, "Language, Gender, and Fascism: Reconstructing Histories in *Three Guineas, Der Mann auf der Kanzel*, and *Kindheitsmuster*," in *Gender, Patriarchy, and Fascism in the Third Reich: The Response of Women Writers*, ed. Elaine Martin (Detroit: Wayne State UP, 1993), 60.

⁷¹ Wilke, "'Ausgraben und Erinnern,'" 35. See also 77.

⁷² Helen Fehervary, "Christa Wolf's Prose: A Landscape of Masks," in *Responses to Christa Wolf*, ed. Marilyn Sibley Fries (Detroit: Wayne State UP, 1989), 165 and 174.

⁷³ See for instance, Sabine Wilke, "Between Female Dialogics and Traces of Essentialism: Gender and Warfare in Christa Wolf's Major Writings," *Studies in Twentieth Century Literature* 17.2 (Summer 1993): 243.

⁷⁴ See for instance, Love's argument that Wolf — especially during the writing of *Nachdenken über Christa T.* — was intent on "chang[ing] the focus of literature in her society from the representation of reality as a realm external to people which has to be mastered to the exploration of possibilities for intersubjective relationship and communication in a given historical situation" (*Christa Wolf: Literature and the Conscience of History*, 81).

[75] For a discussion of this as it relates to autobiography, see Paul John Eakin, *How Our Lives Become Stories* (Ithaca: Cornell UP, 1999), particularly chapter 2.

[76] Gail Finney, *Christa Wolf* (New York: Twayne Publishers, 1999), 57.

[77] This resonates with the work that contemporary feminists ethicists such as Joan Tronto and Fiona Robinson are doing to think through how care ethics applies in a global context. See Fiona Robinson, *Globalizing Care: Ethics, Feminist Theory, and International Relations* (Boulder, CO: Westview Press, 1999).

[78] Wolf, *Die Dimension des Autors*, 812; *The Fourth Dimension*, 43.

[79] Walker, *Moral Understandings*, 109.

[80] "Diskussion mit Christa Wolf," 882.

[81] Walker, *Moral Understandings*, 136–37.

# 5: Grete Weil: The Costs of Abstract Principles

GRETE WEIL IS A PART OF THIS STUDY for three reasons. Similar to both Wolf and Drewitz, Weil came of age during the Nazi era (albeit earlier than the other two since she was born in 1906). Questions of history and collective and individual memory and identity mark her work. Additionally, her experience and articulation of these questions lead her to positions on morality that resonate clearly both with the other two writers examined here and with feminist ethics. Relationships with family and friends also form pivotal points from which the writer constructs key moral positions. On the other hand, her experiences as a German Jew during the Nazi era and afterward created an irreparable rupture in her sense of collective history. As readers, therefore, we must explore how she depicts this rupture and the consequences it had both for her understanding of German Jewish identity for people of her generation, as well as for her sense of individual and collective responsibility.

Grete Weil saw herself as German. Both in her own words and in those of her narrative stand-ins, she stresses her self-identification as German from childhood on and her affinity with what she saw as the centerpieces of German culture.[1] She certainly shared many of the cultural traditions and collective memories that Drewitz and Wolf did. However, after the Nazis stripped her of her public identity as German and cast her out of the German collective, her relationship to those cultural traditions and collective memories was ruptured, a breach she attempts repeatedly to repair in her fiction. The literary works that form the focus of this chapter explicitly address her efforts to reconnect somehow to a shared collective past.[2] In her 1980 novel *Meine Schwester Antigone,* Weil works through the tradition of Greco-Roman mythology as part of the cultural heritage of the German bourgeoisie. Her 1988 novel *Der Brautpreis* (The Bride Price), on the other hand, represents her efforts to find a space for herself in the collective history of the Jews. This chapter examines these two works as experiments in locating her own relationship to the collective histories from which she had been expelled or into which she had been forced. Because her relationship to these histories was called into question — either by the culture in which she lived or by her own misgivings — this chapter's approach to the questions of self-positioning in history differs from that in the chapters on Drewitz and Wolf. Both questions of memory for trauma victims and the construction of ethnic identity will be key to understanding how Weil reaches conclusions about community boundaries and ethical responsibilities. This chapter will return to the problematic distinction that Nora and Halbwachs draw between memory and history as two separate and distinct activities. As noted in chapter 1, Halbwachs and Nora both see history as an objective discipline that studies events that have receded so far into that past that they no longer have personal meaning for people alive today. However, Halbwach's own understanding of collective memory and the differing ways in which individuals participate in it can further an examination of how Weil's characters understand their place in collective history.

Of course, Weil's experiences as a victim and survivor of Nazi persecution also make her vantage point on questions of ethics considerably different from either Drewitz or Wolf. Yet despite the very great distance between their respective starting points, Weil comes to remarkably similar conclusions about the inherently relational character of human nature as well the struggle to define the limits of our responsibilities. The way Sara Ruddick, Virginia Held, and Peta Bowden articulate mother/child relationships and Walker's argument about how flexibly we need to construe the boundaries between or around various communities offer critical insights for understanding Weil's provisional conclusions on personal responsibility.

Weil survived the Third Reich by going underground in Holland. She then returned to Germany in 1947. The difficulties of survival in occupied Holland had provided her little opportunity to develop her writing career early in life. Although she had published a short story in 1949 about lovers deported together from Amsterdam called "Ans Ende der Welt," an opera libretto in 1951 titled *Boulevard Solitude*, a novel about the situation of Jews in Holland during the occupation entitled *Tramhalte Beethovenstraat* (Tramstop Beethovenstrasse, 1963), as well as a short-story collection, *Happy, sagte der Onkel* (Happy, Said the Uncle, 1968), her work was not well known in Germany.[3] The publication much later of *Meine Schwester Antigone* (1980) did, however, finally bring her broader recognition among critics and readers. To a certain extent then, one could argue that Weil's career as a writer was not really fully established until she was already in her mid-seventies.

After this rather late success, there followed a number of largely autobiographical texts,[4] including *Generationen* (Generations, 1983) and *Der Brautpreis* (1988), as well as a short-story collection entitled *Spätfolgen* (Delayed Consequences, 1992). Although her work has not received the critical attention that many of her contemporaries' works have, her style and thematic concerns echo other voices of her generation, such as Christa Wolf and Ingeborg Drewitz, but also Alfred Andersch, Heinrich Böll, and Stefan Heym — to name just a few. While a thorough comparison of Weil's work to other German Jewish authors has yet to appear, Moray McGowan has offered a limited exploration of how Weil's works relate to other German Jewish writers in his article "Myth, Memory, Testimony, Jewishness in Grete Weil's *Meine Schwester Antigone*."[5] Pascale Bos has also written about Weil and Ruth Klüger as examples of the function of autobiographical expression for the Holocaust survivor. Since Weil's society labeled and defined her as Jewish and the truly traumatic moments of her life owed to this definition, she was forced to grapple with what being Jewish and German meant for her.

## German? Jewish? Both?

In the introduction to their collected volume *Reemerging Jewish Culture in Germany: Life and Literature since 1989,* Sander Gilman and Karen Remmler make the claim that "the reciprocal instability of Jewish and German identity is at the very heart of the literary self-representations of the Jewish writer in Germany."[6] Of course, the awareness of this instability has varied historically depending on the level of assimilation, ostracism, government intervention, etc. that pertained to the Jews living in Germany. Grete Weil grew up in a household in Munich that saw itself as thoroughly integrated into German society: her father a successful and influential member of the legal community, her mother a prominent social figure, she and her brother steeped in the traditions of the educated German bourgeoisie. Her narrative stand-ins — the unnamed narrator of *Antigone* and the narrator of *Der Brautpreis,* who is named Grete[7]— both feel bound primarily to the cultural history of Germany with links back to classical antiquity via Germany's own classicist traditions. Although Weil's father insisted on retaining formal connections to the Jewish community, Weil herself felt little need to do so. In fact, until she published *Der Brautpreis* in 1988 she had not focused on her personal connections to Judaism or Jewishness in her work — at least not as her main topic, which it surely is in this work. While one could certainly argue that the Holocaust and her experiences of it were of central importance to everything she had previously written, she did not take what it meant for her to be called Jewish — or to call herself Jewish — as the primary theme of a major text until she was eighty-two years old. Why is this? The answer to this question provides a portrait of Weil's sense of collective and individual history, which in turn leads us to the question of ethics. Since the opening chapter of *Der Brautpreis* addresses precisely the issue of the narrator's Jewish identity, this discussion will begin with it, moving later to address problems of collective history and individual identity in *Meine Schwester Antigone.*

At the end of the Second World War, Grete, the narrator of *Der Brautpreis* tells us, "Ich möchte das Wort Jude nie mehr hören" (52; I don't want to hear the word Jew anymore: 37).[8] Weil herself shared with Jean Améry and many others of her generation a definition of her Jewish identity as not not-Jewish ("nicht Nichtjude").[9] However, as mentioned above, and in contrast to a number of her contemporaries and younger German Jewish authors, Weil did not move to explore her Jewishness (or anyone else's for that matter) in a systematic fashion until very late in her life. And when she did so, she did it reluctantly. Had the Nazis not legislated her Jewish identity, and had they not then murdered over six million people they defined as Jews, what it means to be Jewish would not have been her question. However, she recognized and, in a sense, acquiesced to the fact that certainly no later than 1933 and continuing until the present — to paraphrase Esther Dischereit — the Jew in public perception is a Jew and nothing but a Jew.[10] In other words, the world around her had decided that she was Jewish and this fact needed to be addressed.

Three contributions to David Theo Goldberg and Michael Krausz's edited collection *Jewish Identity* give us a sense of how fraught Jewish self-definition can be; they can also provide clues to the struggles that Weil faced as she attempted to define it for herself. Asa Kasher, Berel Lang, and Michael Krausz all attempt to offer flexible ways to define Jewishness as both individual and collective identity.[11] Each author addresses a different aspect of the process of identification — or self-identification: various ways to designate different levels of Jewish identity; the significance of asking the question about Jewish identity; and the ways in which individuals can make Jewish identity personally meaningful. These essays can help us understand what it means to say that Grete Weil is a Jewish writer and part of a complex collective history that both overlaps with but is by no means identical with that of non-Jewish Germans like Drewitz and Wolf. A short description of *Der Brautpreis* will provide the necessary background.

The novel contains two first-person narratives that are clearly separated by chapter divisions. One is told by Grete, the other by Michal, the first wife of the biblical King David. Grete begins the book by describing her fascination with Michelangelo's sculpture of David (from ca. 1501–4 CE). Instead of pinning up pictures of the latest hot movie star, Grete tells the reader that she had hung in her bedroom pictures of the warrior David, with his sculpted curls and muscular body. On one level, she knew of course, that King David was a Jew, but for her — at first — he was a Florentine. Thus, her initial fascination was not with the man who is considered to have united the Jewish kingdom and founded the city of Jerusalem, but rather with an excellent example of Renaissance sculpture in Greco-Roman style.

The narrator contrasts this idolization with her first visit to the Mauritshuis in Amsterdam. Here she comes across a very different image of David, namely Rembrandt's painting of David the boy, playing his harp for the mentally anguished King Saul (from ca. 1650/55 CE). Here David is a small figure in the lower right-hand corner, while Saul, a physically much more imposing figure, tearfully watches him play from behind a curtain. The mood and hues of the portrait are dim and brooding. Both drawn to and repulsed by Rembrandt's dark, subservient musician, Grete buys herself a poster version of the Rembrandt and pins it up at home next to his Florentine relative. Throughout the following years, the narrator is torn in her affections between the Hellenized, warlike David, and the harp-playing and singing shepherd, whose music enthralls and soothes all those who hear it.

*Der Brautpreis* embodies this conflict in the characterization of David, who is in Michal's narrative both the blond warrior and the ultimate singer. To represent David as the central character of Weil's novel would, however, be a mistake, since we come to know David only through Michal's narrative. She falls in love with the youthful shepherd musician, convinces her father Saul to give her to David in marriage, but loses him shortly thereafter when he has to flee because of Saul's paranoid rages and his plots to have David killed. David eventually becomes king of the Israelites and commands Michal's return to him. Nonetheless, the sexual passion of their early relationship has been lost, and she watches David's life unfold before her with a critical eye. Michal struggles throughout to reconcile in her own heart the seemingly incongruous facets of David's character: the angelic singer/poet and tender lover and the power-hungry political and military leader.

In relation to Weil's (or — more specifically — the narrator's) German-Jewish identity, the novel pursues a twofold strategy: first, the narrator takes up a personal search for a relationship to "Jewishness"; and second, she continues to resist the social and historical pressures that define her with terms that hold very little meaning for her. She does this however, while at the same time questioning her relationship to Germany, a relationship that had at one time seemed much more straightforward to her than her Jewishness.

In his book *Jewish Identity in the Modern World*, Michael Meyer describes both Sigmund Freud's and Martin Buber's views of what it means to be Jewish as "manifestly present in individual consciousness, but darkly beyond definition."[12] Instead of rehashing the reasons why this would be true for many Jews, Weil included, I would rather look at three recent efforts to shine some light in the dim, definitional corners. Asa Kasher, Berel Lang, and Michael Krausz offer alternative approaches to the questions pertaining to Jewish identity that will constitute our starting point. From there the discussion moves to the specific case of Grete Weil and her own attempts at a definition of Jewishness.

Asa Kasher, for instance, argues that there are multiple versions of Jewish self-definition and breaks the broader community of Jews down into several smaller groups.[13] The smallest subset would be what Kasher terms "an incontrovertible core" of Jews, who both see themselves and are seen by others as unambiguously Jewish. Individuals who do not think of themselves as Jewish, but are defined as such by others would still belong to the "collective union" of Jews, but would not be part of the "incontrovertible core." Similarly, individuals who define themselves as Jewish, but are not recognized as such by all members of the incontrovertible core might, again, belong to a broader collective, but not be part of the core.

On one level, Kasher's spectrum of affiliation to Judaism seems to offer us the possibility of dealing with what appear to be contested identities. It also allows us to highlight the shifting relationship individuals have to a broader and often only loosely related collective. The existence of various subsets within Judaism makes it clear how individual identities intersect also with other collectives, making it impossible to label individuals with one designation. This in turn shows that Kasher's efforts to specify Jewish identity through multiple subgroups are aimed more at a designatory practice than at addressing the question of how Jewish identity becomes significant for individuals. In this sense his model does not help us to categorize people like Weil, who can openly and unambiguously declare herself to be Jewish, and who would be considered part of Kasher's "incontrovertible core," but who have little idea how to make such a designation personally meaningful.

Furthermore, such definitions reinforce what many non-religious Jews in Germany perceived as a coercion to make the designation meaningful. Like Weil and Esther Dischereit, Jurek Becker, a prominent writer and cultural figure in postwar literature and in East Germany's cultural landscape, emphasizes the power external identification has for individual Jews, particularly in Germany. In his contribution to a collection of essays on Jewish identity he writes:

> Ich weiß wohl, dass man nicht nur der ist, der zu sein einem vorschwebt, sondern dass man wohl oder aber auch der zu sein hat, für den die anderen einen halten. Das ist ja das Unglück. Und so gesehen bin ich in drei Teufels Namen der, der ich nach dem Urteil vieler gefälligst zu sein habe: Jude.[14]

> [I know full well that one is not only the person one imagines oneself to be, but rather that one also is required to be the one that others consider one to be. That's the problem. And thus I am in the last instance that person that many people believe I must be: a Jew.]

Becker, however, is willing to see the question of his Jewishness as a kind of puzzle or mystery. He does not attempt to specify a personal, emotional definition for himself, as does Weil.[15]

In this way, Becker's essay more closely resembles the work of Berel Lang.[16] Rather than positing several subsets of Jewishness, Lang stresses that Jewish identity is problematic not because it makes no sense or even too little sense, but because "it makes too much sense."[17] He asserts that an individual, to achieve a meaningful Jewish identity, would have to resolve at least three antinomies: self-definition versus external definition, historical versus present identification, and exclusivity versus inclusivity. He concludes by emphasizing that while the resolution of these antinomies will be individual rather than universal, how the questions are resolved will have consequences for more than just specific individuals. The fact that Weil feels compelled to make sense of her Jewishness would support Lang's notion that the antinomic character of Jewishness requires individuals to make a decision about how they will define it. In its emphasis on the persistent antinomies of Jewish identity, his argument also implies that identifying oneself as Jewish is a process that is unlikely to find a conclusion at the end of any one novel.

How individuals can resolve the antinomies of Jewish identity forms the subject of Michael Krausz's essay "On Being Jewish," which I find most compelling for understanding Weil's literary project in *Der Brautpreis*.[18] In their introduction to the book, *Jewish Identity*, in which Krausz's essay appears, Krausz and his co-editor David Theo Goldberg insist that "to be Jewish simply by way of descent will differ from assuming a Jewish identity, from *affirming one's Jewishness* as a matter of choice."[19] Krausz argues further that the distinction between being a Jew by *descent* and being Jewish by *assent* is critical to self-identification strategies. It is also crucial to the project with which Weil struggles in *Der Brautpreis*. While the question of descent does not lie within the power of the individual being so described, the question of assent clearly does.

Krausz acknowledges that one form of assent lies in accepting certain religious tenets related to monotheism and to the observance of any number of religious practices. However, he also identifies another form of assent, one that involves accepting and identifying oneself with Jewish history.[20] Ultimately, Krausz asserts that such identification "involves embracing certain beliefs and seeing oneself as a character in a valued Jewish narrative that one both occupies and fashions."[21] Drawing on Krausz's conclusion, I argue that it was not until Weil wrote *Der Brautpreis* that one could fairly call her a Jewish author by *assent*. For it was not until then that Weil, through her rewriting of Jewish history, created a space within it for herself, or in other words, a personal relationship to Jewish history. At least she did so for Grete, her narrative stand-in, but even then Weil limited the scope of that identification.

Over the years, as Weil struggled with what it meant for her to be Jewish, she laid out four criteria for Jewishness, some of which she can accept as valid, some of which she rejects entirely. The first is a religious criterion based on belief in the god Jahwe. The second rests on a personal or emotional connection to the land of Israel. Both of these first two criteria take assent as the basis of Jewish identity. Of course, she is also fully aware of the Nazi definition of an incontrovertible Jewish core: four Jewish grandparents and eight Jewish great-grandparents, a designation based solely on descent, or in Nazi terms, "race." While she rejects emotionally the Nazi definition of Jewishness, she cannot apply the first two criteria to herself either, as valid as they might be for other Jews. She settles finally — as did many of her contemporaries — on a fourth way to define Jewishness, namely as a "Leidensgemeinschaft" or community of suffering.

Younger German Jewish authors, such as Rafael Seligmann and Richard Chaim Schneider have rejected such a definition as too negative to sustain identity.[22] Yet the history of collective suffering is the only aspect of Jewish identity that Weil can embrace. This aspect of her self-constructed connection to Judaism also plays a crucial role in the discussion of morality to which her work contributes. Nonetheless, Weil's efforts to find herself even in this history required a great deal of creativity. Other Jewish authors of Weil's generation also identified with the history of Jewish suffering, but few of them chose to think through the connections via a character like King David or more importantly Michal, opting often instead for the more obvious figure of Job.[23]

What made Michal attractive to Weil? As a Holocaust survivor, Weil's reception of Jewish suffering is filtered through that event. Like Job, Michal is in one sense, of course, a fellow sufferer. She is cast aside both by Saul and then by David, and must watch from the outskirts as Solomon consolidates the reins of power. On the other hand, the cause of her suffering differs markedly from Job's. Weil, however, isolates as a common denominator for both Grete and Michal their position within patriarchally defined societies. Through a feminist critique of nation-building, Weil manages to connect Grete to Michal's story. In this way *Der Brautpreis* establishes a different kind of foundation for the suffering that the two characters experience, and contributes to Weil's vision of international ethics, which the chapter lays out later. She does this in part by traveling an alternate route through history. Whereas traditional historiography has focused on the great men and the great institutions of society, as Pierre Nora points out, women and minorities seeking to create connections between themselves and those who have gone before them turn to voices that have been excluded from historical accounts. Although Weil is not writing an actual history of the Jewish people, she is attempting to forge meaningful connections by centering her creative energy on a woman who sat at the margins of that history.

In sum, *Der Brautpreis*, structured in the form of two first-person narratives, interweaves the stories of Grete and Michal. At the end, it is only through the figure of Michal (whom she identifies culturally, but not religiously as Jewish) that the narrator feels any bond to her Jewish heritage. As mentioned above, Weil had never before focused explicitly on either Jewish history or Jewish culture, however the narrator's efforts to fill the gaping holes in the biblical Michal's story have brought her much closer to the people with whom she felt she had so little in common. At the novel's conclusion, Grete continues to feel that her ties to a Greco-Roman tradition are stronger than the connection she feels to Jewish history. Nevertheless, she has definitely constructed through the character of Michal a link for herself to that history and to a collective identity to which she previously had no compelling ties. Grete muses:

> Bin ich jüdischer geworden, seitdem ich mich mit David und Michal beschäftige? Ja sicher, irgendetwas hat angefangen, das vorher nicht da war.
> Ein neues Thema in meinem Leben, ein neuer, mir bisher unbekannter Stoff. Warum aber beschäftige ich mich mit David?
> Die jüdische Wurzel, natürlich. (168)

> [Have I become more Jewish since I've been involved with David and Michal? Yes, surely, something has started that was not there before.
> A new theme in my life, new material, previously unknown to me.
> But why am I preoccupied with David?
> Jewish roots, naturally. (128)]

Borrowing again from Krausz's definition of Jewishness by assent, it is not until *Der Brautpreis* that Weil sees herself "as a *character* in a valued Jewish narrative that [she] both occupies and fashions" (277, my emphasis). Her emplotment in Jewish history allows her to straddle collective identities, which then also gives her the ability to view history from multiple collective perspectives and to question her role within them. In this last respect, *Der Brautpreis* closely resembles the project of Weil's earlier *Meine Schwester Antigone*.

At this point, the analysis transitions from the discussion of Weil's relationship to the concept of Jewishness and to Jewish history to her much stronger sense of belonging to the classical Western cultural history into which German intellectuals inscribed themselves. However, first I will return briefly to the discussion in chapter 1 about the distinction between history and memory on which both Halbwachs and Nora insist. In that chapter, I suggested that the distinction is problematic at best and fails to account for how individuals conceive of their relationship to cultural traditions and events that go much further back in time than their collective memory reaches, which Halbwachs maintained generally includes the cultural memories of a few generations. I argued at that point that such chronologically distant events as the Reformation and the American Revolution still figure into the collective memory of many US citizens and shape the normative and interpretive lenses through which we view the present. In Weil's case, she struggled to create such interpretive structures in her confrontation with Jewish history.

Clearly, Weil did not write anything resembling an academic history of the Jewish people in Palestine, so in that sense Halbwachs and Nora's distinction still stands. On the other hand, Weil's efforts to understand her place in a historical trajectory that goes so far back in time represents a modification of Halbwachs's understanding of collective memory. The cultural traditions that previous generations created and then passed on, as well as the traces that the historical events of their own lifetimes left in their cultural perspectives offer a way to expand Halbwachs's delimitation of collective memory and problematize his and Nora's definition of history.

Jan Assmann's revision of Halbwachs's basic terminology could be helpful here. Assmann works with the concepts of communicative memory and cultural memory. Communicative memory, in Assmann's sense, is generated in active communication with other people and, thus, generally does not reach further back in time than three to four generations. It is the form of collective memory from which both Drewitz and Wolf draw. Cultural memory, which is what interests Assmann particularly, both maintains a storehouse of cultural knowledge from which groups draw their sense of belonging, and works to connect tradition to contemporary reality.[24] Cultural memory in this sense is somewhere between collective memory and historiography. It is also related to Nora's unique definition of memory in the sense that he saw memory as tying individuals to a community's past and giving the present a significance beyond its specific historical moment. Weil's narrator in *Der Brautpreis* struggles to connect to the cultural memory of a broadly defined Jewish community. Her relationship to German cultural memory, which had essentially annexed the cultural repositories of Greco-Roman history, is much more readily available to her — indeed, her approach to Antigone, a prominent character in Greek mythology, reveals a greater familiarity and ease with this cultural heritage than with Jewish history. What Weil does in both novels, then, is examine ways in which cultural memory functions and can be engaged by members of a collective who share in a particular cultural tradition.

## *Meine Schwester Antigone*

Like *Der Brautpreis, Meine Schwester Antigone* also consists of a series of first-person reflections on the narrator's own life: growing up in Germany as a member of a privileged, educated Jewish family, being forced to flee to Holland, losing her young husband to the labor camp Mauthausen, returning to Germany, marrying a German, and having constantly to explain her decision to live in Germany to her German and Jewish friends and acquaintances. The narrator's autobiographical reflections are interwoven with an extensive exploration of Antigone, the outspoken and ill-fated daughter of Oedipus, who refused to stay silent and passive in the face of what she considered to be an unjust law.[25]

Weil constructed *Meine Schwester Antigone* as a series of loosely related reflections on the life of an older female narrator, who is in her seventies. The style of the novel reminds one particularly of Ingeborg Drewitz's *Eis auf der Elbe*, but also of Christa Wolf's much more expansive work, *Kindheitsmuster*. Similarly to Drewitz and Wolf, Weil does not plot a story that leads from point A to point B. Instead, we confront fragments that together create a mosaic of memories spanning from the early years of the twentieth century through to the early eighties, creating a portrait of the century's torturous history.

The autobiographical reflections of the narrator and her musings about the biography of Antigone, so central to this analysis, are intertwined with one another to such an extent that it proves difficult to unravel them in a cogent way. This entanglement, however, constitutes one of the book's greatest achievements. At times parallel, at times inseparable, and at other times quite distinct from one another are the narrator's autobiographical considerations and her interrogation of the guilt she feels she bears as a Holocaust survivor, her attempt to write a biography for Antigone, and finally her reflections on the individual's impact on and resultant responsibility to collective history. She examines these issues not to exonerate herself of the sense of guilt she has toward those who did not survive, but rather to explore how, when, and why an individual stands up and says no to injustice, oppression, and persecution.

Weil builds into this work of literary fiction a report written by Friedrich Hellmund, a German soldier, which he wrote after witnessing the clearing of the Jewish ghetto in Petrikau on July 26, 1943. Hellmund's descendents gave the report — otherwise unpublished — to Weil for use in the Antigone book. Her decision to include the report and the way she has the narrator reflect on it illustrate not only how strongly Weil self-identified as German but also that there was a struggle within her between that identity and her identity as the Germans' self-posited other — both German and Jewish, both victimizer and victim, both agent and passive spectator, both powerful and powerless. A good twenty pages before the narrator inserts the report itself, she writes an imaginary letter to Hellmund in which she thinks through all of the things they had in common:

> Wir sind uns nie begegnet, aber ich bin überzeugt, daß wir eine Menge gemeinsamer Bekannter hatten, wir entstammten der gleichen Schicht. Weder Sie noch ich waren auf Gehorsam gedrillt,

doch hatte uns niemand beigebracht, den Schlagworten zu mißtrauen. So haben wir uns abschaffen lassen. Sie als deutscher Soldat, und ich als Verfolgte.[26]

[We never met, but I am sure we had many acquaintances in common, for we belonged to the same circles. Neither you nor I was trained in obedience, but on the other hand no one has taught us to be wary of slogans, either. And so we allowed ourselves to be destroyed, you as a German soldier, I as one of the persecuted.]

In fact, in anticipating the report, the narrator first imagines herself as standing beside Hellmund, watching Petrikau's remaining Jews be loaded up and driven off to the cemetery where they were to be killed: "Von Zeit zu Zeit sehen wir uns an und senken gleich wieder den Blick; Eingeständnis, versagt zu haben" (135; Now and again we look at each other and immediately lower our eyes: an admission of failure: 124). In the very next paragraph, however, she sees herself on one of the wagons, a mannequin limply allowing herself to be shipped off, shot, and thrown into a mass grave. One minute she emphasizes the guilt she shares with Hellmund, and the next she cites him as the one who threw over her "ein tödliches Gewirr von Stricken" (a deadly [. . .] mesh) in which she will be caught forever.

Of course, the report adds documentary evidence that the narrator herself cannot provide. She never witnessed this kind of ghetto-clearing, and never saw anyone being killed. She was never captured by the Germans, nor interned in a concentration camp. It does more, however, than simply add other evidence of the Nazis' atrocities; Weil's narrative is not a documentary of Nazi war crimes. Instead it explores what survival means in such a context and just how guilty one becomes simply by having survived — in other words, how one is implicated in this series of events as victim or victimizer, or as passive spectator or active participant. Her unique position as a member of these particular intersecting historical collectives brings her to query how responsibility is distributed throughout certain groups. Specifically, Hellmund's report allows the narrator to link his experiences with her own, and for a moment to equate what she sees as her own guilt with his, but she condemns neither him nor herself because of the failure to act, she only asserts their guilt. I will return to this topic later in the chapter in further detail, but of interest here is primarily the way Weil explores the individual's position within different collectives and how these intersecting identities position her narrator to explore the relationship between individual consciousness and collective identity and the consequences of individual action or — for that matter — inaction. She illustrates in examples like this one the way Halbwachs articulates the place of individuals' memories within collective memory. Halbwachs uses the term viewpoints, and suggests that the shifting bonds that individuals have to groups within a larger collective shape the individuals' memories, which remain, nonetheless, part of the larger group's collective memory. Weil's placement of her narrator both next to and opposite the space that the German soldier Hellmund occupies offers a radical instance of how individual memories can both reveal points of contact between the memories of subgroups in a collective and expose contradictions between the memories of subgroups. Despite the Nazis' efforts to excise Germany's Jews from the German collective, Weil's narrator insists uncomfortably on their shared collective memories at the same time that she highlights the divergences.

The narrator's inability to keep her different selves separated and distinct continues throughout *Antigone*. Although the narrator relates to us her own biography, it is striking that this autobiographical gesture is so deeply ambivalent. This aspect becomes visible already in a rather innocuous passage about aging:

> Ich bin alt, eine alte Frau. Nicht sehr alt, ziemlich alt. Ziemlich: Das Loch, durch das ich entkommen möchte. Ein sehr enges Loch. Ist relativ besser? Oder: Man ist so alt, wie man sich fühlt? ... Beim Aufwachen waren es zwanzig, jetzt, nach dem Schock des Erkennens, um die siebzig. (5)

> [I am old, an old woman. Not *very* old, just *quite* old. Quite: my escape hatch. A very narrow opening. Does *relatively* have a better sound to it? Or: *You are only as old as you feel?* ... In the moment of waking it was twenty; and, after the shock of recognition, around seventy. (7; emphasis in translation)]

The narrator cannot bring herself to accept that she is an old woman, so she begins to relativize a fact about her life, about who she is, that should be fairly straightforward. While this particular moment in the text might strike one as simply amusing, the narrator repeatedly catches herself slipping into an identity or identification that on reflection becomes suspect. In addition to the way she identifies with the German soldier, she also speaks of the mistrust in which the younger generation holds people of her generation — that is broadly the generation of Germans that were old enough to be responsible agents during the Third Reich — and she sees this sensation as perfectly justified: "Warum sollten sie auch vertrauen? Ausgerechnet uns? Der Nazigeneration. Der Generation der Sturmbahnführer, Einsatzleiter, KZ-Bewacher. Aber ich bin doch Jüdin. Ein Opfer" (7; And why should they trust us? Us of all people? The Nazi generation. The generation of SS officers, execution squad commanders, concentration camp guards. But I am Jewish. One of the victims: 8–9). As an assimilated, secular Jew, she had always thought of herself primarily as German, a sentiment that finds expression in the first part of the passage. She saw herself only peripherally as Jewish, but world history refused to let her define the "us" in her case independently. Thus, the second part of the passage underscores the unease of her identification with only one group or the other.

Growing up in the world of bourgeois humanist traditions, the narrator felt secure in her sense of self until the dynamics of National Socialist history stripped her of that security forever, leaving her with a perpetual sense of estrangement and distance: "aber plötzlich ist wieder die Fremdheit da, die mich jetzt so oft überfällt. Nicht genau zu definierende Fremdheit, doch ständig stärker werdend. Distanz zu Menschen, Dingen und zu mir selbst" (8; Yet suddenly I am swept by that sense of strangeness that overtakes me so often these days. A strangeness that eludes clear definition but seems to be growing steadily. A sense of distance between myself and others, myself and objects: 9–10). In contrast to other German Jewish writers, Weil does not explicitly link this sense of estrangement to being a Jew in Germany.[27] In fact, Moray McGowan suggests that she rejected an overemphasis on the sense of estrangement that Jews living in Germany perceive, arguing instead that it "excludes the German Jews once again by reidentifying them as the victim group."[28] Rather, it appears a consequence of being unable to heal the wound her experiences during the Holocaust have caused in her. Although she admits to feeling distanced from those around her, she expresses very little anger or frustration with the non-Jewish Germans among whom she has spent the last thirty odd years.

However, Weil's approach to Antigone and the classical tradition from which she arose is also indelibly marked by fragmentation or dislocation — just as is her relationship to Jewish history. The text offers evidence for this in how her use of the Antigone story differs from the way her contemporaries used it. For this context, the most important difference between Weil's Antigone reflections and, for example, the Antigone dramas of Bertolt Brecht (*Die Antigone des Sophokles* from 1947) or Jean Anouilh (*Antigone* from 1944) is that Weil either could not or chose not to recreate Antigone in a consistent and focused manner — there is no drama or cohesive Antigone story, just a collection of loosely related reflections. Although Weil worked for years on another Antigone novel that might have had a different narrative structure, she never completed it, and what remains of it has not been published.[29] As opposed to re-enacting the Antigone story in a modern interpretation, Weil transplants Antigone on occasion into her own reality, allowing the mythological heroine to try very different kinds of roles from the one Sophocles imagined for her. She does not, however, build a plot around the mythological figure, nor does Antigone speak in "her own voice" consistently throughout the book. This distinguishes her Antigone text also from the mythological appropriations and retellings of Christa Wolf. Although both Wolf and Weil query the role of historical consciousness in individuals' lives and the transmission of such consciousness throughout the generations, Wolf has not experienced the same kind of rupture in historical perception that Holocaust survivors feel so intensely. Christa Wolf not only tells stories in both *Kassandra* (1983) and *Medea. Stimmen* (1996) that are thematically very different from Weil's, she is also able to construct a cohesive, continuous narrative in the voice of her mythological heroines. Weil's narrator, on the other hand, needs more distance structurally to the figure of Antigone than such a narrative would provide. She could neither speak as one of the characters from within the Antigone story, as Wolf has various figures from the Medea cycle do, nor could she consistently speak as Antigone herself.

Additionally, the narrator is fully aware that the Antigone she relates to us is her own construct. She can invent romantic interludes with Dionysian shepherds, speculate about further incestuous tendencies in the family, or selectively emphasize and de-emphasize elements of the Sophoclean Antigone just enough to shade the character differently: "Wenn ich sie erzähle, ist sie *meine* Antigone" (26, emphasis added; When I tell her story, she is my Antigone: 25). Along with the freedom the narrator has to reshape Antigone to fit her own needs comes the liberty to deal with the material when she feels she wants to do so, "Die schöne Kunstfigur, die in vielen Stunden — nicht in allen — die Erwartung erfüllt. Die wegschickbar und herbeirufbar ist" (55; The beautiful work of art that in many hours — not all — fulfills my expectations. That can be dismissed and summoned).[30] She does not have such freedom with her own autobiography, nor would she have it with a biography of Sophie Scholl or Gudrun Ensslin, in whose lives the narrator sees parallels to the Sophoclean character.[31]

The narrator does not recall when she first came across Antigone, and originally she did not feel anything for the play other than what undoubtedly many readers would feel after reading it — "eine gruselige Story, sonst nichts" (12; a grim story, no more: 13). In her own mind she sees her identification with Antigone beginning only after the Nazis and their extensive network of collaborators tore her out of her own princess-like childhood — in other words: at the moment of rupture. When she loses control over her own life and her place within German society, she moves toward the character of Antigone, whose story offers an essentially finished framework that she can flesh out, running through various options as she tries to explain to herself the quality in Antigone's character that led her to make a choice that the narrator at times feels is the exact opposite of her own choices during the Third Reich.

In fact, she finds in the character's life so many similarities to her life that she occasionally sees Antigone as part of her own self, "bald ist sie ein Stück von mir und bald in allem mein Gegenpart" (13; At times she is a part of me, at other times my exact opposite: 14). These similarities range from the pampered childhoods that they enjoyed, to their deeply-felt love for both father and brother, to the moments waiting for death in a claustrophobic setting (Antigone's imprisonment in the cave, the narrator's narrow hiding place behind bookshelves in a friend's apartment). At times the very structure of the text blurs the boundaries between the narrator and Antigone's voices to such an extent that one cannot easily distinguish between them (see e.g., 19–20, 104–5).

The passage cited above, however, also underscores that the narrator's identification with Antigone cannot completely explain her long-lasting interest in this character's life story. Only the differences between the narrator's and Antigone's biographies can provide the impetus for the former to complete (so to speak) Sophocles' highly abbreviated Antigone story. The narrator describes Antigone as follows: "Traum durch die Zeit, wie ich mir wünsche zu sein, wie ich nicht bin, . . . kompromißlose Widerstandskämpferin, die ihr Leben einsetzt und verliert, . . . für die Leben Haß und Tod Liebe bedeutet, die Entschlossene, nicht von ihrem Gesetz Abweichende" (13; A dream over time, the image of what I wish to be but am not, . . . an unyielding resistance fighter who stakes her life and loses . . . for whom life means hate and death means love, a determined soul who refuses to deviate from her own law: 14). While she is fascinated with Antigone's absoluteness, ultimately she cannot embrace such moralistic rigor (94). Instead, Antigone provides the measure against which she can reflect on her own choices in an ultimately futile attempt to figure out whose choices were best: "Ich möchte ein Buch schreiben über ein Mädchen, das sich von mir nicht schreiben lassen will, meinen Eigensinn an ihrem Eigensinn messen, sehen, wer zum Schluß die Oberhand behält" (23; I should like to write a book about a girl, a book which does not want to let me write it. I should like to compare her stubbornness with my own and see who finally gains the upper hand: 22).

The narrator's relationship to Antigone proves ambiguous in several ways. The title of the book itself speaks to some of this ambiguity. The narrator underscores the many affinities she finds between her own life and Antigone's, and thus offers a portrait of sisterhood that would stress the common bonds between them. On the other hand, in Sophocles' play Antigone and her sister, Ismene, could not be more different from each other. In many ways Ismene provides the antithesis to Antigone's dogmatism. She appears to be the only descendent of Oedipus who survives the curse on the family and the destruction that his fate entails. Depending on which translation a reader consults, Ismene either strikes one as the voice of reason, or as a colorless, moral weakling. Her willingness to think about both the consequences and the perspicacity of Antigone's proposed burial of Polyneices has been perceived by scholars either as only nominally rational, but uncompelling, or as wholesale moral failure. Ismene does not understand what Antigone hopes to accomplish, but, out of love for her sister, she does offer to share the blame with her: "Now that you're in trouble / I'm not afraid to weather suffering with you."[32] In other words, she will risk her life for a living human being whom she loves, but not for one already lost to her since she had refused to help Antigone bury Polyneices and break Creon's law that had forbidden it. Antigone roundly rejects her offer of support: "You will not die, not with me you won't. / You had nothing to do with this; don't try to claim you had" (43). Ismene's choice to live rather than to sacrifice her own life for her dead brother has built an unbreachable wall between them.

Although Ismene is really Antigone's sister, the narrator mentions her only twice in the entire book. Both times she uses the adjective "blass" to describe her (60, 137). Jocasta, Oedipus's wife and mother, is the subject of an extensive excursion by the narrator, but Ismene plays no role whatsoever in the depiction of Antigone's story. Either the narrator has adopted the view of many critics in seeing Ismene as purely incidental to the tragedy, or she has tacitly taken on Ismene's position within Antigone's narrative. When Antigone proposes burying their brother, Ismene insists that she will do no dishonor to her brother's memory, but she will not disobey the laws of the country. Antigone, on the other hand, insists that to obey such a law would make her guilty, would in fact constitute dishonor.

The narrator's attempts to judge herself through Antigone's eyes lead her to recognize that she too said yes and not no. In a sense then, Ismene is at the heart of the narrator's dilemma. She survived, but only because she said yes. The question the reader might ask is whether *Meine Schwester Antigone* is the autobiography of the Holocaust survivor or of Ismene — or both. Upon Antigone's death, Ismene would have had to face similar questions about her sister's choices and her own. However, the striking similarities between the moral positioning of Ismene and the narrator aside, Ismene never takes on any contour as a character. The narrator fashions and refashions her images of Antigone to play through moral alternatives, but the woman who made choices similar to her own remains an empty cipher. In essence, the narrator casts further doubt on her own choices through her relationship to the title character's sister Ismene. While the narrator tries to hold fast to her belief that Antigone, not Ismene, made the morally proper choice, this proves increasingly difficult for her over the course of the novel.

Indeed, despite the narrator's obsession with Antigone, her attempts to mold and determine the character for her own purposes fail. Her approaches to Antigone are as riddled with doubt and insecurity as is her own autobiography. The blurring of narrative perspective mentioned above, the re-modeling of events from her own life to resemble more closely the life of the Theban princess — or vice versa: the refashioning of Antigone's biography to complement her own life experiences — underscore how inseparably interwoven are Antigone's biography and the narrator's own autobiography. The narrative voice frequently switches from that of the Holocaust survivor to that of Antigone and back again, moving freely as it does so in and out of first-person narratives, third-person narratives, and dialogues. In one dream sequence, Antigone speaks to the text's primary narrator trying to get her to realize that the biography is misdirected: "Du suchst mein Geheimnis, dabei ist es so leicht: Fühle und denke dich und nicht mich. Frage nie: hast du mich auch lieb? Sage immer: Ich bin es, die dich liebt . . . Wehre dich nicht gegen dich selbst" (205; You keep searching for my secret, yet it is so simple: Feel and think yourself, not me. Never ask: Do you love me as I love you? Always say: It is I who love you. . . . Do not resist yourself: 185). The narrator's ability to identify with Sophocles' heroine meets clear boundaries — the path to cultural or emotional identification is no longer freely accessible.

In a sense, one could argue that the rift between Antigone and Ismene was reenacted in the lives of assimilated German Jews as they watched what many believed was a positive and productive symbiosis denied and severed. In such a parallel, one would see the assimilated German Jewish community comply with the irrational and destructive laws that gradually led to their extermination in order to uphold the legal framework of the society they called their own. A much smaller minority would have stood up and said no — as Weil's narrator frequently suggests Antigone would have done. Although Weil wishes to embrace Antigone and what she represents on many levels, ultimately she cannot do so. She, like Ismene, is no longer willing or able to invest herself fully in Antigone's care for the dead Polyneices — who, in the end, may himself represent the connection to the classical tradition that formed such a substantive part of the narrator's pre-Holocaust German identity.

Recent work by Sigrid Weigel on Ingeborg Bachmann's autobiographical gestures might be helpful in understanding the nature of Weil's project in *Der Brautpreis* (indeed across Weil's oeuvre), as positing a collective and public authorial identity. Weigel's 1999 *Ingeborg Bachmann: Hinterlassenschaften unter Wahrung des Briefgeheimnisses* engages the concept of "*Autor*biographie" to discuss Bachmann's gestures of self-representation. Weigel argues that Bachmann's autobiographical gestures reveal less about the person Ingeborg Bachmann than they do about the author and public figure that Bachmann represented, hence the term "*Autor*biographie." Bachmann worked with experiences configured from past events to which she may or may not have had the personal relationship she publicly posits. Instead she constructs of them scenes of memories in a highly symbolic form that she considered crucial to her identity as an author. Weigel refers to such scenes as "*Urszenen* ihrer *Autor*biographie" (primal scenes of her *author*biography).[33] While they may or may not have actually happened as depicted, such scenes acquire through reflection and further experiences the character of "Ursprungsmomente" (moments of origin) for psychologically charged experiences that convey historical significance beyond the specific individual.

Possible examples of such a procedure in Weil's case would be her depiction of the way the narrator came to know both Michelangelo's and Rembrandt's Davids,[34] the introduction of herself as a literary character, and certain key moments in the narrator's biography that acquire a specific charge. One "Urszene" of Weil's "authorbiography" is the moment at which, in both *Meine Schwester Antigone* and *Der Brautpreis*, the speaker relates how she did or did not stand up and say no in the face of orders that — should she comply with them — would implicate her in wrongdoing. Such a scene is multiply enacted in *Meine Schwester Antigone*, both in Antigone's decision to resist Creon's ban on the burial of her brother Polyneices, and in the narrator's recollection of the moments at which she felt she should have, but did not, stand up to the Jews' Nazi persecutors and simply refuse to comply, and in her reflections on Friedrich Hellmund's report. This moment resurfaces in *Der Brautpreis* in Michal's repeated self-questioning about her inability to stand up to David's manipulative drive to power and say no (see for example, 175).[35] The question of resistance becomes a central constituent of the narrator's struggle for self-identification as a Holocaust survivor and a Jew who returned to the land of her persecutors. It links Grete to Michal across historical divides and, for Grete, cultural boundaries. Such a reading would allow us then to see Grete and Weil's other first-person narrators as manifestations of a stylized literary self that explores the quandaries of German-Jewish identity in postwar Germany and how such a self connects to collective historical identities.

Those quandaries entail the painful awareness of rupture and dislocation — both from the community into which Weil's parents had socialized her, and from the historical narrative that had framed her childhood experiences and through which she located herself in the world. However, the moment of rupture, namely precisely this period of human history has held the narrator captive, and against it she measures what came before it, what came after it, and ultimately what will come in the future. A central aspect of the book is its exploration of the ways in which individuals have an impact on and are deeply marked by their historical present. Weil treats this, however, in a markedly different way from Drewitz and Wolf, for whom history (both national and familial) represents a chronological and geographic continuum. Although Weil's narrators recognize the historical continuum that links them to the classical tradition of which Antigone is part, it no longer offers a source for understanding one's own place in history: she continues to feel emotionally and physically distant from the community she has attempted to re-enter.

Because of this, Weil's work becomes in effect an experiment in mental mapping. Having been forcefully disconnected or exiled from the cultural landscape in which she grew up, she searches desperately to reconnect to it via her reception of classical antiquity through Antigone — a cultural tradition that predates considerably the German culture that defined her childhood, but that ultimately also feeds into it. However, she also tries to establish a connection to Judaism, a culture from which she feels removed, in order to make a connection plausible and welcome. Her literary stand-ins are perhaps more successful at this than she was herself, although their conclusions too are nothing more than provisional.

In the end, however, her attempts to locate herself on a cultural map of her own making lead her to the three basic questions that form the foundation of the ethical positions she assumes along the way: 1) how are collective identities formed and at what cost; 2) what role do individuals play in historical developments that seem beyond their control; and 3) how can we define individual responsibility before that backdrop? These questions run through much of Weil's work, although this discussion again will focus on *Meine Schwester Antigone* and *Der Brautpreis*.

## Weil's Ethical Discourse

This chapter has already discussed extensively the ways in which Weil questions and critiques her membership in primarily two social and ethnic groups: German society and culture and various versions of Jewish society and culture. Her expulsion from German culture in the thirties and her somewhat forced inclusion in Jewish culture caused her to note the role that power, oppression, and exclusion play in the construction of collective identities. *Der Brautpreis*, in particular, thematizes and critiques this process of community or nation-building through the figures of Saul (Michal's father) and King David, the biblical uniter of the Jewish people and founder of the Jewish nation. The autobiographical character of the book also tempts us as readers to seek the parallels between Weil's narrative of Jewish history and Germany's history leading up to and during the Nazi era.

One possible "Urszene" in Weil's "authorbiography" that links Grete and Michal is the depiction of the process and the costs of nation-building in a patriarchally stratified society. This narrative represents a connection between the two characters, since both witnessed the birth of new nations through the suppression and oppression of those deemed to be "other." Michal's relationship to David develops against the backdrop of a power struggle — first between Saul and David and then between David and the non-Jewish population groups that shared the same geographic home.

The novel begins just before Michal meets the shepherd musician David. As their passion for one another increases, Saul threatens to give one of his daughters to the soldier in his command who would prove himself victorious against the Philistines, with whom the tribes under

Saul are locked in continuous struggle. Michal becomes desperate at the thought that she and David could thus be separated, but she also chafes at the trade in women's bodies in which her entire male-dominated culture engaged. Finally, she realizes that David could be the one to "win" her and becomes even more horrified that the basis of their life together should be such a transaction between men.

Michal recognizes that even clever manipulation will not make the situation palatable to her and resigns herself to submission (29). This submission becomes a characteristic behavior pattern for Michal. On the one hand, she can easily see how unjust patriarchal control of women's bodies is and how destructive the aggressive, violent, and militaristic lifestyle that supports the patriarchy is. This holds true even for men, as the reader becomes conscious that David's success as a warrior is bound to come at the detriment of his identity as a musician and poet. On the other hand, Michal sees no possibility for acting outside the norms of patriarchal society, reluctantly accepts the situation at hand, and looks pointedly to the future for relief (59, 123).

After David flees from Saul's murderous plotting and Saul banishes Michal from the royal household in a marriage to the stranger Palthi, she finds the space to hone her critical thinking skills. Since Palthi is neither Michal's true husband nor her father, and thus does not occupy a position of socially-sanctioned authority over her, their relationship becomes one of relative equality. Thus, during her years with Palthi, Michal finds some peace. However, once David has solidified his power base and founded his court, he calls her back to him. At that point in the narrative, she feels herself again unable to act freely, to resist becoming complicitous with the nationalist aspirations of the King David. Even though she knows she does not play the role of queen convincingly — something the younger Bathsheba does particularly well — she does not feel she can simply refuse to play the role of royal wife either. Weil's narrative, however, encourages the reader to question Michal's perspective in this matter.

Michal repeatedly wonders at her own inability to say no when asked to comply with either her father's or David's commands. For instance, after discussing Amnon's rape of Tamar with David, Michal rebukes herself, "So schwieg ich in dem Augenblick, in dem ich hätte reden sollen, und ließ dem Verhängnis seinen Lauf. Schweigen als Schuld. Wieder nicht nein gesagt. Warum?" (175; Thus I remained silent at the moment when I should have spoken and let fate take its course. Silence as guilt. Again did not say no. Why?: 134). While we can, as readers, have some sympathy with Michal's frustration both with the social structures into which she was born and with herself, we do not — and I believe this is a deliberate move on Weil's part — ever begin to feel that Michal did not have any other options. Just as in *Meine Schwester Antigone,* Weil insists that while we may have good reasons for not saying no to commands that could implicate us in injustices, having chosen to say yes, we are still complicitous with the wrongs we do not protest openly.

Time after time, Michal watches as men justify their destructive, warring behavior with reference to god's will. In the same breath, Michal notices, they seek to exclude women from access to power. Michal believes that were women to participate in a community's decision-making process, they could effectively dampen male tendencies to aggression (123). This is perhaps a rather naïve belief given Bathsheba's example of how women, too, can thrive in the unscrupulous world of violent power struggles, and maybe doubly naïve since Michal herself is more than once drawn into David's schemes to get what he wants at the cost of another.

In a sense, Weil's text wields a double-sided critique of nation-building. On the one hand, she consistently condemns through Michal the ways in which the Jewish nation is predicated on the extermination of the other groups living in Canaan. First Saul, then David engage in war after war to solidify their power base in the region — purportedly acting always according to the will of Jahwe. On the other hand, although Michal finds this kind of reasoning questionable, she seems too unsure of herself to object:

> Sie alle mußten wir besiegen, zum Teil auch ausrotten, um Fuß zu fassen. Schon unsere Kinder erfahren, dass es sich nicht anders machen ließ. Ich konnte das nie recht einsehen, mit einiger Mühe hätten wir friedlich nebeneinander leben können. Doch vielleicht ist das Land wirklich zu klein, uns alle zu ernähren. (54)

> [We had to conquer them all, in part even exterminate them, in order to gain a foothold. Even our children learn that there was no other way to do it. I could never really see that, with a little effort we could have been able to live in peace with one another. But perhaps the country is really too small to nourish us all. (40)]

The need for *Lebensraum* was, of course, one of the arguments that the Nazis wielded to justify expansionist policies. Here it appears as a tool of the ruling elites during Michal's era. Michal quickly points out how such arguments take root in a society — namely through the indoctrination of its children — and gradually appear to be simple facts: only through the overthrow and repression of the ethnic other can Saul (or David after him) unify the Israelites and secure their future. Even the skeptical Michal finds the argument somewhat persuasive.

Often the process of subjugation involves the emasculation of the enemy, a fact that so disgusts Michal that it irreparably separates her physically from the one she loves the most, David. In Weil's narrative, Saul demands the foreskins of 100 Philistines as the price for Michal's hand; but David goes far beyond this, bringing back a basket full of the severed penises of 200 Philistines and laying them before Saul one by one.

Saul's effort to intimidate the supposedly effete musician David backfires. Instead of a subservient soldier, Saul has created for himself a rival, one who will trade not only in women's bodies, but who also can and will dismember any male obstacle to power.

David's act so appalls Michal that she refuses to have sex with him ever again. Just at the time when she is socially joined to David forever, Michal quite explicitly does say no to such abuse of the human body. Certainly, in one sense, we can thus say that Michal does protest, does stand up and say no. There is, however, an irony in this moment of refusal: by rejecting David after this incident, she also shuts herself off from him and from any influence she might have had in David's quest to unite the Jewish nation. Although David does not manage to rape his new bride, he also shows no understanding for Michal's objections, and she cannot reach him on his narrow path that leads straight to the throne. At first Michal hopes that her disgust will ebb, that she will eventually be able to meet David again physically, but the thought of society's expectations that she bear sons who will then become soldiers so angers her that even her early hopes begin to fade, and David distances himself more and more from Michal (40–49).

Her decision is also problematic in the sense that her refusal to have a sexual relationship with David and to bear his children leaves the door open for the Machiavellian Bathsheba, a woman who knows no scruples when pursuing power. Michal's insistence on her absolute powerlessness rings false and her hope that women's participation in state politics would someday prevent wars of aggression seems naïve when one sees just how much power a figure like Bathsheba wields. Of course, Michal resoundingly rejects Bathsheba's strategies for winning influence, but Michal's decision has left her in a disturbingly ambiguous position.

Uwe Meier, the author of the first monograph on Weil's work, underscores Michal's independent thinking and her refusal to accept things the way they are. He also acknowledges, however, that she does not live up to her own principles in life. Nonetheless, he chooses to emphasize in her character a high degree of independence, a refusal to accept tradition unconditionally, and the insistence on the possibility that the individual can lead a life outside of common social norms.[36] Michal is certainly conscious of the limitations her society places on her choices for action, and — as mentioned above — looks pointedly to the future for positive change. However, Weil portrays Michal against the backdrop of both Bathsheba and Antigone, making it possible for readers to perceive the gap between Michal's beliefs and her will to act. As readers, we can see that her love for David more than once makes her complicitous in his regime, while her sense of women's powerlessness shields her from forming a conscious strategy for participation in David's life (see 54, 153–54, 175). Weil's portrayal of the way women position themselves around power in a patriarchal society shows both the possibilities for female agency and its limitations.

Michal's critique of David's methods as he builds his kingdom is not limited to the beginnings of a Jewish state.[37] Instead, it pertains generally to how collective identities are constructed and asserted, seeking both to unite and to protect the people drawn together in the collective. David's attempts both to differentiate the Jews from the cultures around them and to stabilize the community from within entail the forceful destruction and alienation of those surrounding groups. Similarly, the Nazis' efforts to put forward a unified German collective involved both the internal destruction of what the Nazis defined as Germany's other and the external oppression of the cultures surrounding it. It is tempting, therefore, to consider the possible readings of David in Weil's novel as a kind of parallel to Weil's own biography or, indeed, her "authorbiography."

In an article about Weil's *Der Brautpreis,* Miriam Fuchs reads the novel largely as autobiographical. Although she draws attention to the problems of seeing an analogy between David and Weil's first husband, Edgar, she insists on attempting to do so nonetheless.[38] Such a dilemma provides us a very good reason not to overemphasize the autobiographical character of this novel — despite the fact that Weil and the narrator share first names. It is undoubtedly more productive — not to mention interesting — to see in David a representative of the nationalism patriarchal societies have bred, a reading both Fuchs and Dagmar Lorenz find compelling.[39] In such a reading, Weil's portrayal of David could apply not only to Jewish history, but even more convincingly to German history. Additionally, linking Jewish history to German history in such a way opens up an ambiguous, but intriguing avenue for comparison. In such an interpretation, Weil would be calling attention to the fact that both nation-building projects involved the slaughter of innocents. Such a process of nation-building configures them as enemies via a twisted evocation of a higher cause (Jahwe or racial superiority) and within the framework of a society structured around the struggle for male dominance.

Weil's love/hate relationship with Germany resonates broadly with Michal's love/hate relationship with David. The narrator's identification and preoccupation with the great names and masterpieces of German culture, through which she finds a link to classical antiquity, bind her to a history that was also responsible for the destruction of life as she had known it, and the death of millions of people — including her own husband, Edgar. Similarly, Michal loves and is bound to a man who ultimately ravages her life and robs her of many people she loved: Absalom, Palthi, and in many ways, David himself.

At the end of the novel, Grete wonders again which of the two Davids she admires most — the warrior and king, or the shepherd musician who made both himself and his listeners weep when he performed.

The possible analogies become at this point rather difficult. Is the warrior David Germany's fascist, militaristic past, and the shepherd its rich history in all of the arts? This equation would leave all sorts of unanswerable questions. Is Michelangelo's David then perhaps representative of European culture's nationalist history and Rembrandt's subservient David its powerless victims? Such an analogy would not be satisfying either. I agree with Uwe Meier, who warns us against trying to pin specific labels on the characters in Weil's biblical narrative.[40] Who or what David represents may not be as central to this book as the relationship of the narrator and the author to both David and Michal. For it is through the story of Michal and David that Weil explores from a woman's perspective the costs of nation-building, and what we all lose in societies structured by the dominance of one or more men over all others.

It proved impossible in the previous section to talk about the process of founding a united Jewish kingdom under David without including some reflection on the role that Michal played in this drama. She, of course, sees herself as essentially powerless — a female in a patriarchally-structured society, cast off from the real center of power by her refusal to bear children. Weil's text, however, leaves room to question Michal's acceptance of her own powerlessness. Rather than spending more time on Michal's (in)ability to intervene, however, it will be more useful to talk about how feminist ethics helps us to explicate Weil's confrontation of the individual (through Michal and Antigone) with impersonal structures of violence and oppression.

The act of saying no takes on the contours of a moral dictate in Weil's work. Its importance transcends the distinct cultural traditions Weil tried to establish between classical Greek society and early Jewish history. In fact, Weil jumps through some rather awkward narrative hoops to bring Antigone and her act of refusal into Michal's narrative (62). Although she repeatedly explains to us why her heroines and her narrators were unable to meet the ethical standard she posits as absolute, she never rejects flatly the postulate that the only morally acceptable act open to individuals in situations that call on them to comply with unethical or immoral policies is to refuse and to do so publicly.

In *Meine Schwester Antigone,* the narrator's own sense of having failed morally comes out poignantly when she recounts having read a teenager's essay response to the question: "What do you know about Hitler?" She cannot get the statement the student made, "Hitler schaffte die Menschen ab" (Hitler destroyed human beings), out of her head:

> Zum erstenmal verstand ich, daß ich mich habe abschaffen lassen. Es war nicht allein Hitlers Schuld. Zu so was gehören zwei, einer der's tut, und der andere, der's hinnimmt. Er erließ irrwitzige Gesetze, ich habe sie befolgt. Ich würde mich selbst nicht ernst nehmen,

wenn ich mich darauf berief, daß mir als Jüdin nichts anderes übrigblieb. Ich sagte nicht nein — Neinsagen, die einzige unzerstörbare Freiheit, Antigone hat sie souverän genutzt —, ich sagte ja. Ja, ich verlasse Deutschland, ja, ich bin keine Deutsche mehr, . . . ja, ich nähe mir auf die Kleider den gelben Stern, . . . ja, ich nehme einen fremden Namen an, . . . So rette ich mein Leben, so schaffe ich mich selber ab. (128)

[For the first time it became clear to me that I had let myself be destroyed. It was not all Hitler's fault. It takes two for something like that, one to do it and the other to accept it. He promulgated insane laws, and I obeyed them. How could I take myself seriously if I argued that as a Jew I had no choice? I did not say no. Saying no is the only freedom that cannot be taken from you. Antigone made superb use of it. I said yes. Yes, I shall leave Germany, yes, I am no longer a German, . . . I shall wear the yellow star, . . . yes, I shall answer to a name that is not my own . . . In this way I shall save my life while destroying myself. (118)]

Weil's narrator states that saying no is the one freedom no one can take from us. It is also for her the only ethically acceptable act. In this sense Antigone's refusal to follow Creon's new laws strikes one as the perfect model against which to measure any individual's failure to say no.

The gesture with which the narrator and the author most consistently identify Antigone — refusing to become complicit in injustice — offers an example of the kinds of moral principles that feminist ethicists since Carol Gilligan have seen as characteristic of traditional Western ethics: a rule that one can apply in any relevant situation and feel secure that one is acting morally. Yet *Meine Schwester Antigone* also searches for the many reasons why the one ethically acceptable act was often simply unacceptable. Although Weil's Antigone text appeared in 1980 — the same year as Gilligan's pathbreaking study of moral reasoning, and thus cannot have been influenced by Gilligan's work directly — her interrogation and comparison of the narrator's behavior with that of the Sophoclean heroine reach ultimately the same conclusions. Weil never explicitly rejects the principle of saying no, but her narrator ultimately comes to see that Antigone cannot provide us with a model for our own behavior.

This section looks at various different aspects of how Weil examines the individual's role within history: our ability to understand history, how we decide what is or is not the right thing to do, what the relationship is between action, inaction, and guilt; how broad the individual's space for action is; and finally what kinds of individuals and what kinds of protest interest Weil's narrator. After that is laid out, the discussion draws insights from feminist ethics — familiar from chapter 2 — to lay out the ethical implications of Weil's work.

As mentioned above, the narrator in *Meine Schwester Antigone* does not herself feel capable of answering questions such as: Why did the Jews not offer more resistance? She feels uneasy trying to explain the reasons why large groups of people behaved as they did. She is not, in other words, interested in writing a textbook on the history of the Third Reich and the Holocaust. An individual has no real access to the motives driving the behavior of large groups of people. Instead Weil's narrator feels able only to describe the particular situations and contexts within which individuals make particular choices, and even those explanations are subjected to repeated revisions, doubts, and second-guesses:

> Warum tut man etwas oder tut es nicht, von dem man nacher nicht mehr begreift, daß man es getan oder nicht getan hat? . . .
> Warum sage ich noch heute: wie entsetzlich, furchtbar, nicht zu ertragen? Warum sage ich das stereotyp nach den meisten Zeitungsberichten, Radiosendungen, Tagesschauen? Warum rede ich und tue nichts? Warum weiß ich nicht, was ich tun könnte? . . .
> Ich gehöre weder zu den Herrschenden noch zu den Unterdrückten. Doch was fange ich mit der Unabhängigkeit an? Dem Schlendrian der Gleichgültigkeit verfallen, schließe ich mich der schweigenden Mehrheit an und verdränge mein besseres Wissen. (75)
>
> [What makes a person do a thing or not do it, the kind of thing that later on one cannot understand having done or not done? . . .
> Why do I still say today: How terrible, frightful, intolerable? Why do I trot out this stereotyped response to most newspaper reports, radio broadcasts, television news programs? Why do I talk and do nothing? Why do I have no notion of what I might do? . . .
> I am neither one of the rulers nor one of the oppressed. But what use do I make of my independence? Prey to creeping indifference, I go along with the silent majority, against my own better judgment. (69–70)]

What is so intriguing about this passage is Weil's ability to take the questions the narrator asks herself as a victim of Nazi persecution and draw them into the present by asking them of herself as a witness to persecution and oppression — a witness who does not know what to do, and does not say no.

In order to understand the moral reasoning with which the narrator tries both to explain and accept her own life choices, it is necessary to give a somewhat fuller picture of the narrator's role as a moral agent in the text. Although she would occasionally lead the reader to believe otherwise, we know that she was not passive in the face of Nazi persecution: as a member of the Jewish council in Amsterdam she was able to fulfill certain roles for the underground resistance, for instance smuggling letters and helping to get many individuals out of the Schouwbourg, the Amsterdam theater that served as a collection site for Jews who were to be deported to concentration camps. Weil's narrative stand-in recognized the ambivalent character of the Jewish Council's work quite clearly, and later saw her cooperation with the council as a mistake. This mistake, however, allowed her to keep her mother alive.[41] The narrator also does not avoid being part of the conflicts that plagued Germany in the seventies — even though here too, her involvement is marked by ambivalence. Despite misgivings, she does not, for instance, turn away Marlene, a fugitive from the law. She harbors enough doubts about the state's efforts to vilify the terrorists and to stifle civil liberties in its pursuit of terrorist sympathizers that she cannot turn Marlene, to whom she gives shelter in her apartment, away, even though this might make her complicit in a crime. In fact, the one lesson she does feel comfortable drawing from her own history is that living in history places us before choices that make us guilty regardless of which decision we make: "Wie ich da sitze, vor meinem Antigoneheft, weiß ich wieder, durch welchen Dreck ich gegangen bin, durch welche Eiseskälte, gestellt vor Entscheidungen, die, wie immer sie ausfielen, mich schuldig machten" (99; Sitting here bent over my Antigone notebook, I become aware of the filth I have waded through, the icy coldness when I found myself confronted with decisions that could not but make me guilty, no matter how I chose: 90).

As the narrator sees it, no matter what your intentions and no matter if you were a victim or a passive German witness: if you survived the Holocaust, you did so because at least once you did not stand up and say no. As mentioned above, she believes that saying no is the one indestructible individual freedom, something anyone theoretically could do at any time — if that person was willing to pay the price. For a Jew, saying no would have meant death. For the Germans the consequences were not as clear, or as predictable. Freedom is, however, a concept that causes the narrator a certain amount of discomfort. In the following passage, the narrator expresses her misgivings about freedom and ends by asserting that Antigone's freedom to act independently of others was ultimately fatal:

> Freiheit. Was ist das? Kein Zustand für Lebende. Leben, das unaufhörliche Bemühen, sie zunichte zu machen. Freiheit nach Waikis Tod zerstört durch Urs, Freiheit nach Urs' Tod zerstört durch den Hund, und schon denke ich, wenn ich sicher wüßte, daß er tot ist . . . Nein, keinen neuen. Es sind auch ohne ihn genug Freiheitsvertilger da. Ich muß an Ursula schreiben, an Milia, Loreley, Andreas . . . Jeden flehe ich an: Nimm ein Stück meiner Freiheit. Ein kleines nur, ich will dich nicht belasten, aber eben doch. . . . Hätte ich nur den Mut, allein zu bleiben. Ich habe ihn nicht.
> . . . Die tödliche Freiheit. Antigone. (19)

[Freedom. What is freedom, anyway? No fit state for the living. Life: an unremitting effort to destroy freedom. My freedom after Waiki's death destroyed by Urs, my freedom after Urs's death destroyed by the dog, and already I am thinking: If I were absolutely sure he was dead . . . No, no new dog. Even without one there are enough forces working to curtail my freedom. I must write to Ursula, to Milia, to Lorely, to Andreas . . . I implore each of them: Take a bit of my freedom. Just a little, I don't want to burden you, but still. . . . If only I had the courage to remain alone. But I do not. . . . Deadly freedom. Antigone. (18–19)]

Freedom is only possible if one is not enmeshed in a network of human relationships. Depending on how you look at it, being thus entangled either provides us with ready-made excuses for our actions, or it sets certain limits on our freedom to act. Which interpretation is preferable? Is that even a question one has the ethical space to ask — particularly from the perspective of a reader who has never confronted the same kinds of difficult dilemmas that Weil and her narrator did?

The narrator states early on that she wants to use Antigone as a measuring-stick for her own choices, but Antigone's situation was not similarly constrained. Antigone's father, mother, and two brothers were already dead. She had cut herself off from her sister Ismene, because Ismene did not see the same meaning or urgency in burying Polyneice's body. Thus, she had already lost or had herself severed all of the personal relationships to which she would have been responsible. The narrator then muses:

Wie hätte sie an meiner Stelle gehandelt? Die Integrität bewahrt? Die Mutter beschützt? Beides zugleich war nicht möglich. Voll Neid denke ich an sie, die einen Toten begraben, nicht einen Lebenden retten mußte. Sie war allein. Alleinsein — ungeheuerste Stärke. (94)

[What would she have done in my position? Would she have preserved her integrity? Acted to protect her mother? The two were irreconcilable. I think of her with envy, for all she had to do was bury the dead, not try to save the living. She was alone. Being alone — an incomparable source of strength. (86)]

Only when completely independent from others, or willing to act as if one were completely independent from others, does the individual have unrestricted freedom to say no. In other words, only in a situation of almost complete autonomy can we act solely according to abstract dictates. Once we have responsibilities toward others — particularly others who are dependent on our assistance — our spectrum of choices narrows.

Oddly enough, the narrator chooses not to explore more thoroughly Antigone's decision to abandon her sister Ismene. Initially, Creon is prepared to have both of the sisters killed because of Antigone's actions. She thus could have been responsible for her sister's death. We know, therefore, what the answer to the narrator's question is: yes, Antigone would have maintained her integrity — or at least what she defined as her integrity. The question Antigone does not ask in this situation, but one the narrator is forced to ask herself, is whether preserving one's integrity is an ethically acceptable choice when it could result in the endangerment of others.

One of the main points of emphasis in feminist scholarship on ethics has been the insistence that we must begin rigorously to integrate into our thinking about the nature of the self and the parameters of moral behavior the acknowledgement of how extensively human lives consist in networks of relationships — not just the ones we choose to enter, but also the ones we are born into, the broader ones in which we work and live, and even those networks whose scope goes beyond our personal awareness of them.[42] Early feminist ethicists saw a key to understanding the implications of this in the relationships between mothers and their children. In the work of Nel Noddings, such relationships tacitly constitute the model for caring. Sara Ruddick builds what she hopes will form the philosophical underpinnings of a strategy for working toward world peace on what she sees as the basic tenets of being a mother. Virginia Held tries to make such a relationship the experimental antidote to a moral philosophy that rests on the concept of the autonomous individual. She writes:

> When we bring the experience of women fully into the domain of moral consciousness, we can see that the most central and fundamental social relation is that between mother and mothering person and child. It is mothering persons and children who turn biological entities into human social entities through their interactions. It is mothers and mothering persons who create children and construct with and for the child the human social reality of the child. The child's understanding of language and of symbols and of all that they create and make real occurs through cooperation between child and caretakers. Mothering persons and children thus produce and create the most basic elements of human culture.[43]

Later feminist scholars — such as Sarah Hoaglund and Marilyn Friedman — worried that one should not found basic moral relationships on the basis of relationships in which such a fundamental disequilibrium in both abilities and power obtains.[44] Peta Bowden and others, however, have called our attention to the fact that both these early attempts to use maternal behavior as a guide for moral theory and their critics overlook how the relationship between mothers and children change over time and emphasize instead the aspects of "reciprocity and mutuality."[45] We can see this clearly enough in the narrator's evocation of her relationship with and responsibilities for her mother.

Her mother is — so she at least believes — completely dependent on her protection for survival. The narrator sees this as a handicap in her efforts to act in a morally rigorous manner, a topic to which the analysis will return later. Held notes that "no mapping of the social and moral landscape can possibly be satisfactory if it does not adequately take into account and provide guidance for relations between mothering persons" and those dependent on them.[46] Yet, in the sense that Antigone has cut herself off from her personal relationships, this is the kind of moral model that she offers the narrator. Using feminist ethics to understand the narrator's dilemma clarifies the fundamental conflict in moral reasoning with which the narrator grapples.

She recognizes that her decision to protect her mother is one she voluntarily made. It was not a promise that her mother extracted from her and not something that held a strategic key to underground resistance in Holland, a fact that could have possibly altered the parameters of her decision-making. It is nevertheless a responsibility she feels she must fulfill. This resonates well with Margaret Urban Walker's point that we cannot simply be assigned responsibilities: we must also decide to accept them. Having accepted the responsibility for her mother's survival, the narrator can no longer act freely in response to Nazi acts of violence. In her mind she plays through a certain episode at the Schouwbourg over and over again. A new SS officer had been appointed to run operations there, because his predecessor had been deemed too soft. His first act was to convene the Jewish council members and warn them that they were not to spend too much time with the deportees and that anyone caught doing so would be deported as well. She wants desperately to react and tell him exactly what she thinks, but cannot, because she fears it will endanger her mother:

> Niemand rührt sich, niemand spricht. Ich möchte vortreten und sagen: Ich bin kein Gefangenenwärter. Ich bin dasselbe wie die, die ich bewachen soll, ein Jude, ein Mensch. Ich möchte, aber ich tue es nicht. Denke in rasender Eile. Was würde geschehen, wenn? Vielleicht schlüge er mir ins Gesicht, es wäre Befreiung, mein Haß fände das Bett, in dem er strömen kann. . . . ich ginge mit auf Transport. Aber da ist die Mutter, die freiwillig auf mich genommene Pflicht, sie zu schützen. . . . Ich kann sie nicht ausliefern, darf meinen Haß nicht herausschreien. (98)

> [No one stirs, no one speaks. I want to step forward and say: I am not a prison guard. I am the same as those I am supposed to guard, a Jew, a human being. I want to, but I do not. My mind is racing. What would happen if I did? Perhaps he would strike me in the face — that would be liberating, it would give my hatred a channel into which it could flow . . . toward death, for I would be shipped

out with the others. But then there is my mother and the responsibility I have assumed for protecting her . . . I cannot deliver her into their clutches, must not give voice to my hatred. (90)]

As much as she wishes, however, that interdependence would justify her choices — at the very least to herself — she finds no peace in this explanation. Interdependence explains for the narrator her choice, yet is for her still an excuse: "Wahrheit und Ausrede" (157; Truth and excuse: 143). No matter how compelling the explanation, it will not serve the narrator as clear justification. She is left with a profound sense of guilt toward those who lost their lives.

A crucial separation between public and private lives underlies her assessment of what is or is not moral in such a situation. It seems that regardless of how much one may do underground in the resistance, what counts as protest for Weil's narrator is publically standing up and saying no in a way that will awaken public consciousness, however slowly and incrementally. When she describes Antigone's seizure and audience before Creon, it is the public character of her protest that she underscores:

> Geschmückt zum Opfer, das sie bringen wird, der Stadt, dem Volk, im Namen der Gerechtigkeit, sieht die aus dem spärlichen Staub gezerrte Leiche, sieht sie, sieht sie nicht . . . Alles klappt, sie wird gepackt, vor Kreon gebracht, *der sie vor allem Volk — und das ist das wichtigste — verhört*, und hat endlich Gelegenheit ihren Satz zu sagen: Zum Hasse nicht, zur Liebe bin ich. (15; my emphasis)

> [Adorned for the sacrifice she intends to make for the city, for the people, in the name of justice. She sees the corpse, dragged free of its thin covering of dust, sees it, does not see it . . . Everything goes as she hoped: she is seized, dragged before Creon, *who interrogates her before all the people — and that is the main thing*; now at last she has a chance to say her piece: Not for hatred but for love am I among you. (15–16)]

The efficacy of protest or resistance (that is, the question of how many lives were saved) interests her less than the protest's ability to change public consciousness and her own adherence to what she considers ethically correct precepts. This leads her from Antigone to people such as Sophie Scholl:

> Die Analogie zwischen Sophie und Antigone ist dicht. Menschen, die bis an die Grenze gehen. Die ihr Selbst voll ausschöpfen. Nicht nach dem Erfolg fragen, nur nach der eigenen Notwendigkeit. Unbequeme. Schwierige. Die uns zum Denken zwingen. Unser Bewußtsein wach machen. (162)

[The analogy between Sophie and Antigone is sound. Both of them people who go to the limit. Who give completely of themselves. Who care not for success but for obeying their own sense of necessity. Not comfortable to have around. Difficult. People who force us to think. Who prod our awareness. 147–48]

Joan Tronto's book *Moral Boundaries: A Political Argument for an Ethic of Care* could explain why Weil considers this distinction between public protest and underground resistance or between making her protest public and saving her mother so important. One of Tronto's major concerns is to lay out how Western cultures came to think of morality as a series of rules governing the interaction of autonomous individuals within the public sphere. Chapter 2 of this book discussed her account of how our moral understanding developed from commonly shared, context-driven community values to one that emphasized the application of certain behavioral codes that could be applied theoretically to any like situation regardless of the participants in the interaction or the context in which the interaction occurred. She argues that the changing character of the economy in the eighteenth century with its expanding trade and markets made it difficult to apply a more contextually-determined, community based moral system. Instead, rules were needed to insure that participants in the public sphere were all acting according to similarly predictable moral tenets and were not overly influenced by personal (domestic) attachments. This transformation established a boundary between public and private life, the institutionalization of which eventually erased its own creation. This, in turn, led us to accept for centuries such boundaries as "natural." Weil's narrator subjects herself and others to the same moral expectations: what we do as moral agents is done publicly and according to certain universal rules.

Walker's discussion of traditional Western ethics maintains that an overemphasis on moral dicta creates this kind of coercive moral checklist. So long as we manage to act according to the code, checking our behavior against the list all the while, we can rest assured that we have performed well as moral agents. In chapter 2, however, I called attention to Walker's discomfort with the pressure under which this puts people. The narrator's inability to act in the one way she sees as ethically acceptable what she sees as the one ethically acceptable act — to resist publicly in the face of violence and oppression — leads her to see herself as a moral failure. What she is left with is the lifelong struggle to accept herself despite this failure. Weil's *Antigone* may have been published more than ten years before either Tronto or Walker offered us the tools to understand the nature of the conflict the narrator faced, but the novel nevertheless illustrates the costs to human beings that traditional patterns of moral reasoning have exacted.

On the other hand, Weil's narrator comes to similar, if uneasy, conclusions in thinking through this conflict through her experimentation with the narrative frame that the Antigone story provides. Just because Weil's narrator is still struggling with the moral dictates she considers to be universal, this does not mean that Antigone's choices win out over her own, and this is where Weil's moral reasoning leads her to insights about moral choices that resonate so clearly with later feminist ethicists. The narrator notes that the absoluteness by which Antigone lived marks her character. Hers is an extremely rigid moral code that made her able to abandon her sister to an uncertain fate for the sake of symbolically burying her brother. Late in the book, the narrator suddenly realizes that, as a real person, Antigone would have been pretty unbearable: "Ich ahne, daß die leibhaftige Antigone, die ich nicht nach Lust und Laune herbeirufen und wieder ins Dunkle zurückstoßen könnte, mir schwer auf die Nerven ginge" (140; I surmise that the flesh-and-blood Antigone, not the one I can call forth and send back into obscurity at will, would put quite a strain on my nerves: 128–29). In fact, Antigone is only useful as a model structure, one with which the narrator can tinker to see how the pieces would lie if they were rearranged. Ultimately, Antigone's answer to impersonal violence is no more appropriate than the narrator's own — and certainly not more moral.

Twice the narrator puts Antigone into situations she actually faced herself just to see if Antigone's moral principle could positively effect change — once when she wants to see if Antigone would have shot the SS officer at the Schouwbourg, a situation in which the narrator remained silent. In this experiment, Antigone provokes the SS officer He, in turn, is captivated by this woman who refuses to follow the rules. He is, in fact, almost magically transfixed, a situation Antigone uses to pull out a revolver and shoot him:

> Sehr ernst, sehr feierlich sagt sie. "Nicht mitzulieben, mitzuhassen bin ich da." Dann zieht sie aus ihrem Kleid einen Revolver, zielt auf den starr dastehenden Hauptsturmführer und drückt ab. Kein Blut. Von allen Seiten treten Männer in langen Goebbelsmänteln auf, mit Hüten, die ihre Gesichter verdecken. Sie gehen auf Antigone zu. (219–20)

> [Very seriously, very ceremoniously, she says. "Not for love but for hatred am I among you." Then she pulls a revolver out of her dress, aims it at the SS captain, who stands there rigid, and pulls the trigger. . . . There is no blood. From all sides appear men in long Goebbels-style coats, with hats that cover their faces. They approach Antigone. (199; translation modified)]

The narrator imagines Antigone doing what she herself regrets not having done in that situation. But this act of violence forces Antigone to reverse the principle according to which she had acted in Sophocles' tragedy and brings about no change. In fact, she apparently shoots into thin air; there is no body, no blood. She has shot a symbol, not a human being, and others — equally anonymous, for one does not see their faces — step into his place to take her away. Later in that same dream-like episode, Antigone rushes out of prison — on a cold and frosty night — into the arms of the narrator, who at first tries to comfort her, but finds herself immobile, frozen by Antigone's hotly-shed tears.

Rather than freeing her from her own sense of having failed, Antigone's deed leaves the narrator completely empty and as fearful as she was before:

> Mein Gedächtnis ist ausgelöscht. Woher bin ich gekommen? Wo gehöre ich hin? In welches Land? An welchen Ort?
> Plötzlich lasse ich sie los, sie fällt zu Boden, bleibt liegen wie sie gefallen ist. Ich laufe fort, laufe, laufe. (221)
>
> [My memory is obliterated. Where do I come from? Where do I belong? In what country? In what place?
> Suddenly I let her go, and she falls to the ground, remains lying where she fell. I take to my heels, running, running. (200)]

Antigone, the character from Sophocles' tragedy, does not have the answer to the narrator's questions. As Uwe Meier puts it, the present and the past that the narrator experiences and remembers are hardly eliminated or even softened by the connection to the mythic material: "Das überlebende Opfer bleibt in seiner existentiellen Not allein" (The surviving victim remains in his or her existential need alone).[47] Realizing this, the narrator turns at the end of the book to the mirror, looking at herself. Defined at one and the same time by what she suffered as a victim, by the guilt she feels as a survivor, and by her identity as a German, she sees in her reflection ugliness, and is ready — at least for the moment — to embrace it. "Ich spüre die Häßlichkeit, bin die Häßlichkeit, werde von ihr umströmt, lasse mich von ihr umhüllen, akzeptiere sie, akzeptiere mich, bin glücklich" (223; I feel the ugliness, am one with the ugliness, which swirls around me. I let it wrap itself around me, accept it, accept myself, am happy: 201). After externalizing her own experiences into the character of Antigone, she has come to accept her own choices, to see that she — like Ismene — is more than just a pale shadow in the tragedy of the Holocaust. Unfortunately, the narrator recognizes that her moment of self-acceptance will probably not last, as she concludes with a question mark about tomorrow: "Und morgen?" (223; And tomorrow?: 201).

The narrator's emphasis on her ugliness can lead us in at least two different directions. First, if we read the ugliness as existential rather than purely physical, it can take us back to the notion that morality is about acting according to universally valid moral precepts and that when we do not manage to do that, we fail: we become "ugly." Or alternatively, it can bring us to a discussion of what community comes to mean in Weil's post-Holocaust world. As mentioned above, Weil never managed to embrace fully any connection to Judaism other than as a community of sufferers. There exist at least two different ways to configure the common spaces of such a community: either one can relate to and empathize with those who have suffered or are suffering, that is, one can respond to their long-lasting emotional and physical pain— treating them as sympathetic but powerless victims. Or one can relate oneself to those who do suffer and question to what extent one's own actions — individually or collectively — have an impact on that suffering in the hope of preventing further suffering or trauma. In other words, we can seek the extent to which we are responsible for the suffering of others. This, then, has more to do with the concept of vulnerability, which in turn comes from the Latin word for wound: *vulnus*, a central concept in Weil's work. To what extent do I — either individually or as a member of a certain society — contribute to circumstances in other communities that cause suffering? Or, how are others vulnerable to our actions?

As survivors of traumatic experiences and vast personal loss resulting from the Nazis' persecution of Europe's Jews, Weil's narrators suffer throughout their lives from a wound that will not heal. The narrator in *Meine Schwester Antigone* says, "Meine Wunde, die blutet, wenn man daran rührt und manchmal auch, wenn gar nichts daran rührt, unerwartet, nicht vorauszusehen" (46; My wound bleeds when anyone touches it and sometimes when it is not touched, unexpectedly, unpredictably: 43). What she describes here echoes Lawrence Langer's differentiation between deep memory and common memory, and how — for the survivor — these two forms of memory, these two planes of time coexist. Survival demands of the survivors that they split in two, repressing whenever possible the injuries and humiliations of their Holocaust experiences, in order to function in their everyday lives.[48] Although the narrator can generally function in daily life, has lived "well" for the last forty-some years, her wound and its unpredictable eruptions separate her from those around her. On the other hand, it opens her up to anyone or any group that is vulnerable or suffering. It makes it impossible for her to walk away.

Her reaction to Marlene, whom the narrator's niece has left to her care, provides a good example of this. The police may be after Marlene for harboring a fugitive terrorist. The narrator does not know the details, but suspects the young woman of being a terrorist sympathizer. Characteristically, the narrator's response to Marlene is as ambivalent as is her treatment of Sophocles' Antigone. While she rejects out of hand the methods and the utopias of the terrorists, her liberal sensitivities, her deep suspicion of the state, and her own experiences of persecution make it impossible for her to reject the individuals involved. She wants to wake the sleeping woman in her apartment and yell at her:

> Steh auf und hau ab. Ich bin eine müde alte Frau. Es ist mir egal, was mit dir geschieht. . . . ich weiß, daß du eine Terroristenbraut bist. Ich bin gegen Gewalt und gegen Sympathisanten von Gewalt. . . . Ihr spielt Krieg, einen sinnlosen widerwärtigen Krieg. Und ich will Frieden. Aber ich kann es nicht sagen. Meine Wunde macht es unmöglich. (164)
>
> [Get up and get out of here. I am a tired old woman. I don't care what happens to you. . . . I know you are a terrorist's moll. I reject violence and those who support violence. . . . You are playing war games, meaningless, sickening games. And I want peace. But I cannot say it. My wound prevents me. (149)]

Her time in the Jewish Council, working at the Schouwbourg, and later in hiding at the mercy of those who were willing to help, predispose her to identify with Marlene. By the same token, her upbringing in a liberal household, tolerant of many different views and ideologies also makes her able to identify with individuals whom society and her own experiences would have her see as the enemy: "ich bin noch immer die Tochter aus gutem Hause, eine Scheißliberale. Ich verstehe dich, verstehe jeden, habe eine Geschichte geschrieben, in der ich mich mit einem SS-Mann identifiziere, wir haben beide überlebt, sind beide schuldig" (125; I am still the daughter of a good, solid family, still a bleeding-heart liberal. I understand you, understand everyone, even wrote a story in which I identify with an SS man, for both of us are survivors, both of us are guilty: 114). As much irritation as this ability — one could even say "need" — to identify with others seems to cause her, her description of what she sees as a flaw is also one of the book's greatest strengths. The narrative's repeated efforts to look at history and human suffering from different vantage points and to understand fully the context of other people's behavior brings Weil's work into agreement with feminist ethicists who argue that understanding moral choices and meeting human needs requires us to be able to think outside of our own cultural spaces. Her own experiences of persecution and state violence make her feel protective of those possibly subject to the same kinds of irrational, systemic violence. They bring her to accept responsibility for giving Marlene sanctuary — even when her own personal political convictions would lead her to act otherwise.

Similarly, her response to the suffering of others causes her to query her own responsibility in situations far beyond the boundaries of her immediate community. In a passage quoted previously, Weil — like Drewitz and Wolf — calls the reader's attention to areas of global conflict and oppression. Although she does not do this as extensively in her work as do Drewitz and Wolf, it is clear that she seeks to understand what it means to accept responsibility for suffering of others wherever we see it (75–76).

She responds, she believes, to the suffering of others — to her own and to others' vulnerability — because of her own personal trauma. However, her incessant questioning of responsibility offers us a good example of what Margaret Urban Walker has described as the mapping of responsibility — or the geography of morals. Weil's characters ask how they are or are not responsible for the suffering of others, forcing the reader to rethink the boundaries of responsibility that we have taken for granted. This constitutes a basic element of care ethics as it developed from its earliest articulations. Walker adds,

> This might involve countenancing some new or emerging facts (global interdependencies, new political balances of power) and might involve seeing existing facts anew or with a different emphasis (disproportionate consumption of resources by wealthy nations, citizens' responsibilities in democratic societies for government priorities and policies).[49]

As we have seen in chapter 2, Joan Tronto also urges us to use care as a tool in thinking about relationships that extend beyond our immediate personal spaces (family, community, and nation). She does this by calling attention to one of the hallmarks of caring, namely attentiveness to the needs of others. Tronto engages this specific aspect of caring to think through how care, which has often been criticized as too parochial a concept to apply beyond the domestic sphere, does lead us to rethink our responsibilities — both as individuals and as communities. If we pay attention to the world in which we live, inevitably we will see those aspects of social or collective action that have negative consequences for other communities.[50] While it remains unclear exactly how the individual — that is, someone like Weil's narrator (or for that matter the characters in Drewitz and Wolf's novels) should thus respond, it is clear that we have become implicated in conflicts and systems of exploitation and oppression that occur well outside of our own immediate spheres of action.

Care ethicists maintain that responsibility represents the fundamental concept in care ethics as opposed to obligation, the language of traditional Western ethics. Tronto clarifies by noting that obligations have more to do with "formal bonds, previously stated duties, [or] formal agreements." Responsibility, however, is both more contextual and more nuanced and covers a broader spectrum of both the need for care and the decision to care.[51] The characters in the novels of Wolf, Drewitz, and Weil may have no obligation to care about or for people suffering from political oppression or economic exploitation in corners of the world remote from them, but they assume the responsibility for trying to re-map the lines of connections between individuals and communities. We can think of this process as one of questioning the distribution and negotiation of responsibility within our own communities and across community boundaries. In this sense, Weil's work participates in what Margaret Urban Walker has described as "mapping the structure of standing assumptions that guides the distribution of responsibilities — how they are assigned, negotiated, deflected — in particular forms of moral life."[52]

The various contributions of feminist scholars to discussions of ethics have helped to explain the conundrum that Weil's characters face as Holocaust survivors. Their insistence on the rigid separation of public versus private responsibility and their adherence to a concept of morality as a set of rules for public conduct force them to find themselves guilty. It forces them to pit the needs of individuals dependent on them against the insistence on confronting and opposing systemic forms of violence and oppression. However, it is essential to note that Weil herself saw this as an ineffective, indeed impossible moral system. Unfortunately, her narrative stand-ins are not fully able to think through the alternatives or to find their own conclusions compelling, but they do participate nonetheless in the thoroughgoing re-examination of western assumptions about morality that she and other feminists launched in the last quarter of the twentieth century. Neither Weil's work nor any single ethicist will address all of the complications of and variations to the theme of individual and collective responsibility. It is only through a collective and critically self-reflective examination of ethics that we can develop further as moral agents — both individually and collectively.

## Notes

[1] To give just one example, the opening chapter of *Der Brautpreis* offers an extensive discussion of this topic. *Der Brautpreis* (Zurich: Nagel und Kimche, 1988), 7–12.

[2] Pascale Bos describes this effort on Weil's part as an attempt at "reentry." Pascale R. Bos, *German-Jewish Literature in the Wake of the Holocaust: Grete Weil, Ruth Klüger, and the Politics of Address* (New York: Palgrave Macmillan, 2005). For example, see chapters 1 and 2, pages 1–46.

[3] Pascale Bos discusses at length the sociopolitical climate in which Weil's works appeared and how historical changes in the German public's willingness to think about the experiences that Holocaust survivors needed to share led to a late welcome for her in the German literary landscape.

[4] As noted already in the introduction to this book, many of Weil's works are patently autobiographical. At a minimum, these include *Meine Schwester Antigone* (1980), *Generationen* (1983), and *Der Brautpreis* (1988). However, Weil has insisted on the distinction between her characters' lives and her own and what it means for her to write a literary work rather than an autobiography. For

this reason, I try to respect her understanding of the differences and keep the narrators in her fictional works distinct from Weil, the writer. This is not always possible, and some slippage is unavoidable. For a discussion of Weil's views on the differences between fiction and autobiography, see Carmen Giese, *Das Ich im literarischen Werk von Grete Weil und Klaus Mann: Zwei autobiographische Gesamtkonzepte* (Frankfurt am Main: Peter Lang, 1997).

[5] Moray McGowan, "Myth, Memory, Testimony, Jewishness in Grete Weil's *Meine Schwester Antigone*," in *European Memories of the Second World War*, ed. Helmut Peitsch, Charles Burdett, and Claire Gorrara (New York: Berghahn, 1999), 149–58.

[6] Sander Gilman and Karen Remmler, "Introduction," in *Reemerging Jewish Culture in Germany: Life and Literature since 1989*, ed. Sander Gilman and Karen Remmler (New York: New York UP, 1994), 5.

[7] In order to distinguish clearly between the author Grete Weil and the narrator of *Der Brautpreis*, I use the name Grete only when referring to the narrator in the novel.

[8] Quotations from the novel are from *Der Brautpreis* (Zurich: Nagel und Kimche, 1988). Page references are indicated in parentheses, which also enclose corresponding translations from *The Bride Price*, translated by John Barrett (Boston: David R. Godine, 1991), with page references also within the parentheses.

[9] See, for instance, Jean Améry, "On the Necessity and Impossibility of Being a Jew," in *At the Mind's Limits: Contemplations by a Survivor on Auschwitz and Its Realities*, trans. Sidney Rosenfeld and Stella P. Rosenfeld (Bloomington: Indiana UP, 1980), 94.

[10] Esther Dischereit, "No Exit from This Jewry" in Gilman and Remmler, *Reemerging Jewish Culture in Germany*, 269.

[11] See David Theo Goldberg and Michael Krausz, eds., *Jewish Identity* (Philadelphia: Temple UP, 1993).

[12] Michael A. Meyer, *Jewish Identity in the Modern World* (Seattle: U of Washington P, 1990), 4.

[13] Asa Kasher, "Jewish Collective Identity," in Goldberg and Krausz, *Jewish Identity*, 56–78.

[14] In Hans Jürgen Schultz, *Mein Judentum* (1978; Stuttgart: Kreuz Verlag, 1991), 14. My translation.

[15] Becker writes, "ich fühlte mich nicht als Jude, bin aber in hunderterlei Beziehungen einer. Na und? Wozu, frage ich mich, muss ich einem solchen Rätsel unbedingt auf den Grund kommen wollen? Wäre ich hinterher klüger? Ich fürchte: nein. Ich fürchte: ich würde nur vergeblich versuchen, ein Geheimnis aufzuklären, ohne das mein Leben ärmer wäre" (18; I didn't feel like a Jew, but in hundreds of ways I am one. So what? Why, I ask myself, must I necessarily try to figure out what the source of this puzzle is? Would I be smarter afterwards? I fear not. I fear that I would only try in vain to reveal a secret without which my life would be poorer.).

[16] Berel Lang, "The Phenomenal Noumenal Jew. Three Antinomies of Jewish Identity," in Goldberg and Krausz, *Jewish Identity*, 279–90.

17 Lang, "The Phenomenal-Noumenal Jew," 279.

18 Michael Krausz, "On Being Jewish," in Goldberg and Krausz, *Jewish Identity*, 264–78.

19 Goldberg and Krausz, *Jewish Identity*, 6.

20 Krausz, "On Being Jewish," 274.

21 Krausz, "On Being Jewish," 277.

22 See, for instance, Rafael Seligmann, "What Keeps the Jews in Germany Silent?" in Gilman and Remmler, *Reemerging Jewish Culture in Germany*, 173–83, and Richard Chaim Schneider, "In der Haut der Eltern," in *Zwischen Antisemitismus und Philosemitismus: Juden in der Bundesrepublik*, ed. Wolfgang Benz (Berlin: Metropol, 1991), 73, 76.

23 See Uwe Meier, *"Neinsagen, die einzige unzerstörbare Freiheit." Das Werk der Schriftstellerin Grete Weil* (Frankfurt am Main: Peter Lang, 1996). Meier gives examples such as Margarete Susman and Karl Wolfskehl, 188–89.

24 Jan Assmann, "Collective Memory and Cultural Identity," translated by John Czaplicka, *New German Critique* 65 (Spring/Summer 1995): 126–33; here 130.

25 In Sophocles' account of Antigone's story, she angers Creon, who has become the king of Thebes after an extended civil war over a power dispute between the two sons of Oedipus, Polyneices and Eteocles. Both brothers fall in the conflict, but Creon declares only Polyneices to be an outcast and forbids the burial of his corpse. Antigone sees this prohibition as an affront to the cultural traditions of her people and a dishonor to a member of her family. Twice, she attempts (symbolically) to bury her brother's body. The second time Creon sentences her to a slow death entombed alive in a cave. Sophocles, *Antigone*, trans. Elizabeth Wyckoff, in *Sophocles I*, ed. David Grene and Richmond Lattimore (Chicago: U of Chicago P, 1954), 157–204.

26 Grete Weil, *Meine Schwester Antigone* (Zurich: Benziger, 1980), 134; *My Sister. My Antigone*, translated by Krishna Winston (New York: Avon Books, 1984), 123. Subsequent references will be by page number in parentheses.

27 Friedemann Weidauer, "'Fighting for Defeat': Jewish Identity in Postwar Germany and Austria." *Seminar* 34:3 (September 1998): 290.

28 McGowan, "Myth, Memory, Testimony, Jewishness," 151.

29 Uwe Meier, "'O Antigone . . . stehe mir bei' Zur Antigone-Rezeption im Werk von Grete Weil," *Zeitschrift für Literaturwissenschaft und Linguistik* 26.104 (December 1996): 147–57.

30 My translation.

31 Sophie Scholl was a young student in Munich during the Third Reich. She and her brother Hans founded the non-violent resistance group known as the White Rose. They paid for their resistance with their lives. Gudrun Ensslin was one of the terrorists in West Germany who became known as the Baader-Meinhof group and eventually founded the Red Army Faction in the 1970s. She died in prison in 1977.

32 Sophocles, *Antigone*, trans. Richard Emil Braun (Oxford: Oxford UP, 1973), 42.

[33] Sigrid Weigel, *Ingeborg Bachmann. Hinterlassenschaften unter Wahrung des Briefgeheimnisses* (Vienna: Paul Zsolnay Verlag, 1999), 313.

[34] In an interview with Carmen Giese, Weil talked about the way she manipulated this story to lend a kind of cultural significance to the experience that it did not — at least in her mind — have as she experienced it. See Carmen Giese, *Das Ich im Literarischen Werk von Grete Weil und Klaus Mann: Zwei autobiographische Gesamtkonzepte* (Frankfurt am Main: Peter Lang, 1997), 218.

[35] Michal's relationship to David in *Der Brautpreis* bears some similiarities to Kassandra's relationship to Aeneas in Wolf's *Kassandra*, however, there are also substantial differences. A discussion of this would go beyond the scope of this argument.

[36] Uwe Meier, *"Neinsagen, die einzige unzerstörbare Freiheit": Das Werk der Schriftstellerin Grete Weil* (Frankfurt am Main: Peter Lang, 1996), 28.

[37] Michal's critique of how David goes about creating a Jewish state also applies to the methods Saul used earlier when he established the first Jewish kingship.

[38] Miriam Fuchs, "Recalling the Past and Rescuing the Self: Autobiographical Slippage in Grete Weil's *The Bride Price: A Novel*," *Shofar* 17.2 (Winter 1999): 81.

[39] Dagmar Lorenz, *Keepers of the Motherland: German Texts by Jewish Women Writers* (Lincoln: U of Nebraska P, 1997), 283.

[40] Meier, *Neinsagen*, 300.

[41] Meier, *Neinsagen*, 221.

[42] In some ways, the feminist position overlaps with that of communitarians, but only in some ways. For a critique of communitarian philosophy from a feminist standpoint, see for example: Penny A. Weiss, "Feminism and Communitarianism: Comparing Critiques of Liberalism," in *Feminism and Community*, ed. Penny A. Weiss and Marilyn Friedman (Philadelphia: Temple UP, 1995), 161–86. This emphasis on relationality pervades feminist scholarship in other disciplines as well — from literary theory to psychology.

[43] Virginia Held, *Feminist Morality: Transforming Culture, Society, and Politics* (Chicago: U of Chicago P, 1993), 70.

[44] Sarah Hoagland, "Some Thoughts about 'Caring,'" in *Feminist Ethics*, ed. Claudia Card (Lawrence, Kansas: U of Kansas P), 246–63 and Marilyn Friedman, *What Are Friends For? Feminist Perspectives on Personal Relationships and Moral Theory* (Ithaca: Cornell UP, 1993).

[45] Peta Bowden, *Caring: Gender-Sensitive Ethics* (London: Routledge, 1997). 35.

[46] Held, *Feminist Morality*, 72.

[47] Uwe Meier, *Neinsagen*, 273.

[48] Lawrence Langer, "Remembering Survival," in *Shapes of Memory*, ed. Geoffrey Hartman (Boston: Beacon Hill, 1994), 1–6.

[49] Margaret Urban Walker, *Moral Understandings: A Feminist Study in Ethics* (New York: Routledge, 1998), 98.

[50] Joan Tronto, *Moral Boundaries: A Political Argument for an Ethic of Care* (London: Routledge, 1993), 128–29. See also in this context Virginia Held, *Feminist Morality*, 73.

[51] Tronto, *Moral Boundaries,* 132.

[52] Walker, *Moral Understandings,* 99.

# Conclusion

IN THE INTRODUCTION TO THIS BOOK, I asserted that the narrative spaces of novels create something like laboratories for thinking through moral choices. Of course, they don't always do so. Indeed world literature is replete with examples of novels that would seem to have little relevance to conceptualizing or reflecting on the moral choices individuals make. There are, however, moments in history that seem to demand such moral reflection from us. They call on us not only to reflect self-critically on our own behavior and on that of the groups to which we belong, but also to come to terms with how we structure our choices. The Third Reich and its efforts to exterminate Europe's Jews represent just such a colossal moment in human history.

Social psychologists tell us that it may take as many as twenty-five to thirty years before we have the emotional and intellectual distance to a particular crises that is necessary to engage with them collectively in an effective way — "effective" in the sense of causing lasting changes to how we as groups view the world. Thus, it should not surprise us that Christa Wolf, Ingeborg Drewitz, and Grete Weil all published works about the Nazi era that found particular resonance with readers in the 1970s and 1980s. They had published other works, of course, that included this time period and even explicitly questioned personal responsibility in the face of these overwhelmingly catastrophic events. Weil's *Ans Ende der Welt* (To the Ends of the Earth, 1949) or *Tramhalte Beethovenstraat* (Tram Station Beethoven Street, 1963) as well as a number of her short stories addressed these issues. Drewitz was also an early pioneer in dealing with the Holocaust. In fact, she wrote one of the first dramas about the topic in Germany, *Alle Tore werden bewacht* (All the Gates are Guarded, 1955). Wolf, too, incorporated the recent history of the Nazi era into her novels of rebuilding. Yet it wasn't until *Gestern war heute* (1978) for Drewitz, *Meine Schwester Antigone* (1982) for Weil, and *Kindheitsmuster* (1976) for Wolf, that their literary agendas and the interests of the reading public seemed to merge. Indeed, each of these novels went on to receive widespread public and critical acclaim.

In a recent study of both Weil's and Ruth Klüger's accounts of their experiences during this period, Pascale Bos details the changes that were necessary within the reading public before the work of these two German-Jewish authors could get the kind of reception that they undoubtedly deserved.[1] Bos ties these questions directly to the reception of Jewish authors who returned to Germany after the war and the difficulties that they faced in getting the German population to hear their voices. While there is certainly no reason to take issue with her account, one could also clearly call upon the work of social psychologists who tell us that efforts to address events of such great social impact generally occur in twenty- to thirty-year cycles and are often led by those who were between the ages of twelve and twenty-five when the events happened. So it should in a sense follow that these authors writing at this particular time in history stirred intense collective emotional responses. That resonance depended on both the willingness — indeed eagerness — of the authors to engage these questions and on the openness of the reading public to participate in their process of critical self-reflection.

Another important aspect of their work — its genesis and reception — lies in the historical context in which they wrote these novels, in particular in the development of two "new" social discourses, both of which also had their origins in the broad-based student movements that swept Europe and the US in the late 1960s and early 1970s. In the wake of the Vietnam war and against the backdrop of a new critical attitude toward the German past, the period witnessed a marked increase in interest among Germans in the social and political crises of geographically remote countries, often referred to as the "dritte-Welt-Bewegung" (third world movement). At the same time, in Western Europe and the US, the rise of the second women's movement brought with it a whole set of questions and answers to the topics of interpersonal relationships and responsibility. The coincidence of these three historical phenomena — namely a social readiness to begin an earnest discussion of Germany's fascist legacies, a heightened interest in the social and political struggles of so-called Third World nations, and a burgeoning consciousness of how gender shapes our sense of responsibility and self — represents the backdrop for Weil's, Wolf's, and Drewitz's interrogation of individual and collective responsibility. At this historical juncture, it became possible to look at responsibility — both contemporary and historical — through a set of different social filters or lenses.[2]

The fresh perspective they bring to the topic is their focus on locating responsibility in the lives of women who are devoted to the survival of their families and who must constantly negotiate the spectrum of responsibilities that they feel called to accept. This call to responsibility begins with the immediate care needs of aging parents and grandparents, young children, and ailing spouses. It includes planning birthday parties, shaving elderly men, going to school recitals, changing the bedding of the sick, helping children struggle toward adulthood, and — of course — doing the dishes. Yet none of these activities takes place in a historical vacuum. Each author takes pains to expand the horizon of responsibility that confronts us. The final pages of this book summarize and contrast directly the ways each author tries to map morality and to explore how we can come to agreement in society on the distribution of responsibility.

Ingeborg Drewitz's series of novels centers on the lives of educated, middle-class women who of necessity and choice spend most of their lives caring for the needs of others: primarily family members, but also clients and friends. They have stable careers and are at the forefront of women's entry into a whole new array of occupations, such as journalism, social work, and the law. Their level of education and the nature of their work make them socially engaged, and politically aware individuals. For these characters and their primary social circles, everything that happens in their lives becomes part of the chain of questions that radiate out from Berlin of the late twentieth century (or back into Berlin) both geographically and chronologically.

In the chapter on Drewitz, I used the extended metaphor of mapping to talk about these question chains as routes laid out between events and spaces — sometimes clearly and smoothly, and sometimes with halting, punctuated lines. In a practice similar to that of Christa Wolf, Drewitz ensconces her characters within concentric circles. Generally, she moves in toward her characters' immediate lives and local spaces from more remote times and places. We can see this in the opening structure of *Gestern war heute*, which begins with the reflections of the main character's great-grandmother and gradually moves chronologically through the generations in toward the protagonist. This structure comes out, too, in her frequent choice to begin a passage in a distant place, moving in geographically until her focus tightens on Berlin. However, the process must also follow the opposite path, since her characters need actively to question the connections between themselves and distant times and places in order to contextualize their own life choices.

Drewitz offers her readers few answers to the question of personal and collective responsibility in the wake of the Third Reich and in the face of increasing global tensions, but she demonstrates clearly the processes in which we engage in order to think about responsibility. Similar to the diachronic and synchronic concentric circles that she draws around her characters' lives, she envisions the negotiation of responsibility as one that begins — indeed has its anchors — in those immediate relationships of caring that constitute our daily lives. In other words, asking what our responsibilities are toward broader social groups is contingent upon learning what responsibility is and bearing responsibility for others on a more intimate level.

Of course, caring for others in our more immediate environs does not necessarily generate an interest in questions of responsibility beyond that. Drewitz's characters, however, draw from their shock and confusion over Germany's recent past and their part in it the imperative to extend their questioning of responsibility from intimate personal relationships outward. One of the best examples of this process is a passage from *Eis auf der Elbe* that I cited in the chapter on Drewitz in which the narrator and her future husband walk through the ruins along the Spree, asking each other interrelated key questions: What did you know about what happened here? When did you know it? How does that relate to what happened in places far removed from here such as Paris and Tokyo? Unable to answer those questions at that moment, they turn their attention to helping some young children who have just lost a balloon. Indeed, this is the process they go through repeatedly. They care for those in their immediate families, which leads to an openness to responsibility and care in general. The recent past causes them to question in what other situations and settings they can meaningfully offer to give care. While caring globally takes on more abstract forms, they reach out past their families to occupations that engage them in caring relationships for students, clients, and impoverished, illiterate people at the margins of their own society. Nonetheless, the levels of responsibility that — as Margaret Urban Walker says — we accept or refuse remain objects of collective deliberation (94); we don't resolve these issues and move on, but rather continue to question our own position within numerous intersecting communities. Drewitz's work asks us to question our own role in history, to reflect critically on our responsibilities, to recognize the limits of our agency, but not to give ourselves over to resignation and defeatism.

Christa Wolf and Ingeborg Drewitz have much in common when it comes to these issues as well as — to a certain extent — in questions of style. Wolf's literary-aesthetic agenda is much more complex as it wraps narrative layers in and around each other, while still essentially telling a story chronologically. Thus, while Drewitz's novels move forward in a fairly linear fashion, Wolf's work weaves each chronological moment into a multi-layered tapestry of the present and the past. Drewitz can tell us that the present is never free of the past and that the past informs our life choices, the way we understand our surroundings, and how we relate the two, but Wolf makes the readers feel this multi-layered entanglement of past and present through the narrative structures themselves.

Nonetheless, Wolf's questioning of individual and collective historical imbrication leads her along similar paths. Instead of a pattern of concentric circles, she creates triangular structures that link different times and different places through emotional, personal, social, historical, and political commonalities. From situations that are either chronologically or geographically closer to her characters, she moves on to geographically or chronologically distant places, but always with the intent of exposing the oppression, violence, and the acceptance of the responsibility for them that have informed human behavior throughout human history. Wolf asks how individuals outside of formal power structures are placed — or place themselves — in relation to those structures.

Wolf's main characters in the novels are generally well-educated young to middle-aged women who do not exhibit the same level of social engagement as do Drewitz's. Or more precisely, they do not connect their reflections on history and responsibility as closely to their work in a broader social context as do Drewitz's characters. However, this could reflect the fact that her characters are often — at least in *Nachdenken über Christa T.*, *Kindheitsmuster*, *Kassandra*, and *Medea. Stimmen* — occupationally positioned as social observers: namely as writers (*Kindheitsmuster*), intellectuals generally (*Nachdenken über Christa T.*), or figures marginalized from the centers of power (*Kassandra* and *Medea.Stimmen*).

Rather than seeking to address social injustices concretely, for example through journalistic reporting or working pro bono for immigrants charged with crimes — as do Drewitz's characters — Wolf's narrators assume more the role of social conscience. Anke Pinkert has pointed out that Wolf's particular form of dissidence generally did not lead to open defiance or political activism, but in a culture like that of the German Democratic Republic that had no real public sphere, we could interpret generating dialogue about a subject that the state had officially rejected as a form of social activism.[3] As David Carr points out, authors can — should their work find resonance in the reading public — act as the public spokespersons of their generation, clarifying the crucial questions and attempting to formulate answers, however provisional.[4]

Wolf's narrators have no more answers to the questions of moral responsibility than do those in Drewitz's novels — or, for that matter, than Weil's main characters. When pressed, for instance by her daughter Lenka, the narrator in *Kindheitsmuster* retreats into a kind of cynical irony.[5] Despite the absence of compelling answers, the narrator constantly pushes herself and those around her to think through the issues of moral responsibility, to insist that we exercise a faculty she calls "moralisches Gedächtnis," or moral conscience, to use the past actively and intentionally in sorting through present conflicts. This strikes me as a good example of how individuals constantly engage in a give-and-take over who is responsible for what or whom.

Grete Weil takes a remarkably different path in her reflections on responsibility. At first, her narrator fixates on what she perceives to be a universal moral truth: if we do not protest injustice publicly, we have failed to act morally. The narrator of *Meine Schwester Antigone* repeatedly scrutinizes her experiences through the filter of this precept and finds her own behavior inexplicably morally unacceptable. However, Weil's narrative stand-in refuses to accept this conclusion. The narrator asks: how could I have stood up and said no when doing so would most likely have caused not only my own death, but also that of my mother? She acknowledges that accepting responsibility for her mother was her choice, one Antigone did not make. However, once she had made that choice, it constrained her options for action. The narrator's deliberations on her own behavior during the occupation of Holland resonate solidly with care ethics' call for establishing deep context when laying out situations of moral choice. Weil's narrator subjects her own behavior and her own choices to multiple angles of scrutiny, using Antigone as a kind of game-piece that she can move in and out of test scenarios. Ultimately, it is the rigidity of universal moral precepts that Weil's *Antigone* attacks. Her conclusions at the end of *Meine Schwester Antigone* contain both a sense of peace with her own choices and the intimation that thinking about moral conflict, issues of responsibility, and one's own behavior is a never-ending process, one that will yield different conclusions at different times. Weil's work challenges head-on some of the moral truths that her society considered self-evident, and she enriches our understanding of moral choice by examining the relationships through which we construct our moral spaces.

Weil's novels differ from those of Wolf and Drewitz, however, in how she structures her historical perspective. Rather than establishing historical continuities, she examines historical ruptures. This refers both to how Nazi Germany severed her connections to the classical traditions of German culture and to her non-existent place within the historical narrative of Judaism. The Nazi past and the suffering of the Jews at German hands become the historical focal point for her reflections on responsibility. Rather than using the Third Reich and its many crimes as the motivation for interrogating responsibility — as do Wolf and Drewitz — Weil instead interprets the present from within the trauma victim's locked chronological spaces of her traumatic experiences. Of course, that doesn't mean that her characters live in the past. Instead we could say that her characters seek answers to unanswerable questions about the Holocaust, their own experiences during it, and the creation of healing strategies that they can apply not only to themselves, but to all the sufferers whom they meet.

Indeed, Weil's own suffering functions as the impetus for establishing caring relations. Because of it, she feels a deep-seated need to reach out and tend to others who suffer. In *Meine Schwester Antigone*, the narrator questions her own inaction in the face of media reports about suffering in the world. Her desire to care collides with the structural complexities of global boundaries and the limits of individual intervention. Although Weil comes at the issue of responsibility from a different historical position, she runs into the same series of individually unanswerable questions of responsibility cutting across community boundaries that Wolf and Drewitz encounter.

Thus, despite their many — sometimes subtle, sometimes substantial — differences, the three authors share a common thematic focus as well as the urgency to foster a collective rehearsal of the Nazi past. They do not, however, limit their agenda to interrogating the past, but rather use it as a launching pad to discuss how we negotiate responsibility in the present, both as a society and as individuals. Since they have no satisfactory answer to the question of how differing levels of responsibility can or should be balanced against each other, every aspect of their inquiry resembles something of an experiment — a "let's try this" approach. As they move from novel to novel, thus, the terms of the experiment vary — sometimes by conceptual, structural or thematic increment (as in the shift from *Gestern war Heute* to *Eis auf der Elbe*) and sometimes in more radical steps (as in Wolf's move from *Kindheitsmuster* to *Kassandra*).

Their insistence, furthermore, on the centrality of family relationships to the broader discussion of responsibility moves us beyond the focus on autonomous individuals responding to or interacting with other autonomous individuals in a manner based on the application of universal principles. As I mentioned in the introduction to this book, traditional western ethicists have tended to use short, situational examples to highlight moral conflicts and to reason through possible resolutions. One such example of a moral dilemma (made famous by the developmental psychologist Lawrence Kohlberg) can help clarify the differences between the depiction of moral decision-making in more traditional Western moral paradigms and feminist ethics.[6] The example to which I refer asks us to take the perspective of a man (Heinz) whose wife is dying. If he can get her a specific medication, she will live. Unfortunately, he does not have the money to procure this medication and faces a choice between letting his wife die or stealing from a local pharmacist, thus jeopardizing theoretically the pharmacist's livelihood. This moral dilemma pits the man with the sick wife against a (presumably male) pharmacist. In its most basic form, the dilemma presents a conflict between a private relationship (man/wife — in which the wife is little more than a chiffre for male economic responsibility, that is, in which she never achieves the status of an equal player) against a relationship from the public sphere that involves fulfilling or breaching socially sanctioned rules for economic interaction, rules that serve to insure the smooth functioning of a capitalist economy. In traditional Western ethics, there are different ways to justify stealing or not stealing the medication; yet the basics of the story remain the same. Feminist ethicists could also justify different outcomes for the situation. However, they would object that the brevity of the narrative and the relative dearth of detail (although I have seen slightly more embellished versions than the one I gave above) are an inadequate basis for forming a choice.

Both the feminist ethicists whose moral theories I discussed in chapter 2 and the novelists whose work stands at the heart of this book would take a different tack. Feminists ethicists would begin by asking more questions about the context and by giving each person affected by the dilemma a voice — above all the wife herself, but also the pharmacist, the wife's medical caregivers, and perhaps her children. Obviously, that would require much more time and space as a narrative than the Heinz story in its basic form offers. In contrast, literature — particularly the long, expansive narratives of the novel — provides the narrative breadth to engage in such in-depth interrogation.

Drewitz's, Wolf's, and Weil's novels all enact exactly such an extensive effort to explore the different perspectives and sets of responsibilities that each person brings to the negotiation of moral choices. They also, however, add a dimension to our moral reasoning that does not factor into the scenario of Heinz and his sick wife. One could, of course, easily change Heinz's name and the money at stake to reflect local currencies and/or inflation rates, thus making the story relate more to specific environments. However, using a story as truncated and lacking in detail as this one assumes that the situation in and of itself should resonate with all human beings regardless of their historical and cultural positioning. Drewitz, Wolf, and Weil, on the other hand, insist on including precisely those coordinates in space and time. Our sense of both determine how we reflect on moral choices and the spectrum of behavioral options available to us.

The process-character of moral deliberation and its embeddedness in specific historical and cultural spaces also explain why these authors reach so few conclusions, but instead repeatedly go back over similar situations. They always construct first the personal relationships that will form the moral foundation of their reflections on responsibility. They never ignore the day-to-day tasks that a human being enmeshed in relationships must fulfill. Drewitz, Wolf, and Weil bring moral reflection from the world of abstractions and generalizations home to the family — to specific families that live in specific cultures and at specific points in history. From this "you are here" point, they struggle to map out differing relationships of responsibility. The topography shifts — generally only gradually, but sometimes cataclysmically — so that their maps reveal faint, fragile routes between us. Nonetheless, they insist that we must continue our cartographic efforts to map responsibility *ad infinitum* with four questions: where have we been, where are we now, where shall our next steps take us, and who will be there with us?

## Notes

[1] Bos, *German-Jewish Literature in the Wake of the Holocaust: Grete Weil, Ruth Klüger, and the Politics of Address* (New York: Palgrave Macmillan, 2005), 1.

[2] See here also, Michael Kinney, "A Place for Memory: The Interface between Individual and Collective History," *Comparative Studies in Society and History* 41.3 (July 1999): 420–37.

[3] Pinkert, "Pleasures of Fear: Antifascist Myth, Holocaust, and Soft Dissidence in Christa Wolf's *Kindheitsmuster*," *German Quarterly* 76.1 (Winter 2003): 34.

[4] Carr, *Time, Narrative, and History* (Bloomington: Indiana UP, 1986), 156 and 158.

[5] See for instance, chapter 13, page 348.

[6] Lawrence Kohlberg, *Essays on Moral Development*, vol. 1: *The Philosophy of Moral Development* (San Francisco, CA: Harper & Row, 1981).

# Bibliography

## Primary Texts

Drewitz, Ingeborg. *Eis auf Elbe*. Düsseldorf: Claassen Verlag, 1982.
———. "Gespaltenes oder doppeltes Leben? Gedanken über die Frau als Künstlerin." In *"Die ganze Welt umwenden": Ein engagiertes Leben*, ed. Uwe Schweikert, 147–53. Düsseldorf: Claassen, 1987.
———. *Gestern war heute*. Düsseldorf: Claassen Verlag, 1978.
———. *Lebenslehrzeit*. Stuttgart: Radius, 1985.
———. *1984 — am Ende der Utopien: Literature und Politik, Essays*. Munich: Goldmann, 1984.
———. *Oktoberlicht*. Munich: Nymphenburger Verlag, 1969.
———. "Wege zur Frauendramatik." *Neue deutsche Hefte* 2 (1955–56): 152–55.
———. *Wer verteidigt Katrin Lambert?* Stuttgart: Verlag Werner Gebühr, 1974.
———. *Die zerstörte Kontinuität: Exilliteratur und Literatur des Widerstandes*. Vienna: Europaverlag, 1981.
Weil, Grete. *Ans Ende der Welt*. Wiesbaden: Limes Verlag, 1962, 1949.
———. *Der Brautpreis*. Zurich: Nagel und Kimche, 1988.
———. *The Bride Price*. Translated by John Barrett. Boston: David R. Godine Publisher, 1991.
———. *Generationen*. Zurich: Benziger, 1983.
———. *Happy sagte der Onkel*. Wiesbaden: Limes Verlag, 1968.
———. *Leb ich denn, wenn andere leben*. Zurich: Nagel und Kimche, 1998.
———. *Meine Schwester Antigone*. Zurich: Benziger, 1980.
———. *My Sister. My Antigone*. Translated by Krishna Winston. New York: Avon Books, 1984.
———. *Spätfolgen: Erzählungen*. Zurich: Nagel und Kimche, 1992.
———. *Tramhalte Beethovenstraat*. Wiesbaden: Limes Verlag, 1963.
Wolf, Christa. *The Author's Dimension: Selected Essays*. Translated by Jan van Heurck. New York: Farrar, Straus and Giroux, 1993.
———. "Dienstag, der 27. September." In *Erzählungen*. Munich: Luchterhand Verlag, 1999, 2002. 366–82.
———. *Die Dimension des Autors: Essays und Aufsatze Reden und Gespräche 1959–1985*. Darmstadt: Luchterhand, 1987.
———. "Diskussion mit Christa Wolf." *Sinn und Form* 28.4 (July/Aug. 1976): 861–89.
———. *The Fourth Dimension: Interviews with Christa Wolf*. Translated by Hilary Pilkington. London, New York: Verso, 1988.

———. *Im Dialog: Aktuelle Texte*. Frankfurt am Main: Luchterhand, 1990.
———. "Juninachmittag." *Erzählungen: 1960–1980*. Munich: Luchterhand Verlag, 1999, 2002. 87–110.
———. *Kassandra*. Darmstadt: Luchterhand, 1983.
———. *Kindheitsmuster*. Berlin and Weimar: Aufbau Verlag, 1976.
———. *Lesen und Schreiben: Aufsätze und Prosastücke*. Darmstadt und Neuwied: Luchterhand, 1972.
———. *Medea. Stimmen*. Darmstadt: Luchterhand, 1996.
———. *Nachdenken über Christa T.* Frankfurt am Main: Luchterhand, 1971; Halle: Mitteldeutscher Verlag, 1968.
———. *Patterns of Childhood*. Translated by Ursule Molinaro and Hedwig Rappolt. New York: Farrar, Straus and Giroux, 1976.
———. *The Quest for Christa T.* Translated by Christopher Middleton. New York: Farrar, Straus & Giroux, 1970.
———. *The Reader and the Writer: Essays, Sketches, Memories*. Translated by Joan Becker. New York: International Publishers, 1977.

## Works Consulted

Abel, Elizabeth, ed. *Writing and Sexual Difference*. Chicago: U of Chicago P, 1982.

Adams, Jeffrey, and Eric Williams, eds. *Mimetic Desire: Essays on Narcissism in German Literature from Romanticism to Post Modernism*. Columbia, SC: Camden House, 1995.

Adelson, Leslie. *Making Bodies, Making History: Feminism and German Identity*. Lincoln: U of Nebraska P, 1993.

Alcoff, Linda. "Cultural Feminism versus Post-Structuralism: The Identity Crisis in Feminist Theory." *Signs* 13 (Spring 1988): 405–36.

Allen, Ann Taylor. *Feminism and Motherhood in Western Europe, 1890–1970*. New York: Palgrave MacMillan, 2005.

Améry, Jean. *At the Mind's Limits: Contemplations by a Survivor on Auschwitz and Its Realities*. Translated by Sidney Rosenfeld and Stella P. Rosenfeld. Bloomington: Indiana UP, 1980.

Anz, Thomas, ed. *"Es geht nicht um Christa Wolf": Der Literaturstreit im vereinten Deutschland*. Munich: Spangenberg, 1991.

Asher, Evelyn Westermann. "The Fragility of the Self in Virginia Woolf's *To the Lighthouse* and Christa Wolf's *Nachdenken über Christa T.*" *Neohelicon* 19.1 (1992): 219–47.

Assmann, Jan. "Collective Memory and Cultural Identity." Translated by John Czaplicka. *New German Critique* 65 (Spring/Summer 1995): 126–33.

Aulls, Katharina. *Verbunden und gebunden: Mutter-Tochter-Beziehungen in sechs Romanen der siebziger und achtziger Jahre*. Frankfurt am Main: Peter Lang, 1993.

Bal, Mieke, Jonathan Crewe, and Leo Spitzer, eds. *Acts of Memory*. Hanover, NH: Dartmouth College, 1999.

Bar On, Bat-Ami, and Ann Ferguson, eds. *Daring to Be Good: Essays in Feminist Ethico-Politics*. New York: Routledge, 1998.

Becker-Cantarino, Barbara, and Inge Stephan, eds. *"Von der Unzerstörbarkeit des Menschen": Ingeborg Drewitz im Literarischen und Politischen Feld der 50er und 80er Jahre*. New York: Peter Lang, 2005.

Beddow, Michael. "Sources of Identity: Reflections on the Pronoun 'Wir' in Christa Wolf's Fiction." *London German Studies* 5 (1993): 173–86.

Benhabib, Seyla. "The Generalized and the Concrete Other: The Kohlberg-Gilligan Controversy and Moral Theory." *Praxis International* (1986): 38–60.

———. *Situating the Self*. Cambridge: Polity Press, 1992.

Benjamin, Jessica. "A Desire of One's Own: Psychoanalytic Feminism and Intersubjective Space." In *Feminist Studies, Critical Studies*, ed. de Lauretis, 79–101.

Benstock, Shari, ed. *The Private Self: Theory and Practice of Women's Autobiographical Writings*. Chapel Hill: U of North Carolina P, 1988.

Benz, Wolfgang, ed. *Zwischen Antisemitismus und Philosemitismus: Juden in der Bundesrepublik*. Berlin: Metropol, 1991.

Bird, Stephanie. *Recasting Historical Women: Female Identity in German Biographical Fiction*. Oxford: Berg Publishers, 1998.

Boa, Elizabeth, and Janet Wharton. *Women and the* Wende: *Social Effects and Cultural Reflections of the German Unification Process*. Amsterdam: Rodopi, 1994.

Bordo, Susan. "Feminism, Postmodernism, and Gender-Scepticism." In *Feminism/Postmodernism*, ed. Nicholson, 133–56.

Bos, Pascale. *German-Jewish Literature in the Wake of the Holocaust: Grete Weil, Ruth Klüger, and the Politics of Address*. New York: Palgrave Macmillan, 2005.

Bossinade, Johanna, "Haus und Front. Bilder des Faschismus in der Literatur von Exil- und Gegenwartsautorinnen. Am Beispiel von Anna Seghers, Irmgard Keun, Christa Wolf, und Gerlind Reinshagen." *Neophilologus* 70 (1986): 92–118.

Bouson, J. Brooks. "The Politics of Empathy and Self in Christa Wolf's *The Quest for Christa T*." In *Mimetic Desire: Essays on Narcissism in German Literature from Romanticism to Post Modernism*, ed. Adams and Williams, 187–204.

Bowden, Peta. *Caring: Gender-Sensitive Ethics*. London: Routledge, 1997.

Braham, Randolph, ed. *Reflections of the Holocaust in Art and Literature*. New York: Columbia UP, 1990.

Brenner, Rachel Feldhay. *Writing as Resistance: Four Women Confronting the Holocaust*. University Park: Pennsylvania State UP, 1997.

Brink-Friederici, Christl. "Von der Selbstfremdheit zur Selbstwerdung Dargestellt am Beispiel von Christa Wolfs Erzählung 'Kassandra.'" In *Begegnungen mit dem "Fremden,"* ed. Schichiji, 282–87.

Brodzki, Bella. "Mothers, Displacement, and Language in the Autobiographies of Nathalie Sarraute and Christa Wolf." In *Life/Lines*, ed. Brodzki and Schenck, 243–60.

Brodzki, Bella, and Celeste Schenck, eds. *Life/Lines: Theorizing Women's Autobiography.* Ithaca: Cornell UP, 1988.

Brogan, Kathleen. *Cultural Haunting: Ghosts and Ethnicity in Recent American Literature.* Virginia: U of Virginia P, 1998.

Brüggemann Rogers, Gerhild. *Das Romanwerk von Ingeborg Drewitz.* New York: Peter Lang, 1989.

Bruner, Jerome. "Life as Narrative." *Social Research* 54 (1987): 11–32.

Burkhard, Marianne, ed. *Gestaltet und gestaltend: Frauen in der Deutschen Literatur.* Amsterdam: Rodopi, 1980.

Bürner-Kotzam, Renate. "'Mein Fragen ist von Mitleid aufgesogen.' Indien im respektlosen Blick des Mitgefühls. Ingeborg Drewitz: 'Mein indisches Tagebuch.'" In *"Von der Unzerstörbarkeit des Menschen,"* ed. Becker-Cantarino and Stephan, 269–81.

Card, Claudia. "The Feistiness of Feminism." In *Feminist Ethics*, ed. Card, 3–34.

———, ed. *Feminist Ethics.* Lawrence: UP of Kansas, 1991.

Carr, David. *Time, Narrative, and History.* Bloomington: Indiana UP, 1986.

Caruth, Cathy, ed. *Trauma: Explorations in Memory.* Baltimore: Johns Hopkins UP, 1995.

———. *Unclaimed Experience: Trauma, Narrative and History.* Baltimore: Johns Hopkins UP, 1996.

*The Christa Wolf Controversy.* Special issue of the *GDR Bulletin* 17.1 (Spring 1991).

Claussen, Jeanette. "The Difficult of Saying 'I' as Theme and Narrative Technique in the Works of Christa Wolf." In *Gestaltet und gestaltend: Frauen in der deutschen Literatur*, ed. Burkhard, 319–33.

Cocks, Joan. *The Oppositional Imagination: Feminism, Critique, and Political Theory.* London: Routledge, 1989.

Connerton, Paul. *How Societies Remember.* Cambridge: Cambridge UP, 1989.

Conway, Martin. "The Inventory of Experience: Memory and Identity." In *Collective Memory of Political Events*, ed. Pennebaker, Paez, and Rimé, 21–45.

de Lauretis, Theresa, ed. *Feminist Studies, Critical Studies.* Bloomington: Indiana UP, 1986.

Dischereit, Esther. "No Exit from This Jewry." In *Reemerging Jewish Culture in Germany*, ed. Gilman and Remmler, 266–82.

Drescher, Angela, ed. *Christa Wolf — Ein Arbeitsbuch: Studien — Dokumente — Bibliographie.* Berlin und Weimar: Aufbau, 1988.

DuPlessis, Rachel Blau. *Writing Beyond the Ending: Narrative Strategies of Twentieth-Century Women Writers.* Bloomington: Indiana UP, 1985.

Eakin, Paul John. *How Our Lives Become Stories.* Ithaca: Cornell UP, 1999.

Ebbinghaus, Angelika, ed. *Opfer und Täterinnen: Frauenbiographien des Nationalsozialismus.* Schriften der Hamburger Stiftung für Sozialgeschichte des 20. Jahrhunderts. Hamburg: Delphi Politik, 1987.

Eysel, Karin. "History, Fiction, Gender: The Politics of Narrative Intervention in Christa Wolf's *Störfall*." *Monatshefte* 84.3 (1992): 284–98.
Fehervary, Helen. "Christa Wolf's Prose: A Landscape of Masks." *New German Critique* 27 (1982): 57–87.
Felman, Shoshana, and Dori Laub. *Testimony: Crises of Witnessing in Literature, Psychoanalysis, and History*. New York: Routledge, 1992.
*The Female Autograph*. New York: New York Literary Forum. Vol. 12–13, 1984.
Fentress, James, and Chris Wickham. *Social Memory*. Oxford: Basil Blackwell, 1992.
Finckh, Renate. *Mit uns zieht die neue Zeit*. Baden-Baden: Signal Verlag, 1978.
Fine, Ellen S. "Women Writers and the Holocaust: Strategies for Survival." In *Reflections of the Holocaust in Art and Literature*, ed. Braham, 79–95.
Finney, Gail. *Christa Wolf*. New York: Twayne Publishers, 1999.
Fischer-Lüder, Yvonne-Christiane. *An den Rand gedrückt — zum Opfer gemacht — Subjekt geworden: die Entwicklung der Frauenfiguren in den Romanen von Ingeborg Drewitz*. Frankfurt am Main: Peter Lang, 1990.
Fraser, Nancy, and Linda Nicholson. "Social Criticism without Philosophy: An Encounter between Feminism and Postmodernism." In *Feminism/Postmodernism*, ed. Nicholson, 19–38.
Fredericksen, Elke P. and Martha Kaarsberg Wallace, eds. *Facing Fascism and Confronting the Past. German Women Writers from Weimar to the Present*. Albany: SUNY P, 2000.
Frieden, Sandra. "'Falls es strafbar ist, die Grenzen zu verwischen': Autobiographie, Biographie und Christa Wolf." In *Vom Anderen und vom Selbst*, ed. Grimm and Hermand, 153–66.
———. "A Guarded Iconoclasm: The Self as Deconstructing Counterpoint to Documentation." In *Responses to Christa Wolf*, ed. Fries, 266–78.
———. "'In eigener Sache': Christa Wolfs *Kindheitsmuster*." In *Der Widerspenstigen Zähmung*, ed. Wallinger and Jones, 281–93.
Friedlander, Judith, ed. *Women in Culture and Politics*. Bloomington: Indiana UP, 1986.
Friedlander, Saul. *Memory, History, and the Extermination of the Jews of Europe*. Bloomington: Indiana UP, 1993.
———, ed. *Probing the Limits of Representation: Nazism and the "Final Solution."* Cambridge: Harvard UP, 1992.
Friedman, Marilyn. *What Are Friends For? Feminist Perspectives on Personal Relationships and Moral Theory*. Ithaca: Cornell UP, 1993.
Fries, Marilyn Sibley, ed. *Responses to Christa Wolf*. Detroit: Wayne State UP: 1989.
Fuchs, Miriam. "Recalling the Past and Rescuing the Self: Autobiographical Slippage in Grete Weil's *The Bride Price: A Novel*." *Shofar* 17.2 (Winter 1999): 73–83.

Gaskell, George, and Daniel Wright. "Group Differences in Memory for a Political Event." In *Collective Memory of Political Events*, ed. Pennebaker, Paez, and Rimé, 175–89.

Gättens, Marie-Luise. "Language, Gender, and Fascism: Reconstructing Histories in *Three Guineas, Der Mann auf der Kanzel,* and *Kindheitsmuster.*" In *Gender, Patriarchy, and Fascism in the Third Reich*, ed. Martin, 32–64.

———. *Women Writers and Fascism: Reconstructing History.* Gainesville: U of Florida P, 1995.

Gardiner, Judith Kegan. "On Female Identity and Writing by Women." In *Writing and Sexual Difference*, ed. Abel, 177–91.

Giese, Carmen. *Das Ich im literarischen Werk von Grete Weil und Klaus Mann: Zwei autobiographische Gesamtkonzepte.* Frankfurt am Main: Peter Lang, 1997.

Gilligan, Carol. *In a Different Voice.* Cambridge, MA: Harvard UP, 1982.

Gilman, Sander. *Inscribing the Other.* Lincoln: U of Nebraska P, 1991.

———. *Jews in Today's German Culture.* Bloomington: Indiana UP, 1995.

Gilman, Sander, and Karen Remmler, eds. *Reemerging Jewish Culture in Germany: Life and Literature since 1989.* New York: New York UP, 1994.

Gilpin, Heidi. "*Cassandra*: Creating a Female Voice." In *Responses to Christa Wolf*, ed. Fries, 349–66.

Goldberg, David Theo, and Michael Krausz, eds. *Jewish Identity.* Philadelphia: Temple UP, 1993.

Goodman, Katherine. *Dis/Closures: Women's Autobiography in Germany between 1790 and 1914.* New York: Peter Lang, 1986.

Goozé, Marjanne. "The Definitions of Self and Form in Feminist Autobiography Theory." *Women's Studies* 21.4 (1992): 411–29.

Gravenhorst, Lerke, and Carmen Tatschmurat, eds. *Töchter-Fragen. NS-Frauen-Geschichte.* Freiburg: Kore Verlag, 1990.

Griffiths, Morwenna. *Feminisms and the Self: The Web of Identity.* London: Routledge, 1995.

Grimm, Reinhold, and Jost Hermand, eds. *Vom Anderen und vom Selbst: Beiträge zu Fragen der Biographie und Autobiographie.* Königstein: Athenäum, 1982.

Groag Bell, Susan, and Marilyn Yalom, eds. *Revealing Lives: Autobiography, Biography, and Gender.* Albany: SUNY P, 1990.

Guthrie, John. "The Reconstructed Subject, Christa Wolf, *Kassandra.*" In *The German Novel in the Twentieth Century*, ed. Midgley, 179–93.

Gutjahr, Ortrud. "'Erinnerte Zukunft.' Gedächtnisrekonstruktion und Subjektkonstitution im Werk Christa Wolfs." In *Erinnerte Zukunft*, ed. Mauser, 53–80.

Halbwachs, Maurice. *The Collective Memory.* Translated by Francis J. Ditter, Jr. and Vida Yazdi Ditter. New York: Harper & Row, 1980.

Hamington, Maurice, and Dorothy C. Miller, eds. *Socializing Care.* Lanham: Rowan and Littlefield, 2006.

Hannsmann, Margarethe. *Der helle Tag bricht an: Ein Kind wird Nazi.* Hamburg: A. Knaus, 1982.

Hansen, Miriam, and Michael Geyer. "German-Jewish Memory and National Consciousness." In *Holocaust Remembrance*, ed. Hartman, 175–90.

Harbers, Henk. "'Widersprüche hervortreiben': Eros, Rationalität und Selbsterkenntnis in Christa Wolfs Erzählung 'Kassandra.'" *Neophilologus* 71 (1987): 266–84.

Hartman, Geoffrey H., ed. *Holocaust Remembrance: The Shapes of Memory.* Oxford: Blackwell, 1994.

———. *The Longest Shadow: In the Aftermath of the Holocaust.* Bloomington: Indiana UP, 1996.

Hartsock, Nancy. "Foucault on Power: A Theory for Women?" In *Feminism/Postmodernism*, ed. Nicholson, 157–95.

Hayes, Peter, ed. *Lessons and Legacies: The Meaning of the Holocaust in a Changing World.* Evanston: Northwestern UP, 1991.

Häussermann, Titus, ed. *Ingeborg Drewitz: Materialien zu Werk und Wirken.* Stuttgart: Radius Verlag, 1988.

Heinemann, Marlene. *Gender and Destiny: Women Writers and the Holocaust.* Westport, CT: Greenwood, 1986.

Held, Virginia. *Feminist Morality: Transforming Culture, Society, and Politics.* Chicago: U of Chicago P, 1993.

Heller, Agnes. *A Theory of History.* London: Routledge, 1982.

Henderson, Cary. "Das diskursive Gegenmodell in *Kassandra.*" *Monatshefte* 86.2 (1994): 172–85.

Herrmann, Anne. "I/She: The Female Dialogic of *The Quest for Christa T.*" In *Responses to Christa Wolf*, ed. Fries, 257–65.

Higonnet, Margaret, Jane Jenson, Sonya Michel, Margaret Weitz, eds. *Behind the Lines: Gender and the Two World Wars.* New Haven: Yale UP, 1987.

Hilberg, Raul. *The Destruction of the European Jews: Student Edition.* New York: Holmes & Meier, 1985.

Hoagland, Sarah. "Some Thoughts about 'Caring.'" In *Feminist Ethics*, ed. Card, 246–63.

Hobsbawm, Eric. *The Age of Empire, 1875–1914.* London: Pantheon Books, 1987.

Holub, Robert C. "Fact, Fantasy, and Female Subjectivity: *Vergangenheitsbewältigung* in Christa Wolf's *Patterns of Childhood.*" In *Facing Fascism and Confronting the Past*, ed. Elke P. Frederiksen and Martha Kaarsberg Wallach, 211–34. Albany: SUNY P, 2000.

Hörnigk, Therese. *Christa Wolf.* Göttingen: Steidl, 1989.

Huyssen, Andreas. *Twilight Memories: Marking Time in a Culture of Amnesia.* New York: Routledge, 1995.

Jackman, Graham. "'Wann, wenn nicht jetzt?' Conceptions of Time and History in Christa Wolf's *Was Bleibt* and *Nachdenken über Christa T.*" *German Life and Letters* 45.4 (October 1992): 358–75.

Jackson, Neil, and Barbara Saunders. "Christa Wolf's *Kindheitsmuster*: An East German Experiment in Political Autobiography." *German Life and Letters* 33 (1980): 319–29.

Jonker, Gerdien. *The Topography of Remembrance: The Dead, Tradition and Collective Memory in Mesopotamia.* Leiden: E. J. Brill, 1995.

Kaes, Anton. "New Historicism and the Study of German Literature." *The German Quarterly* 62.2 (1989): 210–19.

Kane, B. M. "In Search of the Past: Christa Wolf's *Kindheitsmuster*." *Modern Languages* 59 (1978): 19–23.

Kant, Immanuel. *Werke.* Vol. 7. Ed. Wilhelm Weischedel. Frankfurt am Main: Suhrkamp, 1968.

Kasher, Asa. "Jewish Collective Identity." In *Jewish Identity*, ed. Goldberg and Krausz, 56–78.

Kaufmann, Eva. "'. . . schreiben, als ob meine Arbeit noch und immer wieder gebraucht würde': Überlegungen zur Utopie bei Christa Wolf." *Monatshefte* 84.3 (1992): 274–83.

Kinney, M. G. "A Place for Memory: The Interface between Individual and Collective History." *Comparative Studies in Society and History* 41.3 (July 1999): 420–37.

Kirkham, Pat, and David Thoms, eds. *War Culture: Social Change and Changing Experience in World War Two.* London: Lawrence & Wishart, 1995.

Kittay, Eva Feder, and Diana Meyers, eds. *Women and Moral Theory.* Totowa, NJ: Rowan and Littlefield, 1987.

Kohlberg, Lawrence. *Essays on Moral Development*, vol. 1, *The Philosophy of Moral Development.* San Francisco, CA: Harper & Row, 1981.

Komar, Kathleen. "The Communal Self: Remembering Female Identity in the Works of Christa Wolf and Monique Wittig." *Comparative Literature* 44.1 (1992): 42–58.

Koonz, Claudia. *Mothers in the Fatherland.* New York: St. Martin's Press, 1987.

Köpnick, Lutz. "Rettung und Destruktion: Erinnerungsverfahren und Geschichtsbewußtsein in Christa Wolfs *Kindheitsmuster* und Walter Benjamins Spätwerk." *Monatshefte* 84.1 (1992): 74–90.

Kraft, Helga. "Zwischen Traditionalismus und Fortschritt: Frauengenerationen im Werk Ingeborg Drewitz.'" In *"Von der Unzerstörbarkeit des Menschen,"* ed. Becker-Cantarino and Stephan, 329–48.

Kraft, Helga, and Elke Liebs, eds. *Mütter-Töchter-Frauen: Weiblichkeit in der Literatur.* Stuttgart: Metzler, 1993.

Kramer, Jane. *The Politics of Memory.* New York: Random House, 1996.

Kramer, Nicole, et al., ed. *Sei wie das Veilchen im Moose . . . Aspekte feministischer Ethik.* Frankfurt am Main: Fischer Verlag, 1994.

Krieger, Gerd. "Ein Buch im Streit der Meinungen: Untersuchungen literaturkritischer Reaktionen zu Christa Wolfs *Kindheitsmuster*." *Weimarer Beiträge* 31 (1985): 56–75.

Kuhn, Anna. "'Eine Königin köpfen ist effektiver als einen König köpfen': The Gender Politics of the Christa Wolf Controversy." In *Women and the Wende*, ed. Boa and Wharton, 200–215.

———. "The 'Failure' of Biography and the Triumph of Women's Writing: Bettina von Arnim's *Die Günderode* and Christa Wolf's *The Quest for Christa T.*" In *Revealing Lives*, ed. Groag Bell and Yalom, 13–28.

Kuhn, Annette. *Family Secrets: Acts of Memory and Imagination*. London: Verso, 1995.

LaCapra, Dominick. *Representing the Holocaust: History, Theory, Trauma*. Ithaca: Cornell UP, 1996.

Lang, Berel. "The Phenomenal-noumenal Jew. Three Antinomies of Jewish Identity." In *Jewish Identity*, ed. Goldberg and Krausz, 279–90.

Langbehn, Volker. "Vom Feminismus zum Post-Marxismus? Christa Wolfs *Nachdenken über Christa T.*" *New German Review* 5–6 (1989–90): 43–55.

Langer, Lawrence. *Holocaust Testimonies: The Ruins of Memory*. New Haven: Yale UP, 1991.

———. "Remembering Survival." In *Shapes of Memory*, ed. Hartmann, 1–6.

———. *Versions of Survival: The Holocaust and the Human Spirit*. Albany: SUNY P, 1982.

Laplanche, J., and J.-B. Pontalis. *The Language of Psycho-Analysis*. New York: Norton, 1967, 1973.

Lejeune, Philippe. "Autobiography in the Third Person." *New Literary History* 9 (1977): 27–49.

Lennox, Sara. "Christa Wolf and Ingeborg Bachmann: Difficulties of Writing the Truth." In *Responses to Christa Wolf*, ed. Fries, 128–48.

Lorenz, Dagmar. *Keepers of the Motherland: German Texts by Jewish Women Writers*. Lincoln: U of Nebraska P, 1997.

Loster-Schneider, Gudrun. "'Du darfst nie wieder so reden!' GeNarrations-Risiken in Ingeborg Drewitz' Roman *Gestern war Heute. Hundert Jahre Gegenwart.*" In *"Von der Unzerstörbarkeit des Menschen,"* ed. Becker-Cantarino and Stephan, 315–28.

Love, Myra. "Christa Wolf and Feminism: Breaking the Patriarchal Connection." *New German Critique* 16 (1979): 31–53.

———. *Christa Wolf: Literature and the Conscience of History*. DDR-Studien/East German Studies, vol. 6. New York: Peter Lang, 1991.

Lützeler, Paul Michael, ed. *Schriftsteller und "Dritte Welt."* Tübingen: Stauffenberg Verlag, 1998.

MacIntyre, Alasdair. *After Virtue*. Notre Dame: U of Notre Dame P, 1981.

Maier, Charles S. *The Unmasterable Past: History, Holocaust, and German National Identity*. Cambridge: Harvard UP, 1988.

Macciocchi, Maria-Antonietta. "Female Sexuality in Fascist Ideology." Translated and edited by Michèle Barrett et al. *Feminist Review* 1(1979): 67–82.

Maltzan, Charlotte von. "'Man müsste ein Mann sein.' Zur Frage der weiblichen Identität in Erzählungen von Kirsch, Morgner und Wolf." *Acta Germanica* 20 (1990): 141–55.

Martin, Elaine, ed. *Gender, Patriarchy, and Fascism in the Third Reich*. Detroit: Wayne State UP, 1993.

———. *Uncommon Women and the Common Experience: Fiction of Four Contemporary French and German Women Writers.* Diss. Indiana University, Bloomington, 1982.

Maschmann, Melita. *Fazit: Kein Rechtfertigungsversuch.* Stuttgart: Deutsche Verlagsanstalt, 1963.

Mattson, Michelle. "Searching for Missing Pieces Around Us: Christa Wolf's *The Quest for Christa T.* and Ingeborg Drewitz's *Who will defend Katrin Lambert?*" *Women in German Yearbook* 19 (2003): 159–78.

Mauser, Wolfram, ed. *Erinnerte Zukunft: 11 Studien zum Werk Christa Wolfs.* Würzburg: Königshausen und Neumann, 1985.

Meier, Uwe. *"Neinsagen, die einzige unzerstörbare Freiheit": Das Werk der Schriftstellerin Grete Weil.* Frankfurt am Main: Peter Lang, 1996.

———. "'O Antigone . . . stehe mir bei' Zur Antigone-Rezeption im Werk von Grete Weil." *Zeitschrift für Literaturwissenschaft und Linguistik* 26.104 (December 1996): 147–57.

Meyer, Michael A. *Jewish Identity in the Modern World.* Seattle: U of Washington P, 1990.

McDonald, W. E. "Who's Afraid of Wolf's Cassandra — or Cassandra's Wolf? Male Tradition and Women's Knowledge in *Cassandra.*" *The Journal of Narrative Technique* 20.3 (1990): 267–83.

McGowan, Moray. "Myth, Memory, Testimony, Jewishness in Grete Weil's *Meine Schwester Antigone.*" In *European Memories of the Second World War*, ed. Peitsch, Burdett, and Gorrar, 149–58.

Midgley, David, ed. *The German Novel in the Twentieth Century: Beyond Realism.* Edinburgh: Edinburgh UP, 1993.

Mill, John Stuart. *Utilitarianism.* Oxford: Oxford UP, 1998.

Moody-Adams, Michelle. "Gender and the Complexity of Moral Voices." In *Feminist Ethics*, ed. Card, 195–212.

Nägele, Rainer. "The Writing on the Wall, or Beyond the Dialectic of Subjectivity (The Quest for Christa T.)." In *Responses to Christa Wolf*, ed. Fries, 248–56.

Nicholson, Linda, ed. *Feminism/Postmodernism.* New York: Routledge, 1990.

Noddings, Nel. *Caring: A Feminine Approach to Ethics and Moral Education.* Berkeley: U of California P, 1984, 2003.

Nora, Pierre, ed. *Realms of Memory: Rethinking the French Past.* Vol. 1. Translated by Arthur Goldhammer. New York: Columbia UP, 1996.

Nunner-Winkler, Gertrud, ed. *Weibliche Moral: Die Kontroverse um eine geschlechts-spezifische Ethik.* Frankfurt am Main: Campus Verlag, 1991.

Olney, James, ed. *Autobiography: Essays Theoretical and Critical.* Princeton, NJ: Princeton UP, 1980.

———. "Some Versions of Memory/Some Versions of *Bios*: The Ontology of Autobiography." In *Autobiography: Essays Theoretical and Critical*, ed. Olney, 236–67.

Özdamar, Emine Sevgi. *Das Leben ist eine Karawanserei hat zwei Türen, aus einer kam ich rein, aus der anderen ging ich raus.* Cologne: Kiepenheuer & Witsch, 1999.

Paez, Dario, Nekane Basabe, and Jose Luis Gonzales. "Social Processes and Collective Memory: A Cross-Cultural Approach to Remembering Political Events." In *Collective Memory of Political Events*, ed. Pannebaker, Paez, and Rimé, 147–74.
Paserini, Luisa, ed. *Memory and Totalitarianism*. International Yearbook of Oral History and Life Stories, vol. 1. New York: Oxford UP, 1992.
Peitsch, Helmut, Charles Burdett, and Claire Gorrara, eds. *European Memories of the Second World War*. New York: Berghahn Books, 1999.
Pennebaker, James, and Betsy Banasik. "On the Creation and Maintenance of Collective Memories: History as Social Psychology." In *Collective Memory of Political Events*, ed. Pennebaker, Paez, and Rimé, 3–19.
Pennebaker, James, Dario Paez, and Bernard Rimé, eds. *Collective Memory of Political Events: Social Psychological Perspectives*. Mahwah, NJ: Lawrence Erlbaum Associates Publishers, 1997.
Pieper, Annemarie. *Gibt es eine feministische Ethik*. Munich: Wilhelm Fink Verlag, 1998.
Pinkert, Anke. "Pleasures of Fear: Antifascist Myth, Holocaust, and Soft Dissidence in Christa Wolf's *Kindheitsmuster*." *German Quarterly* 76.1 (Winter 2003): 25–37.
Postl, Gertrude. "The Silencing of a Voice: Christa Wolf, Cassandra, and the German Unification." *differences* 5.2 (1993): 92–115.
Radstone, Susannah. *Memory and Methodology*. Oxford and New York: Berg Books, 2000.
Rawls, John. *A Theory of Justice*. Cambridge: Harvard UP, 1971.
Rechtien, Renate. "The Self and Other: Images of Men and Women in Christa Wolf." In *The Individual, Identity and Innovation*, ed. Williams and Parkes, 149–64.
Rehmann, Ruth. *Der Mann auf der Kanzel*. Munich: Hanser, 1979.
Rey, William H. "Christa Wolf — vor und nach der Revolution." *Monatshefte* 84.3 (1992): 260–73.
Ries, Wolfgang. "Bewundert viel und viel gescholten, Aischylos Christa Wolf auf der Suche nach der historischen Kassandra." *Wirkendes Wort* 35.1 (January 1985): 5–17.
Rimé, Bernard, and Véronique Christophe. "How Individual Emotional Episodes Feed Collective Memory." In *Collective Memory of Political Events*, ed. Pennebaker, Paez, and Rimé, 131–46.
Ringelheim, Joan. "Women and the Holocaust: A Reconsideration of Research." *Signs* 10.4 (1985): 741–61.
Robinson, Fiona. *Globalizing Care: Ethics, Feminist Theory, and International Relations*. Boulder: Westview Press, 1999.
Ruddick, Sara. *Maternal Thinking: Towards a Politics of Peace*. Boston: Beacon Press, 1989.
Ryan, Judith. *The Uncompleted Past: Postwar German Novels and the Third Reich*. Detroit: Wayne State UP, 1983.
Samuel, Raphael. *Theatres of Memory*. Vol. 1: *Past and Present in Contemporary Culture*. London: Verso, 1994.

Samuel, Raphael, and Paul Thompson, eds. *The Myths We Live By*. London: Routledge, 1990.
Saunders, Barbara. *Contemporary German Autobiography: Literary Approaches to the Problem of Identity*. London: University of London, Institute of Germanic Studies, 1985.
Schilling, Donald, ed. *Lessons and Legacies: Teaching the Holocaust in a Changing World*. Vol. 2. Evanston, IL: Northwestern UP, 1991.
Schlant, Ernestine. *The Language of Silence: West German Literature and the Holocaust*. New York: Routledge, 1999.
Schmidt, Ricarda. "History Reflected in the Imaginary: Pre-revolutionary Attitudes Towards the Process of History in Works by Christa Wolf, Helga Königsdorf, Angela Krauss and Irina Liebmann." In *The Individual, Identity, and Innovation*, ed. Williams and Parkes, 165–81.
Schneider, Richard Chaim. "In der Haut der Eltern." In Benz, *Zwischen Antisemitismus und Philosemitismus*, 71–86.
Scholz, Hannelore. "Gedächtnis Berlin: Anmerkungen zum Verhältnis von Individual- und Zeitgeschichte in Texten von Ingeborg Drewitz." In *"Von der Unzerstörbarkeit des Menschen,"* ed. Becker-Cantarino and Stephan, 379–99.
Schuman, Howard, Robert Belli, and Katherine Bischoping, "The Generational Basis of Historical Knowledge." In *Collective Memory of Political Events*, ed. Pennebaker, Paez, and Rimé, 47–77.
Schumann, Klaus. "Blickwechsel: Christa Wolf und Ingeborg Bachmann: Drei Begegnungen." *Acta Neophilologica* 23 (1990): 63–74.
Schichiji, Yoshinori, ed. *Begegnungen mit dem "Fremden." Grenzen — Traditionen — Vergleich*. Munich: iudicium Verlag, 1991.
Schultz, Hans Jürgen, ed. *Mein Judentum*. Stuttgart: Kreuz Verlag, 1978, 1991.
Seligmann, Rafael. "What Keeps the Jews in Germany Silent?" In *Reemerging Jewish Culture in Germany*, ed. Gilman and Remmler, 173–83.
Sevenhuijsen, Selma. *Citizenship and the Ethics of Care: Feminist Considerations on Justice, Morality and Politics*. London: Routledge, 1998.
Shafi, Monika. "Entdeckung und Entfremdung. Ingeborg Drewitz: *Mein indisches Tagebuch*." In *Schriftsteller und "Dritte Welt,"* ed. Lützeler, 243–62.
———. "'Montagdienstagmittwochdonnerstagfreitag...' Zur Darstellung des Alltags in Ingeborg Drewitz' Romanprosa." In *"Von der Unzerstörbarkeit des Menschen,"* ed. Becker-Cantarino and Stephan, 297–314.
———. "Die überforderte Generation: Mutterfiguren in Romanen von Ingeborg Drewitz." *Women in German Yearbook* 7 (1991): 23–41.
Shirer, Robert. *Difficulties of Saying "I": The Narrator as Protagonist in Christa Wolf's* Kindheitsmuster *and Uwe Johnson's* Jahrestage. New York: Peter Lang, 1988.
Shrage, Laurie. *Moral Dilemmas of Feminism: Prostitution, Adultery, and Abortion*. New York: Routledge, 1994.
Singer, Peter, and Renata Singer, eds. *The Moral of the Story: An Anthology of Ethics Through Literature*. Oxford: Blackwell, 2005.

Smith, Sidonie. *A Poetics of Women's Autobiography*. Bloomington: Indiana UP, 1987.
———. *Subjectivity, Identity, and the Body: Women's Autobiographical Practices in the Twentieth Century*. Bloomington: Indiana UP, 1993.
———. *Writing New Identities: Gender, Nation, and Immigration in Contemporary Europe*. Minneapolis: U of Minnesota P, 1997.
Smith, Sidonie, and Julia Watson, eds. *Women, Autobiography, Theory: A Reader*. Wisconsin: U of Wisconsin P, 1998.
Sobchack, Vivian, ed. *The Persistence of History: Cinema, Television, and the Modern Event*. New York: Routledge, 1996.
Sophocles. *Antigone*. Translated by Richard Emil Braun. Oxford: Oxford UP, 1973.
Stanley, Liz. *The Auto/Biographical I: Theory and Practice of Feminist Auto/Biography*. Manchester: Manchester UP, 1992.
———. "From 'Self-made Women' to 'Women's Made-Selves? Audit Selves, Simulation and Surveillance in the Rise of Public Woman." In *Feminism and Autobiography: Texts, Theories, Methods*, ed. Tess Cosslett, Celia Lury, and Penny Summerfield, 40–60. London: Routledge, 2000.
Stanton, Domna. "Autogynography: Is the Subject Different?" In Stanton, *The Female Autograph*, 5–22. Chicago: U of Chicago P, 1984.
Stephens, Anthony. "'Die Verführung der Worte' — von 'Kindheitsmuster' zu 'Kassandra.'" In *Wolf: Darstellung, Deutung, Diskussion*, ed. Manfred Jurgensen, 127–47. Bern: Francke, 1984.
Stern, Carola. *Doppelleben*. Cologne: Kiepenheuer & Witsch, 2001.
———. *In den Netzen der Erinnerung*. Reinbek bei Hamburg: Rowohlt Verlag, 1986.
Szepansky, Gerda. *"Blitzmädel" "Heldenmutter" "Kriegerwitwe": Frauenleben im Zweiten Weltkrieg*. Frankfurt am Main: Fischer, 1986.
Tetzner, Gerti, and Christa Wolf. *Was zählt ist die Wahrheit: Briefe von Schriftstellern der DDR*. Halle: Mitteldeutscher Verlag, 1975.
Trebilcot, Joyce, ed. *Mothering: Essays in Feminist Theory*. Totowa, NJ: Rowman & Allanheld, 1983.
Tronto, Joan. *Moral Boundaries: A Political Argument for and Ethic of Care*. London: Routledge, 1993.
Thürmer-Rohr, Christina. *Mittäterschaft und Entdeckungslust*. Berlin: Orlanda Verlag, 1989.
Vanhelleputte, Michael, ed. *Christa Wolf in feministischer Sicht*. Frankfurt am Main: Peter Lang, 1992.
Vinken, Barbara. *Die deutsche Mutter: der kange Schatten eines Mythos*. Munich: Piper, 2001.
Walker, Margaret Urban. *Moral Understandings: A Feminist Study in Ethics*. New York: Routledge, 1998.
Wallinger, Sylvia, and Monika Jones, eds. *Der widerspenstigen Zähmung: Studien zur bezwungenen Weiblichkeit in der Literatur vom Mittelalter bis zur Gegenwart*. Innsbruck: Institut für Germanistik, 1986.

Warner, Judith. *Perfect Madness: Motherhood in the Age of Anxiety*. New York: Riverhead Books, 2005.
Weedon, Chris. "Childhood Memory and Moral Responsibility: Christa Wolf's *Kindheitsmuster*." In *European Memories of the Second World War*, ed. Peitsch, Burdett, and Gorrara, 238–46.
Weidauer, Friedemann. "'Fighting for Defeat': Jewish Identity in Postwar Germany and Austria." *Seminar* 34.3 (September 1998): 280–99.
Weigel, Sigrid. *Ingeborg Bachmann: Hinterlassenschaften unter Wahrung des Briefgeheimnisses*. Vienna: Paul Zsolnay Verlag, 1999.
———. "Vom Sehen zur Seherin: Christa Wolf's Umdeutung des Mythos und die Spur der Bachmann-Rezeption in ihrer Literatur." In *Christa Wolf — Ein Arbeitsbuch*, ed. Drescher, 169–203.
Weigel, Sigrid, and Birgit Erdle, eds. *Fünfzig Jahre danach: Zur Nachgeschichte des Nationalsozialismus*. Zurich: vdf Hochschulverlag, 1996.
Weiss, Penny A., ed. *Feminism and Community*. Philadelphia: Temple UP, 1995.
———. "Feminism and Communitarianism: Comparing Critiques of Liberalism." In *Feminism and Community*, ed., Weiss, 161–86.
White, Hayden. *The Content of the Form: Narrative and the Discourse of History*. Baltimore: Johns Hopkins UP, 1987.
———. *Metahistory: The Historial Imagination in Nineteenth-Century Europe*. Baltimore: Johns Hopkins UP, 1973.
———. "The Modernist Event." In *The Persistence of History*, ed. Sobchack, 17–38.
Wiggershaus, Renate. *Frauen unterm Nationalsozialismus*. Wuppertal: Hammer, 1984.
Wilke, Sabine. "Between Female Dialogics and Traces of Essentialism: Gender and Warfare in Christa Wolf's Major Writings." *Studies in Twentieth Century Literature* 17.2 (Summer 1993): 243–62.
———. "'Dieser fatale Hang der Geschichte zu Wiederholungen': Geschichtskonstruktionen in Christa Wolfs *Kindheitsmuster*." *German Studies Review* 13.3 (October 1990): 499–512.
———. "'Kreuz- und Wendepunkte unserer Zivilisation Nach-denken': Christa Wolfs Stellung im Umfeld der zeigenössischen Mythos-Diskussion." *German Quarterly* 60 (1988): 213–28.
———. "'Rückhaltlose Subjektivität': Subjektwerdung, Gesellschafts- und Geschlechtsbewußtsein bei Christa Wolf." *Women in German Yearbook* 6 (1991): 27–45.
Williams, Arthur, and Stuart Parkes, eds. *The Individual, Identity and Innovation: Signals from Contemporary Literature and the New Germany*. Bern: Peter Lang, 1994.
Winter, Hans-Gerd. "Ingeborg Drewitz' Bild der frühen Nachkriegszeit," In Becker-Cantarino and Stephan, eds., *"Von der Unzerstörbarkeit des Menschen,"* ed. Becker-Cantarino and Stephan, 161–84.
Wood, Nancy. *Vectors of Memory: Legacies of Trauma in Postwar Europe*. Oxford: Berg Publishers, 1999.

Yates, Frances. *The Art of Memory.* Harmondsworth: Penguin, 1978.
Young, James. *At Memory's Edge: After-images of the Holocaust in Contemporary Art and Architecture.* New Haven: Yale UP 2000.
———. *The Texture of Memory: Holocaust Memorials and Meaning.* New Haven: Yale UP, 1993.
Zelizer, Barbie. *Remembering to Forget: Holocaust Memory Through the Camera's Eye.* Chicago: U of Chicago P, 1998.
Zeller, Eva. *Nein und Amen.* Stuttgart: Deutsche Verlagsanstalt, 1986.
———. *So lange ich denken kann.* Stuttgart: Deutsche Verlagsanstalt, 1981.
*Zerstörung des moralischen Selbstbewusstseins: Chance oder Gefährdung. Praktische Philosophie in Deutschland nach dem Nationalsozialismus.* Edited by Forum für Philosophie Bad Homburg. Frankfurt am Main: Suhrkamp Verlag, 1988.
Zur, Judith. *Memories: Mayan War Widows in Guatemala.* Boulder, CO: Westview Press, 2001.

# Index

Adelson, Leslie, 87, 94
Adorno, Theodor, 32
American Civil War, 28
Améry, Jean, 145, 181
Anacker, Heinrich, 128–29
Andersch, Alfred, 143
Anouilh, Jean, 155
Anz, Thomas, 9
Assmann, Jan, 24, 37, 151, 182
attentiveness, 48, 84, 179
Aulls, Katharina, 65, 91–92
authorbiography (Autorbiographie), 159–61, 165
autobiography, 3–4, 8–9, 20, 33, 60, 80, 108, 141, 143–44, 152, 154, 156, 158, 159, 161, 165, 180–81, 183
autogynography, 9

Bachmann, Ingeborg, 139, 159, 183
Bal, Mieke, 37
Banasik, Betsy, 19, 36–37, 96, 105
Bar On, Bat-Ami, 58
Becker, Jurek, 147–48, 181
Becker-Cantarino, Barbara, 91–94
Benjamin, Walter, 99, 135
Bird, Stephanie, 136, 139
Bloody Sunday, 79, 93
Böll, Heinrich, 1, 71, 143
Borchert, Wolfgang, 1
Bos, Pascale, 5, 10, 144, 180, 185
Bowden, Peta, 143, 171, 183
Brecht, Bertolt, 139, 155
Brodzki, Bella, 55, 60
Brogan, Kathleen, 35
Brüggemann Rogers, Gerhild, 71, 89, 92, 95
Buber, Martin, 146
Bürner-Kotzam, Renate, 93

Butler, Judith, 59

Card, Claudia, 41–42, 58–59, 183
care ethics, 10, 42–43, 45–50, 54–59, 66–67, 141, 174, 179, 189
cared-for, 42–44, 66–67
caregiver, 65–68, 191
Carr, David, 79–80, 88–89, 93–94, 105, 189, 192
Chile, 7, 61, 112, 114, 130–32
Christophe, Véronique, 21, 37
communicative memory, 24, 151
Crewe, Jonathan, 37
Cuba, 75
cultural memory, 151

Dischereit, Esther, 145, 147, 181
documentary literature, 71
dritte-Welt-Bewegung, 186
Durkheim, Émile, 15

Eakin, Paul John, 141
engrossment, 43
Ensslin, Gudrun, 156, 182
Enzensberger, Hans Magnus, 1
ethics: contractarian, 57; expressive-collaborative model, 49, 52, 134; justice, 45; Kantian, 39–40; neo-Kantian, 57; theoretical-juridical model, 49; utilitarian, 39, 57–58

Fehervary, Helen, 129, 140
Ferguson, Ann, 58
Finckh, Renate, 8
Finney, Gail, 131, 141
Fischer-Lüder, Yvonne-Christine, 92
Fisher, Berenice, 48
Flax, Jane, 58
Freud, Sigmund, 146

Frieden, Sandra, 108, 120, 137, 139
Friedman, Marilyn, 171, 183
Frisch, Max, 1
Fuchs, Miriam, 165, 183
Gastarbeiter, 81
Gättens, Marie-Luise, 140
geography of morals, 46, 55–56, 96, 179
geography of responsibility, 61, 64, 88
Geyer, Michael, 116, 138
Giese, Carmen, 8, 181, 183
Gilligan, Carol, 42, 58, 65, 92, 129, 167
Gilman, Sander, 144, 181–82
Goebbels, Joseph, 99
Goldberg, David Theo, 145, 148, 181–82
Grenz, Jacqueline, 97
Grimm, Hans, 107

Halbwachs, Maurice, 14–18, 25–26, 30–31, 36–37, 77, 79, 96–97, 100, 143, 150–51, 153
Hamington, Maurice, 59
Hannsmann, Margarethe, 8
Hansen, Miriam, 116, 138
Held, Virginia, 39–40, 54, 58–59, 66, 70, 92, 124, 143, 171–72, 183–84
Heller, Agnes, 35
Hellmund, Friedrich, 152–54, 160
Heym, Stefan, 143
Hilberg, Raul, 8
historical present, 1, 5, 7, 11–12, 18, 35, 61–62, 71, 76, 79–80, 88–91, 104, 160
Hoagland, Sarah, 59, 183
Hochhuth, Rolf, 1
Holocaust, 1, 4, 10, 12, 20, 22, 34, 36, 56, 78, 107, 138–39, 144, 149, 152, 155–56, 158–60, 168–69, 176–77, 180, 185, 190, 192
Holub, Robert, 124, 140
Horkheimer, Max, 32
Hörnigk, Therese, 106–8, 111–12, 120, 137–39
Hume, David, 57
Hutcheson, Frances, 57

Huyssen, Andreas, 12–13, 29, 35

Indian Schools (Canada), 22–24, 32

Japan, 7, 134
Job, 149
Jonker, Gerdien, 26, 36–37

Kant, Immanuel, 40, 58
Kasher, Asa, 145–47, 181
Kaufmann, Hans, 102
Kinney, Michael, 22–24, 32, 37, 137, 192
Klüger, Ruth, 10, 144, 180, 185, 192
Kohlberg, Lawrence, 191–92
Köpnick, Lutz, 116, 135–36, 138
Korean War, 18–19
Kraft, Helga, 84, 92–94
Krausz, Michael, 145–46, 148, 150, 181–82
Kroetz, Franz Xaver, 93

Lang, Berel, 145, 148, 181
Langer, Lawrence, 177, 183
Lebensraum, 163
Leidensgemeinschaft (community of sufferers), 149
*lieux de mémoire*, 12, 26–28
Lorenz, Dagmar, 165, 183
Loster-Schneider, Gudrun, 93
Love, Myra, 106, 116, 120, 125, 129, 137–40

MacIntrye, Alasdair, 90
Martin, Elaine, 8, 140
Maschmann, Melita, 8
McGowan, Moray, 144, 155, 181–82
medallions, 99, 101, 135
Meier, Uwe, 164, 166, 176, 182–83
Meyer, Michael, 146, 181
Middle East, 61, 114, 130
Mill, John Stuart, 40, 58
Miller, Dorothy, 59
Mittäterschaft (Mittäter), 122–23, 139
mnemonography, 100, 102–4, 106, 116, 121, 124, 128
Moody-Adams, Michelle, 59
moral laboratory, 5, 54, 89

mother (motherhood), 42, 44–47, 54–58, 60, 65–70, 72, 84, 93–94, 103–4, 107, 118, 121, 126, 128, 131, 140, 143–44, 158, 169–74, 183, 189

Nägele, Rainer, 138
National Public Radio, 27
Nicaragua, 114, 117
Noddings, Nel, 42–47, 54, 56, 58, 65–67, 171
Nora, Pierre, 12–14, 25–28, 31, 35, 37, 64, 79, 91, 96, 103–4, 136, 143, 149–51

one-caring, 43–44
Özdamar, Emine Sevgi, 7

Paez, Dario, 36–37
PEN, 4, 9
Pennebaker, James, 18–19, 36–37, 96, 105
Pinkert, Anke, 119, 139, 189, 192

Radstone, Susannah, 36
Rawls, John, 40, 58
Reformation, 28, 151
rehearsal, 19–24, 30, 73, 82, 96, 105–11, 137
Rehmann, Ruth, 3, 8
Remmler, Karen, 144, 181–82
Rimé, Bernard, 21, 36–37
Robinson, Fiona, 59, 141
Ruddick, Sara, 42, 44–46, 54–55, 58, 65, 67–69, 92, 94, 143, 171
Rudolph, Ekkehart, 86

Samuel, Raphael, 13, 36–37
Schneider, Richard Chaim, 149, 182
Scholl, Hans, and Sophie Hans, 99–100, 156, 173, 182
Scholz, Hannelore, 91
Schultz, Hans Jürgen, 181
Second World War, 1, 3, 5, 18–20, 62, 72, 77–78, 80, 96, 113, 134, 137, 144, 181
second-wave feminism, 63
Seligmann, Rafael, 149, 182

Sevenhuijsen, Selma, 41, 48, 58–59, 84
Shafi, Monika, 84, 91, 93–95
Shirer, Robert, 103, 106, 111, 121, 128, 136–40
Shrage, Laurie, 58–59
Sidgwick, Henry, 57
silent events, 19
Singer, Peter, and Renate Singer, 6, 10
Smith, Adam, 57
Sophocles, 33, 155–57, 159, 167, 176–77, 182
Spitzer, Leo, 37
Stephan, Inge, 91–94
Stern, Carola, 3, 8
Story Corps, 27
Susman, Margarete, 182

Taylor, Charles, 58
Third Reich, 2, 4, 8, 19–20, 32, 80, 90, 92, 97, 99–100, 107, 109, 116, 123, 140, 143, 154, 156, 168, 182, 185, 187, 190
Thürmer-Rohr, Christina, 122–23, 139
trauma, 19–20, 82, 143–44, 177, 179, 190
triangulation, 114–15, 130–31, 188. *See also* Zeitdreieck
Tronto, Joan, 46–49, 55, 57, 84, 141, 174, 179, 184

Ullrich, Gisela, 95
unification, 3

Verband deutscher Schriftsteller, 4
*Vergangenheitsbewältigung*, 80, 140
Vietnam War, 7, 18–19, 61, 118, 131–32, 186
Vinken, Barbara, 58

Walker, Margaret Urban, 6, 10, 41, 46, 49–53, 55–61, 64–66, 75–77, 84, 88, 90–91, 93, 96, 105, 120–21, 124–25, 130–31, 134–35, 140–41, 143, 172, 174, 179–80, 183–84, 188

Walser, Martin, 1
Weedon, Chris, 104, 106, 137–38
Weidauer, Friedemann, 182
Weigel, Sigrid, 159, 183
Weiss, Penny, 183
Wilke, Sabine, 106, 108, 116, 129, 135–38, 140
Williams, Bernard, 58
Winter, Hans-Gerd, 92

Wolfskehl, Karl, 182

Yates, Fraces, 36
Yir Yoront, 22–24
Young, James, 36

Zeitdreieck, 130. *See also* triangulation
Zeller, Eva, 3, 8
Zur, Judith, 35